POWER, DISCOURSE AND RESISTANCE

Advances in Criminology
Series Editor: David Nelken

Titles in the Series

Power, Discourse and Resistance
A Genealogy of the Strangeways Prison Riot

EAMONN CARRABINE
University of Essex

ASHGATE

Published by
Ashgate Publishing Limited
Gower House
Croft Road
Aldershot
Hants GU11 3HR
England

Ashgate Publishing Company
Suite 420
101 Cherry Street
Burlington, VT 05401-4405
USA

Ashgate website: http://www.ashgate.com

British Library Cataloguing in Publication Data
Carrabine, Eamonn
   Power, discourse and resistance : a genealogy of the
   Strangeways prison riot. - (Advances in criminology)
   1.Strangeways Prison 2.Prison riots - England
   I.Title
   365.6'41

Library of Congress Cataloging-in-Publication Data
Carrabine, Eamonn.
   Power, discourse, and resistance : a genealogy of the Strangeways prison riot / Eamonn Carrabine.
      p. cm. -- (Advances in criminology)
   Includes bibliographical references and index.
   ISBN 0-7546-2172-3
   1. Strangeways (Prison) 2. Prison riots--England--Manchester. 3. Prison discipline--England--Manchester. 4. Imprisonment--Sociological aspects. 5. Imprisonment--Psychological aspects. I. Title. II. Series.

HV9650.M62S743 2004
365'.641--dc22

2004054433

ISBN 0 7546 2172 3

Printed and bound in Great Britain by Antony Rowe Ltd
Chippenham, Wiltshire

Contents

List of Figures

List of Tables

Acknowledgements

Many people have helped me throughout the research and the writing of this book. The biggest thanks go to Brian Longhurst who, right from the start, gave a level of advice, encouragement and support that has proven to be invaluable. Funding from the Economic and Social Research Council, Grant No: R00429334064, made the research possible. Joe Sim and Greg Smith examined the doctoral thesis on which this book is based and their comments helped me to conceive it as a book and many thanks are due to David Nelken who gave me the opportunity to be part of this important criminological series at Ashgate.

While this research was being carried out in the mid-1990s both the Home Office and Prison Service proved to be considerable obstacles as they refused access to some important material. However, particular individuals have been exceptionally helpful and I express my thanks to them here. Michael Poole at the Home Office provided me with an enormous amount of contextualising data, often at very short notice. Simon Boddis, Paul Hobson and Anne Maguire at HM Inspectorate of Prisons gave freely of their time and always passed on various reports and papers when they were requested. In the Prison Service, Mike Jenkins and Brendan O'Friel opened some doors and the time spent in conversation with them is greatly appreciated. The staff of Greater Manchester Probation Service willingly agreed to participate in the research and their insights on the workings of Strangeways provided invaluable material.

I owe thanks to the academics, colleagues and friends who I have either discussed aspects of this work with or who have kindly taken the time to read and comment on papers arising from this research. Mary Bosworth, Chris Bryant, Hilary Faulkner, Paula Grange, Bob Jessop, Alison Liebling, Rod Morgan, Ray Pawson, Elaine Player, Joe Sim, Richard Sparks, Jason Rutter, Ian Taylor and Pat Walters all helped in this way. Big debts of gratitude are due to Pam Cox and Christine Rogers who read the final draft of the book and offered indispensable feedback. Only I am responsible for the weaknesses in the final arguments advanced in the book. The Research Endowment Fund of the Department of Sociology at the University of Essex paid for the manuscript to be transformed into camera ready copy by Pat FitzGerald while Andrew Hawkey carefully proof read the final copy.

I would also like to thank Nicki Jameson for generously providing me with materials collected in her research and for putting me in contact with a number of prisoners involved in the protest at Strangeways. The prisoners I have discussed this work with and who have written to me have supplied important insights. Moreover their correspondence served to put whatever I was worrying about at the time into perspective. Eric Allison and John Sutton, who have both spent time inside Strangeways (John in a uniform) gave me chilling and thought provoking accounts of their experiences. My family and friends have always been supportive during the research. In addition they have, in their own unique and inimitable ways, indicated that there is quite a bit more to life than books and stuff. Finally, special thanks are due to Christine Rogers and Sherrie Tuckwell who made the last stages of writing more fun than it really ought to have been.

I would like to thank the Home Office and News International for permission to reproduce figures and Sage for allowing material that first appeared as 'Discourse, Governmentality and Translation: Towards a Social Theory of Imprisonment' in *Theoretical Criminology*, Vol. 4, No. 3, pp. 309–31 to be reproduced in the book in a revised form.

Eamonn Carrabine
Department of Sociology
University of Essex

Series Preface

Eamonn Carrabine's study, *Power, Discourse and Resistance*, well exemplifies the theoretically innovative sort of work that we seek to publish in this series. The author begins by offering a wide ranging and closely argued survey of the literature on prison riots. He shows the need to combine macro and micro sociological perspectives ('what prisons are for' and 'what prisons are like') and the need to distinguish different types of power, discourse and struggle which are sited there. This is followed by a careful case study of the events which led up to the disturbances in Strangeways. His research method here offers a non-deterministic, 'genealogical' account which is supported by reference to qualitative interviews, documentary materials and official statistics. It illustrates the significance both of background conditions and the various more immediate emotions which affect those involved in rioting.

The lessons of this book are not limited to increasing our understanding of how riots come about and how they may be avoided. Indeed in many respects the author casts doubt on explanations of riots which see them as linked to a combination of particularly severe situations of deprivation, organisational incompetence and perceived injustice. He sees these 'background' factors as unfortunately too widespread in any prison system to serve as the key to why certain situations get 'out of control'. His approach seeks instead to elucidate the conditions which characterise a breakdown in the type of fatalistic acceptance of prison life – nurtured by routines and rituals – which is the alchemy through which power persuades itself of its legitimacy. For Carrabine the marvel is 'how a prison the size of Strangeways, with all its problems of overcrowding, chronic conditions and so forth was able to achieve a semblance of order for most of the time'. His argument seeks to show how regimes of practice operate, how forms of domination, relations of power and kinds of freedom and autonomy are linked, how such regimes are contested and resisted, and, not least, why riots are so often avoided.

DAVID NELKEN
Series Editor

Chapter 1

Introduction: Locating Prison Discontent

The month of April 1990 was a time of unprecedented prison unrest in England and Wales. During these four weeks the state lost control of over 20 institutions and the term crisis, which all too frequently has been employed to describe the condition of the prison system over the last three decades, became both highly visible and genuinely acute. The catalyst and symbol of this tumultuous moment in British penal history was the 25-day occupation of Strangeways prison,[1] situated in the inner-city of Manchester in the North West of England. This Victorian prison is one of the largest in Europe, yet the scenes that surrounded it then were more reminiscent of a medieval siege. It seemed as if the dark knights of the state – in their black protective armour, helmets and shields – were involved in the starvation of a peasant revolt, defiantly perched on the ramparts of some ancient fortress. Such images dominated the nation's television screens and newspaper pages. In the first few days tales of barbarism, butchery, and torture were associated with the primitive rebels, yet as the weeks passed the lurid stories became hard to sustain as it emerged that no prisoners perished in the prison.

Five days into the siege the then Conservative government announced the setting up of an independent inquiry under the direction of a high court judge, Lord Justice Woolf. This decision marked a decisive departure from previous state responses to prison disorder. The publication of the subsequent report[2] (Woolf and Tumim, 1991) was greeted with almost universal acclaim across the political spectrum as the most important examination of the prison system in the last 100 years. Moreover, the recipe of reform contained in the report was widely understood as one which would take the system out of the nineteenth century and into the twenty-first.

The primary purpose of this book is to revisit this era of insurgency through providing a detailed sociological account of the events at Strangeways. The *sociological* focus is emphasised here not merely for the purposes of distancing or elevating my interpretation over Woolf's *judicial* inquiry, but because the analysis is directed to the fundamental issue of how order is possible in society. Of course, this was not Woolf's explicit problem when he, and subsequently Judge Tumim undertook their examination, which to all intents and purposes was framed around the questions of why the state lost control of its penal system and what action ought to be taken to prevent any future militancy against the rule of law. Nevertheless, the question of why human beings endure the unequal social situations in which they frequently find themselves is also the key to understanding the fracturing of order in less certain times of upheaval and discontent. Consequently, this book is concerned with how power operates and the versatile ways in which human beings enact their agency, as this ranges from relations of acquiescence to strategies of resistance in the face of institutional power – so that a central question becomes: Why are major prison riots such rare events? Especially since the pains of confinement documented in this book were by no means unique to Strangeways. The analysis, like any other work in the social sciences or humanities, can also be read as a statement on how to study action and what might be learnt from such an enterprise, as its distinctive arguments are based on the understanding that whilst existence is made possible through discourse, this is not the same thing as claiming that social practice is language. The overall point is driven toward generating a sociology of imprisonment that locates the analysis of institutional life in central problems in social theory.

In contrast, the Woolf report should be regarded as an influential example of administrative penology. As the term implies, this body of work tends to deal with technical details concerning the day to day running of prisons, accepts that the apparatus of confinement is the appropriate way of dealing with offenders and pursues the business of managing prisons as defined by the prevailing contours of legitimate authority. The kind of problems it seeks to address are, to the sociological imagination at least, impoverished, and include what kind of techniques minimise disorder and maximise security, or what kind of prison regime is best suited to rehabilitate, deter and regulate offenders. Whilst administrative penology can offer critical interpretations of institutions, policies and processes, the important point to recognise is that it is largely a technicist project that does not seek to answer a whole series of crucial questions. These include, why prisons exist in the form that they do; what is the role the institution performs in society; how incarceration is experienced by the confined; and what are the moral justifications for inflicting this form of punishment on offenders as opposed to others. It is these, and other, matters that animate the sociology of imprisonment which I discuss in more detail in the next chapter. Nevertheless, it is important to acknowledge that Woolf did articulate a sophisticated theory of prison riots through implicitly combining two influential sociological explanations of disorder to the extent that it quickly became regarded as 'the standard liberal account of what causes prison riots and what should be done to prevent them' (Cavadino and Dignan, 1992: 24).

However, it needs to be emphasised from the outset that I will be focusing on a central problem in social theory that concerns specifying how the versatility of human action might be related to more enduring social structures that constrain or enable agency. This problem is part of a broader dualism that emerged in the Enlightenment when human beings came to be understood as both knowing subjects and as objects of that knowledge. Philosophical speculations on the nature of the subjective world of experience and sociological disputes over whether there exists an objective domain of reality that lies beyond the unique and particular practices of any cultural formation or human activity pervade any attempt at explaining social practice. For instance, in the twentieth century the structuralist method of inquiry, whether this was deployed in the disciplines of anthropology, linguistics or sociology, came to regard questions of understanding the meaning that particular subjects attach to their action as largely irrelevant, as it aimed to reveal the objective laws and systematic elements that organise all human activity. In contrast, phenomenology was driven by the precisely opposite goal of prioritising lived experience in everyday practices as the key to understanding the fundamental, hidden and transcendental qualities that condition existence.

In prison sociology this dualism is most readily apparent in the analytical division of labour that separates those inquiries which seek to uncover the reasons why the institution came to occupy, and remains at the forefront of, contemporary strategies of crime control, as opposed to those accounts that provide detailed descriptions and challenging commentaries on the predicaments of the confined in particular prisons. In other words, there are analyses that seek to discover what imprisonment is *for*, in the objective and transcendental sense, and those which claim to reveal what prisons are really *like* in terms of a detailed mapping of the interactions in particular institutions. These two approaches explicitly involve different levels of sociological analysis and implicitly invoke disparate pronouncements on what might count as convincing explanations of social practice.

The investigation of what prisons are for has tended to involve a macrosociological approach as it involves looking at the place of punishment in society, and examines the cultural, economic, historical and political reasons why the exclusionary impulse of confinement replaced the highly public rituals of execution and shaming from the seventeenth century across northern and western Europe. Reflecting on the functions of imprisonment can also involve a commitment to understanding the place of the institution in contemporary strategies of symbolic condemnation and social control. In either case, the ways in which the past speaks to the present is a defining feature and consequently, one of the reasons the term genealogy is used in this analysis is to signal both the continuities and contingencies of social practice with earlier forms of governance. However, the issue of what prisons are like involves a more microsociological approach as it is concerned with the daily life of prisoners and staff in the institutions themselves. At its best, the genre brings into sharp relief the complex dimensions of daily interactions in particular prisons and has produced some of the richest ethnographic research in the discipline.

While the achievements of these two sociologies have been widely acknowledged, it is clear that the approaches provide rather divergent statements on how to understand human action and the ways in which social structures might organise existence. Of course, these differences in emphasis could be regarded as simply a matter of analytical bracketing, as it would be futile to suppose that one specific interpretation of imprisonment could make sense of the complexity of the institution in its totality. Such a position is methodologically defensible, but avoids confronting the difficulties that are encountered in bringing together the subjective worlds of experience with the structural obligations that dictate the conditions of imprisonment over time and in space. Similarly, the choice of the contrasting terms of 'resistance' and 'riot' in the title and subtitle of the book is to highlight just two of the words that could be used to describe the events at Strangeways prison in April 1990. The politics of protest is examined in more detail in Chapter 3, as it is clear that whatever terminology is used will provoke a set of moral assumptions and value judgements on those involved in the 'disturbances'. The point that needs to be emphasised here is that any discussion of protest needs to reconcile the question of why it is that some individuals are motivated to participate in dissent with the equally complex issues of how structural conditions shape obedience, endure beyond the personal milieu and are challenged in particular situations by certain people.

One extremely useful way of situating these problems is in relation to the *Methodenstreit* – the acrimonious dispute over methods – that dominated German intellectual life from the 1880s up to the outbreak of the First World War. The most important concerned the relationships between the natural and cultural sciences, which the philosopher Wilhelm Windelband insisted differed on the basis of their methods. The natural sciences, according to Windelband, used a 'nomothetic' or generalising method that sought to uncover law-like general relationships and properties, whereas the social or cultural sciences tended to employ 'ideographic' procedures to investigate the unique and particular aspects of individual phenomenon. On the other hand, Wilhelm Dilthey distinguished between the cultural and natural sciences on the basis of their subject matter, in that a fundamental distinction ought to be drawn between the realms of 'nature' and 'human spirit' (Marshall, 1982:46), especially since he regarded the task of 'human studies' as the empathetic identification of the historian with the subjects of historical reconstruction (Callinicos, 1999: 154).

Although this debate is normally cast as an argument (the position is also referred to as anti-naturalism) for the outright rejection of the aims and methods of the physical sciences by the human and social sciences, the terms of reference can also be used to shed light on differing forms of explanation that seek to make sense of social practice and human conduct. For instance, Max Weber's sociology is usually regarded as a key resource for undermining the 'scientific' pretensions of the discipline through powerfully advocating an 'interpretative' method that seeks to understand 'meaningful' social action in the light of these methodological controversies (see Cahnman, 1964; Marshall, 1982; Parkin, 1982). Yet an equally compelling intellectual force for Weber was Friedrich Nietzsche's perspectivism – the insistence that all interpretation is selective and partial – to the extent that there is a clear tension in his work between 'the privileging of historical contingency ... and the repeated declarations that humanity's imprisonment in the "iron cage" of bureaucratized capitalism is "inevitable"' (Callinicos, 1999: 178). In other words, the issues at stake are how to bring together attentiveness to the detailed, distinctive and unique qualities of particular times and places with a more abstract, systematic and universalising approach to explaining processes and situating contexts.

These difficulties are summarised with characteristic insight by Raymond Aron (1965: 242) where he states that historical events are always 'born of general causes [and] completed, as it were, by accidents'. It is significant that he comes to this conclusion through a consideration of Alexis de Tocqueville's contribution to sociological theory, especially in his unfinished study of the origins of democracy in France that was published after his death as *The Ancien Régime and the Revolution* (1856) where he posed the crucial question of why only France experienced a revolution when, all across Europe, the old regimes were collapsing. In this book Tocqueville attempts to grasp the essence of historical analysis, which lies in reconciling how necessity and contingency weave 'the web of history' (Aron, 1965: 244). The task of this book is not quite as ambitious as explaining the French Revolution. But the crucial issue of why prison riots do not happen more often is of a similar kind. In addressing this issue the argument will follow Nietzsche's genealogical approach to history – which is to demonstrate 'the iron hand of necessity shaking the dice-box of chance' (cited in Foucault, 1984a: 89).

Although these opening remarks are intended to indicate some of the major themes and substantive issues covered in the book it is important to emphasise that few informed commentators deny that prisons are dangerous places and whilst violence is often described in terms of the characteristics of individual prisoners such an understanding leaves much unexplained (Edgar et al., 2003). Consequently, one of the central ambitions of this book is to locate the study of prison riots in the broader problem of order familiar to social and political theorists. The level of violent incidents in prisons indicates that intimidation, assaults and abuse form part of the everyday routine, whereas riots and disturbances are much rarer and pose a '*special problem* of the occasional complete or near-complete breakdown of order' (Sparks et al., 1996: 2, emphasis in original). Riots and disturbances can be further distinguished in the sense that a riot involves the authorities losing 'control of a significant number of prisoners, in a significant area of the prison, for a significant amount of time' (Useem and Kimball, 1989: 4), whereas a disturbance is a step down from a riot as there are fewer prisoners involved and the administrators do not lose control of any part of the institution but can still involve collective protest over conditions, through refusing to eat or stopping work for example. Although these definitions can be criticised for their vagueness they do have the advantage of highlighting the ways in which the problem of order is a daily feature of institutional life for even though major riots are rare events they do not abruptly occur in an otherwise tranquil vacuum and have multi-faceted causes. Moreover, the term riot is a pejorative one summoning images of frenzied mob violence and as will be seen the label has long been used by ruling elites to discredit the revolutionary crowd in European history (Rudé, 1964).

Nevertheless, it is instructive to begin by situating prison riots in their historical context and the chapter will turn to a broad characterisation of four relatively discrete phases of prison protest. There then follows a discussion of the Woolf report, which will concentrate on identifying what he and Judge Tumim took to be the causes of prison disorder. In essence, this is understood as an imbalance between the elements of security, control and justice – an interpretation that echoes an important North American contribution to the literature on prison riots advanced by Bert Useem and Peter Kimball (1989), which stresses that both the breakdown of social control mechanisms and the grievances generated through deprivation were particularly salient features driving prison unrest in their analysis. Although these two accounts offer insightful accounts of prison protest, there are a number of problems in their respective treatments and much of the book will be directed toward overcoming these difficulties. Before discussing the history of prison unrest it is worthwhile to pause here and provide a brief overview of the penal system in England and Wales for the reader unacquainted with the carceral landscape.

The Origins of the Modern Penal Estate

The historian Ralph Pugh (1968) has described how in medieval England imprisonment came to serve three main uses: custodial (detaining those awaiting trial or sentence), coercive (forcing fine defaulters and debtors into making good their misfortune) and punitive (as punishment in its own right). These legal distinctions continue to be significant, yet it is important to recognise that the main purposes of the medieval prison were custodial and coercive, with the sentences likely to have been corporal or capital and it was not uncommon 'for a person to be sentenced and hanged or flogged on the same day' (McConville, 1998: 118). In other words, the punitive function of imprisonment did not achieve prominence until the late eighteenth century.

By the middle of the nineteenth century there were two different types of prison in England, the local and the convict prison. The local prison is the older and stretches back to at least Saxon times and was made up of two historically distinct institutions, the gaol (now usually spelled 'jail') and the house of correction. The former had mainly been used for detention before trial and holding debtors, while the latter sought to suppress idleness and vagrancy – with the Prison Act of 1865 combining the two and, as Seán McConville (1998: 119) argues, it 'abolished a distinction that by this time ceased to denote a difference'. The convict prisons have a much shorter history and date from 1776, when the American War of Independence left the government with nowhere to send those sentenced to transportation. At the same time philanthropic reformers were promoting a new vision of imprisonment that sought to unite the punitive and reformative through hard labour and religious instruction. These two developments led central government to build new prisons known as 'penitentiaries' in an effort to reform the convicted and deter any others (Harding et al., 1985). The two prison systems – convict and local – continued under largely separate administrations until the nationalisation of the prison system in 1877, which brought local prisons under centralised state control to ensure greater uniformity and reduce personal discretion in punishment.

Imprisonment in the twentieth century in England and Wales continued to be dominated by this Victorian legacy. Nevertheless, it is important to recognise that there are now a range of institutions that can be grouped under two main types. First, there are local prisons and remand centres whose primary task is to receive and deliver prisoners to the courts, and to allocate those serving sufficiently long sentences to the second set of institutions. These are Young Offender Institutions and adult training prisons, which emerged out of the convict prison system. These are further subdivided into closed and open institutions for men and women. This sub-division reflects a prisoner security classification and the level of security that institutions provide. All prisoners are classified A, B, C, or D according to a scheme devised in 1966 by Lord Mountbatten (Home Office, 1966) following a series of notorious prison escapes that pushed the issue of security to the top of the political agenda.

Mountbatten's recommendations have done much to shape the penal system of today. Category A prisoners are those 'whose escape would be highly dangerous to the public or police or to the security of the state' and whilst Mountbatten thought that such prisoners would probably number no more than 120, a recent estimate puts the current figure at some 700 (Morgan, 2002: 1143). Category D prisoners are those 'who could be trusted under open conditions' (Home Office, 1966). Category B and C prisoners are those held in closed conditions providing more or less security. Trial and remand prisoners are, with the exceptions of those provisionally categorized as A, all assumed to be Category B.

The allocation of sentenced Category A prisoners has been the subject of a long-running controversy. Mountbatten called for the concentration of all Category A prisoners into one single-purpose maximum security fortress that would not only ensure that high-risk prisoners were to be kept in secure surroundings but that security could be relaxed in other regimes. This proposal was quickly rejected on the basis that concentrating all high-risk prisoners within a single fortress would mean that maintaining order and providing a constructive regime would be near impossible in a prison composed of 'no-hopers'. Instead a policy of 'dispersal' was adopted, in that maximum security prisoners should be spread around amongst a few high-security prisons. There are currently five dispersal prisons plus a further five that have high-security arrangements and it is becoming increasingly common for institutions to have multiple functions. For instance, although Strangeways is a local prison at the time of the disturbance it had, for many years, not only held remand and convicted adult male prisoners but also convicted young offenders on separate wings in the institution. The more recent penal history will be discussed in greater detail in Chapters 4 and 5, so that an outline of prison unrest can now be sketched followed by a discussion of Woolf's influential examination of the disturbances and concluding with an overview of the substantive content of the book.

Prison Protest in Historical Context

It is important to recognise that the siege at Strangeways prison in April 1990 was no isolated event. Over 20 institutions experienced some form of disturbance during that month. Moreover, as Sim (1991: 107–8), and other commentators have noted (Cavadino and Dignan, 1992: 18–19), the previous twenty years had hardly been incident free. Between October 1969 and June 1983 there were ten major disturbances in male, maximum security prisons. By the mid-1980s lower security institutions, remand centres and local prisons experienced widespread dissent, including 22 separate incidents on the evening of 30 April 1986. The causes of these were taken to be deficiencies in the quality of life for prisoners and deteriorating relationships between staff and prisoners wrought by industrial unrest. Indeed in the year prior to Strangeways, Risley remand centre (which had earned the reputation of being known as 'grisly Risley') erupted in May 1989 and the 'rioters' were subsequently acquitted by jury on the grounds that '"reasonable men" might have acted likewise' (Sparks, 1993: 179). Of course, in the years following Strangeways, riots have continued to be a recurring feature across the penal landscape, such as at Wymott – a Category C prison, in September 1993; Everthorpe – a Category C prison, in January 1995; Full Sutton – a dispersal prison, in January 1997 and April 1998; Portland Young Offenders Institution in May 2000, and at Lincoln, a local prison, in October 2002.

It is equally the case that since the birth of the modern prison, prisoners have been involved in riots. For instance, the first recorded prison riot in the United States took place in 1774 in a prison that had been built in 1773 over an abandoned copper mine in Simsbury, Connecticut and it has been estimated that over 1,300 riots occurred in American correctional institutions in the twentieth century. To make sense of the sheer volume of these events, Robert Adams (1992) has distinguished the following four phases in the history of prison riots in Britain and the USA. The four phases are best regarded as terms of convenience rather than an exact characterisation (Sparks, 1993: 178), as there are many riots that do not neatly fit the periodisation.

Traditional Riots

The riots of the nineteenth and early twentieth century were mainly impromptu mutinies by fugitive prisoners trying to escape the harsh conditions of their confinement in an era guided by the twin doctrines of religious reformation and hard labour (Adams, 1992: 41). Of course, the historical record here is especially mute as the experiences and motives of the rioters largely remain undocumented during this period. However, J.E. Thomas and Richard Pooley (1980: 5) have argued that when unrest did occur it 'was usually particular to an individual or group of individuals rather than anything approaching a wholesale uprising'. One exception was a major riot at Chatham convict prison in 1861.

> Chatham was often in trouble and was nicknamed the 'slaughterhouse' by the prisoners. The governor blamed the officers for incompetence and worse. Some had given newspapers to the prisoners, and the latter apparently believed that the officers would support them against the administration. The convicts were controlled at bayonet point, an escape plan was thwarted and the leader of the riot removed. (Thomas and Pooley, 1980: 5)

Nevertheless, Thomas and Pooley (1980: 5) maintain that such events were rare and it was not until 1932 that England 'had its first experience of a full-scale riot'.

The Dartmoor prison mutiny of 1932 attracted more attention than any other event in British penal history up to the 1960s. The riot began on the parade ground and once the prisoners had gained control those who tried to escape were met with gunfire as they appeared on the walls (guns were used at Dartmoor until 1954). Even though two prisoners were hit, none was killed. Staff and police squads shortly drove the prisoners back into their cells – with the whole riot only lasting a few hours (Thomas and Pooley, 1980: 5). Although the riot came as a considerable shock to those who ran the system, Adams (1992: 115) argues that 'its character as an isolated incident associated with an escape attempt which went wrong, in which the grievances of prisoners were to be inferred rather than spelt out and communicated to non-rioters either inside or outside the prison, meant that it had more in common with traditional riots'.

Riots against Conditions

The ascendancy of the rehabilitative ideal from the turn of the twentieth century up to the early 1960s provides a rather different context in which prison unrest occurred. The major wave of prison riots that swept across the United States from April 1952 (over 40 during an 18-month period) was more than had taken place in the previous 25 years, and is significant in three key respects. First, the riots did not undermine faith in rehabilitation, as later ones would. In fact the disorder was taken as firm evidence that more resources should be allocated to the endeavour. Second, the rioters were viewed not as rational actors with legitimate grievances, but as insane thugs. One American penal expert explained that 'the ringleaders are reckless and unstable men ... of the type generally placed in the vague but convenient category of "psychopath"' (cited in Useem and Kimball, 1989: 10). Third, the riots of this period were largely spontaneous demonstrations over living conditions, challenging abuses of power and not the sources of power, both ideological and material, which the riots from the mid-1960s would come to target.

Similarly a wave of riots in more than half a dozen English prisons during 1961 'were noticeable for their peaceful nature although they were generally responded to with disciplinary charges rather than with attention to any expressed grievances about prison conditions' (Adams, 1992: 119–20). At the same time the Home Secretary announced plans to set up a wing at Brixton prison for up to 20 'chronically violent prisoners', for whom 'although discipline will be strict, every attempt will be made to give the regime a diagnostic and therapeutic bias', and insisted that the unit had no 'direct relationship with the recent incidents' (cited in Adams, 1992: 120). What is important about this development is that it clearly illustrates the continuing faith in the ability of rehabilitation to coerce a cure in wayward offenders.

Consciousness-raising Riots

The riots from the mid-1960s up to the mid-1970s possessed clearly defined political agendas with a pronounced dimension of collective action in a spirit of consciousness raising so that the links to be made between the oppressions they experienced inside and those of other groups in the urban ghettoes and the Third World could be made explicit. Moreover, prisoners engaged in such resistance during this period could rely on hitherto unknown levels of support beyond the walls as a result of the civil rights movement and rising expectations of social entitlements. For example, the 'Groupe d'Information sur les Prisons' (GIP) was set up in France in February 1971 on the initiative of Michel Foucault and other campaigners. Their activities included the organisation of demonstrations and meetings outside prisons in support of prisoners' struggles, particularly during the winter of 1971–72, when over 30 prison riots occurred in France.

That it was the general nature of power, rather than specific abuses which the riots of this era targeted, is made abundantly clear in the Folsom Prison riot of 1970. Prisoners produced a 'Manifesto of Demands and Anti-Oppression Platform', which announced that it 'is a matter of documented record and human recognition that the administrators of the Californian prison system have restructured the institutions which were designed to socially correct men into *THE FASCIST CONCENTRATION CAMPS OF MODERN AMERICA*' (emphasis in original, cited in Fitzgerald, 1977: 203). The Folsom demands later provided the blueprint for those advanced a year later at the Attica riot, which would produce the slogan 'The Solution is Unity'. In Britain the early 1970s were especially noteworthy for the birth of a radical prisoners' movement that successfully organised large scale protests in prisons around the country and the characterisation of prison unrest as part of a wider crisis in public order (Adams, 1992: 126). The more general public order crisis gained currency from an increasingly divided Britain that saw a number of challenges to the state's authority over this period – ranging from the conflict in Northern Ireland, escalating student protests, increasing trade union militancy and burgeoning social movements struggling for gay rights, women's liberation and racial equality.

Post-rehabilitation Riots

From the mid-1970s the strangest of alliances emerged amongst disenchanted liberals, a revitalised New Right and radical prisoners' movements each mounting attacks against the soft machine of rehabilitation. The collapse of this ideal has led to a fragmentation of penal discourse and its associated form of opposition. For Adams (1992: 42–5) the shift has been from riots based on collective activity to those based on self-interest and predatory individualism in the last quarter of the twentieth century. Although this characterisation is open to dispute, as there are riots that disobey such a discrete and coherent periodisation, the paradox is nevertheless illustrated by the two most infamous prison riots in US history. The riot at Attica in 1971 was widely regarded as a political struggle against oppression, racism and injustice, whereas the riot at the Penitentiary of New Mexico in 1980 stands in stark contrast as an indication of the 'Balkanisation' of prisoner society. In the British context there is nothing approximating the level of bloodletting, either by the authorities or the prisoners, witnessed at these events. Nevertheless, attention can be drawn to the collective sit-ins organised by PROP ('Preservation of the Rights of Prisoners' – a radical prisoners movement) in the early 1970s, which will be covered in more detail in Chapter 4, and the riot at Strangeways in 1990 that signalled a fragmented and individualised set of responses to the experience of incarceration that illustrates the changing and diverse character of prison unrest, which will now be briefly outlined.

The riot began on 1 April in the chapel of the prison where 309 prisoners were attending a Church of England service that morning and soon spread to most of the prison once the skeletal staff had retreated. Among the 1,600 prisoners remaining in the prison there was one group who were in serious danger. These were the 97 prisoners separated from other prisoners for their own protection under Rule 43 of the Prison Rules and who were either perceived to be guilty of committing serious sexual offences ('nonces') or were considered to have informed to the police or prison authorities ('grasses'). These vulnerable prisoners now had no protection. The following day press reports and broadcast bulletins suggested that between 12 and 20 prisoners had been horrifically murdered and many more gruesomely tortured. While these reports were subsequently found to be untrue, there is no doubt that alleged sex offenders, informers and a former police officer were viciously beaten over these first few hours. By the early morning of 2 April most of the prisoners who did not want to continue had evacuated the prison leaving some 140 prisoners behind to strengthen their position.

In the meantime the governor and his staff developed a plan to recapture the prison later that day. The plan was put to the Deputy Director General at prison service headquarters in London. Controversially he vetoed the plan as he thought staff might die in the assault and experience suggested that the prisoners would give up shortly as they had done in previous uprisings. This was not to happen. Prisoners occupied Strangeways for the next 23 days and their rooftop protest became a global media event. As the days passed prisoners gradually evacuated so that when an operation to retake the prison was launched on 25 April, involving over a hundred staff, there were only five prisoners remaining on the roof. Overall, 147 prison staff were injured during the riot. One prisoner who had received injuries subsequently died. Forty-seven other prisoners were injured. The cost of the damage to the prison was estimated to be £60 million. A series of trials took place in 1992 and 1993 with 23 prisoners receiving long sentences, some of up to ten years, for offences such as riot and conspiracy to commit grievous bodily harm. In many ways the riot was a watershed in penal history. As Vivien Stern (1993: 252) recalls, April 1990 was a 'dangerous moment' for penal reform as:

> there were conflicting pressures. Some people felt the right response would be a crack-down, greater control, more security technology, better riot gear for prison staff, no more occasions when over three hundred prisoners gathered together with fourteen staff in charge. Many felt that law, order and authority had been mocked by the spectacle of prisoners on the roof performing for the cameras of the world. Respect for authority needed to be reasserted.

In an effort to regain credibility and appease liberal opinion the Home Office took the unusual decision of setting up a judicial inquiry five days into the riot.

The Woolf Diagnosis

The announcement on 6 April 1990, by the Home Secretary, David Waddington, that there was to be an independent public inquiry under the chairmanship of Lord Justice Woolf[3] into the events at Strangeways, marked a substantial departure from previous Home Office responses to prisoner unrest: for instance, an in-house investigation without the publication of a full report[4] or delegated to the Prison Inspectorate[5] (though the then Chief Inspector of Prisons, Judge Tumim, joined the second stage of the Inquiry and co-authored Part II of the report with Woolf). Nevertheless, it is clear that the central reason a full and open Inquiry, independent of the Home Office, was deemed necessary was that:

> the events at Strangeways had become so public that only a high profile response on the part of ministers could hope to assuage public anxiety and restore the Government's credibility as an administration committed to law and order. (Player and Jenkins, 1994: 3)

The Judicial Inquiry was charged with open ended terms of reference 'to inquire into the events ... and the action taken to bring it to a conclusion' (Morgan, 1992: 232) at the six disturbances chosen for investigation, which were Strangeways (1 April to 25 April), Glen Parva (6 April to 8 April), Dartmoor (7 April to 8 April), Cardiff (8 April), Bristol (8 April to 9 April), and Pucklechurch (22 April to 23 April). These incidents were the most serious; however discontent was widespread throughout April – in all there was trouble at eighteen prisons that month.

A number of strategies were pursued in order to make the Inquiry open to the public and promote wide scale consultation. These included public hearings and seminars, requests for submissions from individuals and organisations with expertise and experience of prisons, and visiting prisons in the United Kingdom and other countries. It also sought the views of prisoners and staff on what caused and happened during the events, and what action should be taken to prevent such disturbances happening again. This last strategy is to be particularly welcomed, but this evidence is presented in an annexed summary and attends to highlighting general reasons for prison unrest, rather than the specific causes within the individual prisons. This is a serious omission and needs consideration in explaining prison disorder, particularly when the Report stressed the significance of the perception of justice.

There is a missing link to account for why the disturbances happened where they did, which is a problem of *specificity* that this book will be especially concerned with. A number of other commentators (Adams, 1992; Ryan, 1992) have also noted the leap in emphasis in the report from the meticulous detailing of events in Part I to broad causes and recommendations relating to how prisons can be improved in Part II. These relate to a package of measures designed to reduce overcrowding through the promotion of alternatives to custody, and improve conditions through the introduction of 'community prisons' and contracts at all levels of the Prison Service. It would be diversionary here to enter debates regarding the efficacy of the Woolf recommendations (for further commentary and discussion on the prospects of the Woolf agenda, see R. Morgan, 1991, 1992; Ryan, 1992; Player and Jenkins, 1994) or the twin track approach to implementing the proposals (Home Office, 1991) in which the measures to improve security and control were prioritised and the introduction of a new offence, prison mutiny, can be read as part of a strategy to reinforce the law and order credentials of the then Conservative government, whilst the subsequent embarrassingly high profile security lapses of 1994–95 (at Whitemoor and Parkhurst), Michael Howard's regressive proclamation that 'Prison Works' and the spiralling prison population throughout the 1990s have served to knock Woolf's reformist agenda further off course in a political climate of 'populist punitiveness' (Bottoms, 1994). Instead the focus here is geared toward an examination of what Woolf took to be the causes of the unrest.

It should be stressed that no single cause was advanced. Rather, the balance and level of three interrelated elements: *security*, *control* and *justice* are seen to be crucial in the maintenance of order. This is stated in unequivocal terms:

> The April (1990) riots occurred because these three elements were out of balance. There were failures in the maintenance of control. There were failures to achieve the necessary standards of justice. There could easily have been a collapse in security. (Woolf and Tumim, 1991: 17)

The term *security* refers to the obligation of the prison service to prevent prisoners escaping and *control* implies order and the prevention of disturbances. However, it is the stress on *justice* that heralds the importance of the Woolf diagnosis. As R. Morgan (1992: 233) suggests, this term invokes many meanings, which should have been set out in a more systematic manner. For instance, it incorporates fairness and due process in decision-making; maintaining standards of care in line with prison rules 1 and 2;[6] and the subjective interpretation by the prisoners of their situation that can engender grievances. In Woolf's view there has been an overemphasis on security, inappropriate control measures and insufficient weight given to justice. In addition the right balance and level between the three can only be achieved by fundamental changes in the way the prison service structures its relations, both between management and staff, and between staff and prisoners. Some of the proposals and recommendations are orientated towards ensuring that these relations are based on respect and responsibility, such as reforms of grievance and disciplinary procedures and improved training for officers (see Ryan, 1992, for a discussion of the difficulties involved in this).

The central finding is that the prison system must meet the three requirements of security, control and justice if stability is to be achieved. It is clear that the Inquiry regarded justice of paramount importance in the prisoners' interpretation of their situation, 'the Prison Service had *failed* to persuade these prisoners that it was treating them fairly' (Woolf and Tumim, 1991: 226, emphasis in original). A sense of injustice is, in other words, a lack of legitimacy that can make disorder in prisons all the more likely to occur. The report marks a shift (the extent of which is open to debate) in the manner in which prison riots are conceptualised from previous orthodox explanations in the British context through stressing the importance of justice in maintaining order.

In essence, Woolf's verdict (Woolf and Tumim, 1991: 42, paras 3.7 to 3.9) is that a 'combination of errors by the Headquarters of the Prison Service, and the management and staff at Strangeways' led to the riot. It 'could and should have been avoided ... confined to only part of the prison' and 'could and should have been brought to an end long before 25 April 1990'. Yet there is also the acknowledgement that the scale of the disturbance cannot solely be confined to management errors – even if the appropriate measures had been undertaken to prevent the disturbance on 1 April, this would probably only have led to a postponement of the action due to the intolerable conditions that prisoners were placed under.

Organisation of the Book

The problem of specificity identified in the Woolf diagnosis is a direct consequence of the Report's failure to think through the relationships between human agency, institutional history and social structure. Of course, this oversight is not simply restricted to Woolf and is common within the sociology of imprisonment. The next chapter discusses this literature in terms of an analytical division between the internal dynamics within a particular institution and the external functions of imprisonment. Many of the texts considered here are classics in the field and the intention is to indicate the ways in which they illuminate certain aspects of imprisonment whilst obscuring others. This discussion is then grounded in debates which address the macro–micro issue in social theory and uses these attempts at resolution as resources in the subsequent genealogy of the Strangeways prison riot.

The argument will be that a synthesis of structuration theory and discourse analysis can enable the diversity of interactions within prisons to be connected to broader strategies of control. A range of discourses on imprisonment will be discussed in this chapter to demonstrate that penal systems are a composite of diverse forces, techniques and rationalities that seek to regulate the conduct of individuals and groups in relation to certain authoritative criteria. These criteria, and the ability to *act*, are performed through discourse. The concept of discourse is developed in the book to explain how connections can be made between micro-levels of interaction and macro-structures of governance so that a more nuanced understanding of institutional power and social order can be reached and the problem of specificity directly addressed.

The third chapter critically assesses the two main theoretical perspectives on collective protest, which are social disorganisation and relative deprivation and discusses how these approaches have been applied to prison unrest. Particular attention is then paid to Bert Useem and Peter Kimball's (1989) examination of nine prison riots in the United States as it provides a fresh understanding of prison disorder through introducing the issue of legitimacy as crucial to structuring institutional stability. Their argument is that well managed prisons generate conformity, whereas breakdowns in administrative control render imprisonment illegitimate in the eyes of the confined. This study clearly anticipates Woolf's conclusion that the 25-day occupation of Strangeways was due to widely shared feelings of injustice and the explicit argument is that there are variable conditions under which the confined accept or reject custodial authority (Woolf and Tumim, 1991).

However, there are three important limitations in their respective analyses. First, there is a problematic assumption that a sharp distinction can be drawn between 'normal' and 'pathological' prisons. Second, they yield an 'embarrassment of riches' in that there ought to be far more collective disorder than there actually is if their analysis is accepted as broadly correct. Third, in common with other accounts of disorder they succumb to *ex post facto* (retrospective or after the fact) forms of rationalisation that involve correcting the past to make it consistent with the present. It is for these reasons that an alternative genealogical analysis is developed that owes much to Matza's (1964) concept of drift and the seductions of transgression (Katz, 1988). In doing so the book sets out to advance a fresh understanding of prison disorder through defining the limits of orthodox thinking.

The following two chapters are mainly concerned with defining the key concepts of power, discourse, resistance and genealogy that are central to the book whereas Chapter 4 details the condition of imprisonment in a national context so that the reader is introduced to the enduring difficulties faced by the penal system over the last few decades, which is composed of several interweaving components that compromise not only the ability of the state to maintain order but also challenge moral sensibilities on what the purposes of imprisonment might, or ought to, be. In other words, the severe problems in prisons that are the subject of this chapter are as much moral and philosophical matters as practical and material ones.

The second half of the book begins with a discussion of the sources and methods used in the analysis of the Strangeways prison protest. The sources are diverse and include qualitative interviews, documentary materials and official statistics, which taken together permit a detailed institutional portrait to be drawn in Chapter 5 from 1965. There are a number of crucial reasons for taking this historical trajectory – not least because the period 1965 to 1990 covers an important period in the techniques of regulation practised in many countries in the West. On both sides of the Atlantic, the corporate-liberal consensus associated with the long wave of economic expansion and social integration from the postwar period up to the mid-1970s gave way to more coercive and repressive strategies of control directed toward controlling marginal populations. The relentless expansion of the prison system, and the criminal justice system more generally, has been understood as a project of 'regressive modernization' (Hall, 1988).

For some commentators prison building programmes, privatisation, electronic tagging, increasingly repressive changes to sentencing and parole policies are taken as evidence of both the intensifying punitive obsession and the orchestration of consent in civil society through authoritarian programmes that have broad symbolic appeal in the popular consciousness (see Scraton et al., 1991: 158–9; Ryan and Sim, 1998: 202). But the most important reason for charting organisational change is to understand how power is translated in a particular locale over an extended period of time. This is at some distance from the account provided in Woolf, which focuses on the three months before the riot. Consequently his analysis tends to emphasise the exceptional characteristics of the prison, whereas a longer examination of the discourses governing interactions in Strangeways illustrates the important fact that these were rather more matters of routine, and despite the institution's ominous name, it was a 'normal', rather than a 'pathological' prison.

Chapter 6 provides an account of the drift to the events of April 1990 and concludes with a discussion of the initiation of the protest in the Church of England chapel service on Sunday 1 April. The concept of 'drift' is used in the book to emphasise the improvised, provisional and contingent nature of social order. In particular it illuminates the strictures of the genealogical method, for as Hoy (1986: 224) succinctly puts it, 'there is no essence or original unity to be discovered. When genealogy looks to beginnings, it looks for accidents, chance, passion, petty malice, surprises, feverish agitation, unsteady victories and power'. Chapter 7 describes the expansion of the disturbance and the following siege, which lasted for 25 days. The main reason why the disturbance lasted this long is to be explained by the reactions of the authorities to the protest, rather than the activities of the remaining prisoners.

The final chapter draws out the implications of the analysis for an understanding of power and resistance. In doing so one of the central conclusions to be drawn is that prisons generate diverse forms of social order in spite of illegitimate distributions of power and consequently the overlooked contribution that fatalism makes to the maintenance of order in prisons is examined in some detail. There then follows a consideration of the distinctive qualities that the genealogical analysis undertaken in this book offers through addressing the issues of necessity and contingency in historical interpretation and concludes with some comments on the importance of understanding prisons as gendered organisations. The overall argument of the book is geared toward understanding the complexities of prison life and revealing why prison riots do not happen more often.

Notes

1   In official parlance it is referred to as HM Prison Manchester, though it is more commonly known as Strangeways – the name of the inner city district where the institution is located.

2   Although the report was co-authored by the then HM Chief Inspector of Prisons, Judge Tumim (who joined the Inquiry at a later stage) it is conventionally referred to as 'Woolf' in the singular for reasons of brevity rather than denying the Judge's place in penal history.

3   A High Court Judge with a record of judgments against government abuse and administrative powers (Fielding and Fowles, 1990: 283).
4   As on the occasions of the disturbances at Haverigg and Lindholme in 1988, and Risley in 1989.
5   This was the response to the series of disturbances (29 April to 2 May) in 1986.
6   Prison Rules 1964, S.I. No. 1988, as amended: Rule 1 provides that the purpose of training and treatment of prisoners is 'to encourage and assist them to lead a good and useful life'; Rule 2 (3) provides that 'at all times prisoners must be treated so as to enhance their self respect and sense of personal responsibility' (cited in R. Morgan, 1992: 247).

Chapter 2

Prison Sociology and Social Theory

Introduction

The sociology of imprisonment can be characterised as a field of inquiry marked by a range of disparate and largely unconnected studies of particular aspects of imprisonment, and more generally punishment. The sense of disconnection emanates, in part, from the diverse array of intellectual traditions drawn upon and is indicative of the inherent complexity of imprisonment as a social phenomenon. In order to make sense of this literature it is instructive to distinguish two fairly discrete and discontinuous research traditions. One body of inquiry is microsociological in orientation with a focus on the internal dynamics of a particular institution and reveals what the experiences of imprisonment are *like* for the keepers and the kept. In contrast the other tradition is more macrosociological in scope through attending to the external functions of imprisonment, and thereby illustrating what punishment is *for*.

Many of the classic monographs in the former microsociological field (for example, Clemmer, 1958; Sykes, 1958; Goffman, 1961; Mathiesen, 1965; Cohen and Taylor, 1981) have concentrated on particular prisons and, with varying degrees of success, have illuminated the day-to-day routines, struggles and accommodations within institutions. Recent accounts of this nature in England include those studies by Genders and Player (1995), King and McDermott (1995), Sparks et al. (1996) and Bosworth (1999). In many respects the early sociologies of imprisonment were obsessed with prisoner subcultures and drew their inspiration from the Chicago School.[1] Although the later work attends to a broader range of problematics and offers important readings of the literature, the action remains firmly centred on the dynamics of the particular prison(s) chosen for investigation. In contrast, macrosociology tends to dispense with detailed accounts of institutional life as it is lived, and prefers to indicate how penal practices are related to broader social processes, economic relations, political structures, historical formations and cultural sensibilities (e.g. Durkheim, 1983; Rusche and Kirchheimer, 1968; Foucault, 1977; Pashukanis, 1978). Whilst the central contributors in this trajectory of thought differ widely in their interpretations, they each shed light on the different roles that punishment performs in society. For example, while

Durkheim emphasises the sentiment-based, morality-affirming and solidarity-producing functions of punishment, Foucault depicts the disciplinary principles of incarceration implicated in processes of domination and subjectification that stretch far beyond prison walls.

The argument in this book is that the question of what prisons are like cannot be separated from an examination of what imprisonment might be for, at any given historical point, and this chapter is directed toward reconciling these two levels of sociological analysis through the resources of social theory. However, I cannot claim to be the first to have noticed this division, and it would be quite wrong to argue that the recent literature on imprisonment is unaware of the significance of these questions. For instance, Sparks et al. (1996) discuss the literature on the microsociology of prison life, the macrosociology of penal change, and Foucault's examination of the technologies of disciplinary power as important elements in forging an understanding of how order is achieved under conditions of confinement. The authors seem implicitly to accept that there is a worrying division of labour in prison sociology as they turn to Giddens' (1976, 1979, 1984) structuration theory to make sense of the structural and systemic dimensions of order and disorder in prisons 'and their contingent, local occurrence in specific times and places between real people' (Sparks et al., 1996: 69). Although their work attempts to situate the study of prisons in relation to broader concerns in social theory and thereby refresh the tradition, it fails to acknowledge that there are a number of failings in structuration theory. In particular whilst it can yield sophisticated understandings of agency (which is acknowledged below) Sparks et al. (1996) pass over the fact that a conceptual apparatus to deal with more macrosociological issues, such as already existing objective relations of domination and subordinations is absent in structuration theory. The problem is that in Giddens' work these relations are characterised as a practical accomplishment instantiated by actors and consequently, they cannot possess any enduring structure. In his opposition to deterministic approaches that marginalise human agency, Giddens has succeeded in marginalising serious considerations of objective power relations – a shortcoming that is reproduced in Sparks et al.'s (1996) text.

Nevertheless, Sparks et al.'s (1996) study of order in two English maximum security prisons is a key text, not least as it develops Woolf's (1991) insights on legitimacy in a sophisticated fashion and will be returned to below and throughout the book. In these opening remarks comment is restricted to those sociological accounts that attempt to reconcile detailed accounts of prison life with a broader understanding of penal change and continuity. In this context

James Jacobs' (1977) *Stateville*, which charts the transformation of the Illinois prison from a patriarchal organisation driven by charismatic authority to a bureaucratic institution based on rational-legal authority over a 50-year period (1925–75), was the first explicit attempt to combine micro and macrosociology through a detailed institutional analysis. As he put it, he wanted to plot 'the changing relationship of the prison with the larger society and ... [show] how the changing relationship of the prison with the larger society is reflected in the changing patterns of authority within the prison' (Jacobs, 1977: 2). This classic of prison sociology is largely indebted to Max Weber's (1968a and 1968b) influential depiction of the sources of domination in society, which are based on charismatic, traditional and rational-legal types of authority. In Jacobs (1977) the essential shift is from structures of authority based on personal dominance (in the charismatic guise of Warden Joseph Ragen) to a corporatist bureaucratic organisation by the mid-1970s. The internal dynamics of the prison reflect, and are influenced by, broader changes occurring in society, which includes changes in political dominance, the rise of the civil rights movement, as well as transformations in the inmate population (such as the prominence of Chicago street gangs in the 1970s) and transitions in the guard force.

Although his analysis is highly suggestive, and a number of his themes will be developed in this book, such as historically charting organisational change, extending the notion of structures of authority and drawing together micro and macro levels of analysis, there are two problems that arise from his approach to the latter problem. The first is that while the trend at Stateville was toward an 'ever-increasing bureaucratization' (Jacobs, 1977: 11) there is no possibility of an alternative in his account. Consequently, the conceptual work that follows in this chapter can be read as a way of extending his Weberian understanding of structures of authority through a more nuanced account of penal power. The second problem arises from his reliance on Shills' (1975) 'mass society' thesis in charting macrosociological change. This contends that there is an emerging social consensus, based on processes of incorporation and the expansion of citizenship rights to integrate the 'masses' into the dominant value system. The recognition and granting of rights to prisoners and the construction of legal forms of accountability over prison administrators are understood by Jacobs (1977) as particular instances of this trend. This corporate-liberal rationality can be readily associated with the long wave of economic expansion from the postwar period up to the mid-1970s, and in the formulation of specific solutions to the social problems of poverty and crime in the United States. Whilst this characterisation may well have held at the time when Jacobs (1977:

6) was writing, his depiction of 'a heightened sensitivity on the part of the elite to the dignity and humanity of the masses' as the inspiration for such liberal responses to social distress now seems at best misguided. However, the more fundamental point is that Jacobs (1977) was not in a position, neither historically nor theoretically, to anticipate the 'Great Moving Right Show' (see for example, Hall and Jacques, 1983) from the late 1970s. Consequently, the task of this chapter is to advance a conceptual framework that can account for how imprisonment is experienced in particular places without losing sight of the crucial question of what functions incarceration might be performing in broader social formations.

The Macro–Micro Issue in Social Theory

The above discussion pointed to an analytical division of labour between those studies that focus on the internal dynamics of an institution, as opposed to an emphasis on the external functions of imprisonment. This dualism in effect mirrors the macro–micro issue in social theory. The problem, in essence, revolves around the question of how the micro features of existence, such as face-to-face interactions, daily routines, and self-identity are related and connected to macro features of society, such as organisations, unequal distributions of power and resources. At stake is the extent to which the macro features of society determine the agency of human beings, and what are the limits (if any) on human agency.

It could be argued that the division of analytical focus reflects two entirely different domains of social reality, which are independent of each other. It is here that both theoretical and empirical objections should be raised. For instance, it denies the ability of human beings to make a difference to the set of social arrangements in which they find themselves. However, it is more instructive to view the issue in terms of connection, in terms of how the two are related. As Wright Mills (1959: 3) put it, 'neither the life of an individual nor the history of a society can be understood without understanding both'. At stake then, is the relationship between history and biography, which restates Marx's (1963: 15) celebrated assertion that '[m]en make their own history, but they do not make it just as they please; they do not make it under circumstances chosen by themselves, but under circumstances directly encountered, given and transmitted from the past'.

It is important to recognise that the macro–micro issue is the most inclusive of the dualisms in the social sciences as it encompasses the divisions between the individual and society; the objective and the subjective; and the relationships between human agency and social structure. For instance, in the microsociology of prison life attention can be drawn to the structural functionalism of Sykes (1958) as opposed to the phenomenology of Cohen and Taylor (1981). The former subscribed to an objective understanding of the world and argued that the structure and function of prisoner subculture serves to preserve solidarity and acts as a defence against the pains of imprisonment.[2] The latter, however, consciously sought to provide a more subjective interpretation as the traditional studies of the prison had failed to do justice 'to the full psychological effects of imprisonment by concentrating upon the prison as a social system or by merely describing the typical roles played in the prison community' (Cohen and Taylor, 1981: 41–2). Yet the focus, in both accounts, remains on how prisoners adapt to or cope with confinement, hence my preference is for locating the problem in terms of the more inclusive macro–micro issue that incorporates such issues as what might count as a convincing explanation of human action, social structure and institutional analysis.

The individual–society distinction represents the oldest and most basic form of dualism which has received extensive criticism for its 'tendency to see individuals as if they were completely separated from social influences' (Layder, 1994: 3). The agency–structure issue concentrates on the way in which human beings both create social life and, at the same time, the extent to which they are constrained by or remould existing social arrangements. The defining preoccupation is with the connection between human activity and social contexts. On the other hand, the macro–micro distinction is rather more concerned with:

> the level and scale of analysis and the research focus ... it distinguishes between a primary concentration on the analysis of face-to-face conduct (everyday activities, the routines of social life), as against a primary concentration on the larger scale, more impersonal macro phenomena like institutions and the distribution of power and resources. (Layder, 1994: 5)

It is clear that the sociology of imprisonment reflects this distinction, as there are studies that focus on the internal dynamics of an institution, as opposed to an extended consideration of the broader functions of imprisonment. Though most recent writers on the prison contend that both features are intertwined and dependent on each other, it is my intention to make this connection explicit. In prison sociology the most influential has been Giddens' structuration theory that has informed, amongst others, Sparks et al.'s (1996), Jewkes' (2002) and Edgar et al.'s (2003) analyses of prison life.

Agency and Structuration

Anthony Giddens' (1976, 1979, 1984) structuration theory directly addresses the agency–structure distinction through insisting that what 'is at issue is how the concepts of action, meaning and subjectivity should be specified and how they might relate to notions of structure and constraint' (Giddens, 1984: 2). The theory attempts to overcome dualistic approaches to social investigation through putting forward the notion of the 'duality of structure', which refers to his proposition that structure and agency are two sides of the same coin. Social structures are both constituted by human agency, and are at the same time the medium of this constitution. When enquiring into the structuration of social practices explanation is sought in terms of how structures are constituted in and through action, and reciprocally how action is constituted structurally. Thus structures not only constrain, they also enable agency, in which a sharp differentiation is drawn between the terms 'structure' and 'system'. 'Social system' refers to the surface patterns of interaction, whilst 'structure' refers to the 'virtual order' of generative rules and resources that individuals draw upon, yet also change, in their production and reproduction of society.

Where elements of this theory have underpinned studies of imprisonment the emphasis has been on human subjects as knowledgeable agents; the significance of 'practical consciousness'; the importance of 'routines' in managing day-to-day activity; and the 'dialectic of control' in the patterning of social relations. Giddens' understanding of routines, as Bottoms and Sparks (1995) recognise, is particularly relevant for understanding imprisonment. The repetitiveness of activities provides 'mechanisms whereby a sense of trust or ontological security is sustained' (Giddens, 1984: xxiii) and the means by which the structured properties of social life are reproduced and maintained. The phrase ontological security refers to 'the confidence that most human beings have in the continuity of their self-identity and in the constancy of the surrounding social and material environments of action' (Giddens, 1990: 92). These particular concepts, such as ontological security, the importance of routines, practical consciousness, and the dialectic of control, are highly relevant to understanding imprisonment and will be returned to later in this chapter.

Yet, in terms of resolving the agency–structure issue it can be argued that Giddens' thesis lies in the subjective domain of comprehension. This can be made clear with reference to his conception of power which he defines as:

> an integral element of all social life ... this is the significance of the claim that structure can only be analyzed as rules and resources, resources being drawn

upon in the constitution of power relations. All social interaction involves the use of power, as a necessary implication of the logical connection between human action and transformative capacity. Power within social systems can be analyzed as relations of autonomy and dependence between actors in which these actors draw upon and reproduce structural properties of domination. (Giddens, 1981: 28–9)

Barbalet (1987: 9) and Layder (1985: 142) have noted that as a result of Giddens' subjectivist understanding, the depiction of power as a 'transformative capacity' is too tightly coupled to agency, at the expense of a more structural conception of power expressed through already existing objective relations of domination and subordination. In Giddens, structure is understood as a practical accomplishment instantiated by actors. However, as Clegg (1989: 145) observes, 'structures which exist only in conditions where individuals instantiate them are not structures at all: they do not display any enduring relations'. In other words, Giddens has not resolved the agency–structure issue since in his opposition to determinism he has succeeded in effacing serious considerations of objective structure. Whilst Dyrberg (1997: 6) states, quite simply, that the 'problem does not disappear by arguing that structure instead of constraining action also facilitates it'. Nevertheless, the importance of Giddens' work is that it provides a number of concepts that can usefully be employed in the understanding of agency in prisons, and this will be applied in subsequent chapters. It is clear though that for an understanding of structure further conceptual work needs to be undertaken, especially in relation to the diverse forms of power that can be identified.

The Elementary Forms of Power

In Scott's (2001) wide-ranging account of power he usefully distinguishes between two influential traditions, what he terms the 'mainstream' and 'second-stream' that each highlight different aspects of the central features of power. The mainstream has tended to concentrate on the *corrective* forms of state power, whereas the second-stream has emphasised the significance of *persuasive* influence. The mainstream tradition originates in Thomas Hobbes' ruminations in *Leviathan*, written in the aftermath of the English Civil War, where he insisted on the necessity of the state apparatus to regulate the essentially antisocial tendencies of the sovereign's subjects. Max Weber provides the classic analysis of the structuring of authority in modern and pre-modern states through the varying abilities of actors to secure the compliance of others. This corrective understanding of power was subsequently developed in a positivist direction by Dahl (1957, 1961), who maintained that power should be observed in visible instances of concrete decision-making, and initiated an influential debate around 'community power' that led others to argue that there is a whole second face to power that actually prevented issues from reaching the political agenda through processes like 'non-decision-making' (Bachrach and Baratz, 1962).

The mainstream tradition culminates in Lukes' (1974) three dimensions of power and reaches a hiatus in Marxist contemplations on false consciousness – in which the operation of power is held to be so total, pervasive and prohibitive as to mystify the thoughts and actions of those caught within its locus. This tendency confirms a view of power as monolithic and repressive and presents a binary class opposition between those who dominate and the oppressed, which effectively reaches an impasse with Abercrombie et al.'s (1980) critique of the dominant ideology thesis.

The persuasive form of power associated with the second stream of writing is not as well defined as the mainstream, yet it nevertheless has provided important insights into the limitations of orthodox treatments of power. The starting point for this alternative approach can be traced back to Machiavelli's uncompromising, practical advice to 'The Prince' over how to secure order amidst the instability, rivalry and war between sixteenth-century Italian city-states as it emphasises the strategic, contingent and diffused nature of power. Gramsci (1971) is a central figure in the development of this stream through his concept of hegemony that highlights the mechanisms by which a dominant class can secure the consent of subaltern classes without recourse to the direct use of coercion, while Foucault (1977) decentres and disperses the question of power further through arguing that it has no privileged origin emanating from a sovereign nor is it the possession of a dominant class as it diffused throughout the social sphere.

Writing from a very different theoretical vantage point, Arendt (1959) argued that power relations are formed through communicative actions, which include speech acts and shared symbols that enable political communities to coordinate actions, realise collective capacities and overcome conflict through signifying practices. Habermas (1984, 1987a) builds on this consensual understanding in his theory of communicative action that points to how collective decisions are not only produced but are also legitimated. Although these are the broad contours of thinking on power, it does not necessarily follow that only one position is tenable or that they are equally suitable in every instance, which would result in a superficial synthesis of incongruent ideas. Instead, it is important to recognise that each of these approaches has highlighted different aspects of power that, in varying ways, structure practice.

Further analytical distinctions can be made as corrective influence can involve force and manipulation, whereas persuasive influence operates through forms of signification and legitimation as it causes 'subalterns to believe that it is appropriate to act in one way rather than another' (Scott, 2001: 14). The fundamental elements of power can be summarised as force, manipulation, signification and legitimation, which combine in different and variable ways so as to give rise to concrete patterns of domination and resistance. Much prison sociology, influenced by Sykes (1958), has been especially concerned with the corrective dimensions of power – in particular how the naked use of force is rarely relied on in prisons but that ordinarily authorities manipulate order through informal systems of power sharing with prisoners. More recent work, in particular Sparks et al.'s (1996) account of order in prisons, develops the issue of legitimacy in a far more robust manner than has hitherto been attempted, which will be returned to in the following chapter. However, little attention has been given to the signification of power in prison sociology and it is this absence that the remainder of this chapter will be preoccupied with through first outlining a framework that can grasp these elementary forms of power and then detailing the relationships between discourse theory and social practice so that the variable ways in which coercion, expediency, consent and resistance combine in concrete settings can be articulated in the chapters that follow.

Translation and Governmentality

In order to develop an analytical framework that can encompass these elementary forms of power the literature that has developed in the sociology of science and technology and recent, Foucauldian inspired analyses of 'governmentality', to the practices of imprisonment will be outlined.[3] The former work tends to focus on technological innovations and scientific controversies, and has developed an approach known as a 'sociology of translation' or, as it is sometimes referred to, 'actor-network theory' (some key statements would include Callon and Latour, 1981; Latour, 1986; Callon, 1986; Callon et al., 1986; Law, 1994; Latour, 1994). The preference here is for the term translation, as it implies transformations, deformations and dislocations, whereas an actor-network suggests a system that is static, transparent and unmediated.[4] Nevertheless, the importance of this perspective is that it explicitly addresses the macro–micro issue and articulates the fundamental problem involved in analytical bracketing, for we 'should miss the point completely, if we distinguish between "individuals" and "institutions" if we supposed that the first fell within the sphere of psychology, and the second of economic history' (Callon and Latour, 1981: 279). The approach does not imply that there are no powerful actors, but rather that the focus must be on how power relations are constructed and maintained.

The argument is based on the crucial principle of symmetry – both the macro and micro should be approached from the same analytical perspective, rather than switching between 'psychology' and 'economic history' depending on the level of analysis as size is the consequence of struggle. The importance of the principle of symmetry is that it 'suggests that we might treat size as a product or an effect, rather than something given in the nature of things' (Law, 1994: 11). The alternative to this approach is to assume that the macro and micro are fundamentally different, which raises two significant problems. First, it prevents the analysis from examining how macro phenomena *become* macro and are able to *be* dominant. It obscures the fact that domination is a condition that is permanently worked at. Secondly, this division ultimately serves to denigrate micro situations of interactions as they do not address the 'big' questions relating to macro structures.

Such problems may be avoided only if it is accepted that size, inequality, domination and so forth are continually produced and worked at. This labour is captured by the notion of 'translation', which is defined as the way 'we understand all the negotiations, intrigues, calculations, acts of persuasion and violence, thanks to which an actor or force takes, or causes to be conferred on itself, authority to speak or act on behalf of another actor or force' (Callon and Latour, 1981: 279). As a result the relationship between power and structure is conceptualised and constituted in terms of networks, alliances, points of resistance, instability and relative durability. The methodological approach is a form of Machiavellian ethnography in that the interpreter has 'neither fear nor favour of what it is that actors do' (Callon et al., 1986: 5). These are important propositions and they have far-reaching implications. For example, the microsociology of prison life is profoundly *asymmetrical*. In practically every account the analytical gaze is skewed toward prisoners. Whilst this can illuminate the pains, degradations and so forth experienced by the confined, it tells us little about how the powerful are able to *be* powerful. I take this to be a fundamental issue raised by this body of work on science and technology, and one that has guided the thinking on the relationships between power, order and discourse in prisons, that is discussed in greater detail below.

However, the 'governmentality' literature is also useful for understanding imprisonment at both the micro and macro levels of analysis. I initially describe the reasons why Foucault turned to this domain of inquiry and then outline Rose and Miller's examination of 'political rationalities' and 'governmental technologies' as they provide a conceptual vocabulary to make sense of the widely divergent ways of thinking on what imprisonment is for and how it is experienced in particular institutional sites. Foucault's (1991) reflections on governmentality have been read as a response to criticisms from the Left that his (1977) attentiveness to the micro-physics of power failed to address the relations between society and the state, and his suggestion that the disciplinary project produced 'docile bodies' meant that there was no space left for meaningful agency. In reply to such objections Foucault (1979, 1982, 1991) subsequently clarified his position in two crucial ways.

First, it is important to recognise that Foucault's move from a micro- to a macro-physical study of power did not entail a move to state theory as practised by some of his Marxist critics. He insisted that his 'ascending' (or bottom-up) method of analysis was superior to their 'descending' (or top-down) mode of deduction, since he argued that:

> anything can be deduced from the general phenomenon of the domination of the bourgeois class. What needs to be done is something quite different. One needs to investigate historically, and beginning from the lowest level, how mechanisms of power have been able to function. (Foucault, 1980: 100)

His point is that the same methods used to study local arenas could be used to analyse the techniques and practices for governing populations in the territories of nation-states. This argument initially appears in the final chapter of the first volume of *The History of Sexuality*, where Foucault (1979) introduced the term 'biopower' to refer to the administration of populations, which became a distinctly modern phenomenon. This concern is developed in his 1978 and 1979 lecture courses in which he defined a fresh area of inquiry around 'governmentality', in a further effort to distance his work from what he considered to be the reductionist tendencies of Marxist state theory (see Gordon, 1991, for further details). In this new work he argued that it is the 'governmentalization' of the state, or changes in the practice of government that are of prime significance in the project of modernity (Foucault, 1991: 103). Government possesses a general meaning, loosely defined as 'the conduct of conduct', and a more specific definition, which is a system of thinking about the practice of government, for instance, who can govern, what is governing, and who is governed.

Second, Foucault's (1982) essay 'The Subject and Power' offers significant qualifications to his association of disciplinary power with an ability to tame, suppress and reduce individuals to 'docile bodies', through stressing the importance of active subjects in the processes of their own government of conduct. Power offers technologies of the self that can be adopted by individuals who choose to become involved in the programme of 'subjectification', or who contest governmental practice through 'counter-conducts'. Foucault's later work has generated a range of research on a variety of topics (see, for example, Burchell et al., 1991; Barry et al., 1996). The intention here is to demonstrate how elements of this literature can integrate micro and macro levels of analysis. In this respect Nikolas Rose and Peter Miller's (1992; Miller and Rose, 1990a, 1990b; Rose and Miller, 1992; Miller and Rose, 1995; Rose 1996, 1999, 2000) deliberations on problematics of government are particularly instructive, where they state that there are two fields of analysis. The first concerns *political rationalities*, which attend to:

> the changing discursive fields within which the exercise of power is conceptualised, the moral justifications for particular ways of exercising power by diverse authorities, notions of the appropriate forms, objects and limits of politics, and conceptions of the proper distribution of such tasks among secular, spiritual, military and familial sectors. (Rose and Miller, 1992: 175–6)

Rationalities relating to welfarism and neo-liberalism are articulated and elaborated in this field. The second refers to *governmental technologies*, which are 'the complex of mundane programmes, calculations, techniques, apparatuses, documents and procedures through which authorities seek to embody and give effect to governmental ambitions' (Rose and Miller, 1992: 176).

As Garland summarises it, with allusions to the translation perspective outlined above:

> the framework argues that power should be viewed as a matter of networks and alliances through which 'centres of calculation' exercise 'government-at-a-distance'. Power is not a matter of imposing a sovereign will, but instead a process of enlisting the cooperation of chains of actors who 'translate' power from one locale to another. This process always entails activity on the part of the 'subjects of power' and it therefore has built into it the probability that outcomes will be shaped by the resistance or private objectives of those acting 'down the line'. (Garland, 1997: 182)

The point is not so much the power of the centralised state, but rather how various local arenas are able to act. Moreover, Stenson (1999: 55) suggests that the recent work on governmentality 'seems to provide an agenda for strictly grounded, empirical avenues of investigation of how governing practices at the "molecular" level (in schools, prison cells and so on) connect to the "molar", organizing level in strategic centres such as state ministerial offices'. My argument is that the penal system can be regarded as an articulation of diverse forces, techniques, rationalities and devices that seek to regulate the actions and decisions of individuals and groups in relation to certain authoritative criteria. It is my claim that these criteria and the ability to *act* are performed through discourse. In other words, discourses constitute the social through processes of signification.

Discourse Theory and Social Practice

It would be impossible to provide an extensive overview of all the developments in discourse theory that have occurred in the humanities and social sciences over the last four decades in this chapter.[5] Instead, what will be provided here is an indication of the theoretical assumptions that inform the understanding of the concept used in this book. It is important to recognise that I am not using the term as conventionally conceived in linguistics, which tends to define a discourse as a passage of speech or written language. Instead, I am using it as a way of structuring knowledge and organising practice. Of course, Foucault (1972: 49) originally formulated this definition in his initial archaeological studies, where he argued that we should no longer just treat 'discourses as groups of signs (signifying elements referring to contents or representations) but as practices that systematically form the objects of which they speak'. The implication of this assertion is that discourses do not simply reflect or represent social meaning, rather they not only constitute what can be meaningfully thought and said but they also organise conduct within particular discursive formations.

A discursive formation can be defined as the horizon of possibilities within which the being, or essence, of objects are constituted and transformed through a series of regularities that link activity, representation and meaning across many different sites. The suggestion that objects cannot be treated as something external to discourse, or that nothing can exist beyond discourse, is not to deny that things can have a material existence in the world but that their conditions of existence are given meaning through discourse. Laclau and Mouffe (1985: 107) radically develop this insight and call for the rejection of a distinction between discursive and non-discursive practices (a separation that Foucault tried to maintain in the archaeologies of madness and grammar, but sought to bypass in his later genealogies of punishment and sexuality through focusing on the impossibility of knowledge without power[6]). In a frequently misunderstood passage they insist that:

> The fact that every object is constituted as an object of discourse has *nothing to do* with whether there is a world external to thought, or with the realism/ idealism opposition. An earthquake or the falling of a brick is an event that certainly exists, in the sense that it occurs in the here and now, independently of my will. But whether their specifity as objects is constructed in terms of 'natural phenomena' or 'expressions of the wrath of God', depends upon the structuring of a discursive field. What is denied is not that such objects exist externally to thought, but the rather different assertion that they could constitute themselves as objects outside any discursive condition of emergence. (Laclau and Mouffe, 1985: 108, emphasis in original)

This is not to say that society is 'a totally open discursive field' as Hall (1996a:146) argues, but that a discourse will include certain possibilities whilst excluding others. The point is that whilst material objects and social entities exist, they have no fixed meaning and that they only become meaningful once they are defined within discourse. But the crucial point, and one that Foucault came to make, is that power lies in discourse as it both constrains and enables what can be known. So whilst 'things' might have a pre- or extra-discursive existence, they only acquire a social and historical *meaning* through discourse.

Amongst the important questions that this definition of discourse raises, in the context of the overall discussion in this chapter, is how do individuals live identity and assert agency within particular institutional confines? In this regard, Howarth and Stavrakakis (2000: 12–14) make a significant distinction between subject positions and political subjectivity (see also Laclau, 1990: 60–61). In the former, attention is drawn to the location of subjects within a particular discursive formation, whilst the latter seeks to account for the agency of subjects. The notion of subject position is central to Foucault's (1972: 55) understanding of discourse, as he maintains that 'discourse is not the majestically unfolding manifestation of a thinking, knowing, speaking subject, but, on the contrary, a totality, in which the dispersion of the subject and his discontinuity with himself may be determined'. In other words, the subject is not something that exists prior to, or outside of, discourse, instead the subject is created in and through discourse (Williams, 1999: 85). One of the implications of this formulation is that subjects fill a number of different positions within particular networks of signifiers. For instance, an 'agent at any given point in time might identify herself, or be simultaneously positioned, as "black", "middle class", "Christian", and a "woman"' (Howarth and Stavrakakis, 2000: 13).

As I shall argue below, this conceptualisation of subject positions within discursive formations is particularly salient for understanding imprisonment. However, it is far from being unproblematic. In particular, it can involve viewing 'the identities inhabited by historical individuals as simply the mirror-image of the subject-positions produced within particular discursive regimes' (Nixon, 1997: 316). The notion of political subjectivity is one way of establishing the means by which social actors are able to act, and here Lacanian psychoanalysis has been particularly influential with respect to the relationships between his concepts of 'lack' and 'identification'. The argument is that at times of social and political crisis, structures have to be recreated and the agent is forced into identifying with certain political projects and the discourses that they articulate. This has been succinctly put:

> In Lacanian terms, the emergence of political subjectivity is the result of a lack in the structure. It is this lack in the structure that 'causes' subjects to identify with those social constructions that seem capable of suturing the rift in a symbolic order. (Howarth and Stavrakakis, 2000: 14)

This does not mean that the subject is determined by political or social structures, nor does it simply imply that the subject constitutes structures, but rather that it is through the process of identification that subjectivities are created and formed.

Whilst this characterisation of subjectivity might hold during times of social crisis and political upheaval, it is not particularly well suited for understanding how it is that agents are able to act creatively, or even think of themselves as subjects, in their daily practices and routine encounters. One potentially productive way of addressing this lacuna is through a consideration of Foucault's later work on technologies of the self, which he argues 'permit individuals to effect by their own means or with the help of others a certain number of operations on their own bodies and souls, thoughts, conduct and way of being, so as to transform themselves in order to attain a certain state of happiness, purity, wisdom, perfection or immortality' (Foucault, 1988: 18). I have already alluded to the significance of this work, as it emphasises the importance of active subjects in the processes of their own government of conduct, but there is also the possibility that technologies of the self can offer a sense of the dynamic ways in which subject positions might be lived.

Subjectivity can then be understood as a performance that draws on discursive regularities and is expressed through specific techniques and practices (Butler, 1993), yet I would add that subjectivity will always involve a process of translation and is never a straightforward enaction, or imitation, of a discursive subject position. In fact, the very notion of translation can render visible the historically contingent nature of discursive formations.

This last point is of central importance, as a defining feature of discourse theory is the insistence that the analysis 'investigates the way social practices systematically form the identities of subjects and objects by articulating together a series of contingent signifying elements in a discursive field' (Howarth and Stavrakakis, 2000: 7). The key concept here is articulation, which can be characterised as a post-Marxist means of addressing both class reductionism and economic determinism in orthodox understandings of Marx. Slack (1996) provides a cogent mapping of the origins and application of the theory in Cultural Studies, and in particular the work of Laclau (1977), Laclau and Mouffe (1985) and Hall (1980, 1996a). She argues that it arose as a means of confronting the twin problems of reductionism and determinism when Marxism was faced with the difficulties of explaining the non-revolutionary culture of the working class, the contradictions of existence, how these are lived and understood, whilst also accounting for how factors other than class (as expressed in such things as age, ethnicity, gender and sexuality) complicate relations of domination and subordination (Slack, 1996: 116).

Put simply, the term articulation implies the composition of parts to make a unity. Unity refers to the concrete practices which constitute a social formation so as to make the case that whilst power operates contingently, this is not the same thing as arguing that it operates arbitrarily. It also emphasises that there is a partial fixing of meaning that is both possible and necessary, for otherwise all social practice is reduced to an essential logic of discontinuity. This is clearly an untenable position, as it would involve claiming that there is no continuity or fixing of meaning. Instead, the '*practice of articulation ... consists in the construction of nodal points which partially fix meaning; and the partial character of this fixation proceeds from the openness of the social*' (Laclau and Mouffe, 1985: 113, emphasis in original).   Nodal points are, in a sense, privileged moments that bind together a particular system of elements into discursive formation. Hall (1996a) defines articulation as:

> the form of the connection that *can* make a unity of two different elements, under certain conditions. It is a linkage which is not necessary, determined,

absolute and essential for all time ... So the so-called 'unity' of a discourse is really the articulation of different, distinct elements which can be re-articulated in different ways because they have no necessary 'belongingness'. (Hall, 1996a: 141, emphasis in original)

The notion of articulation can, I want to argue, explain how the diverse elements which constitute and sustain the social formation of the prison are not simply reduced to relations of correspondence (such as the ways in which the institution is implicated in strategies of symbolic condemnation, carceral discipline and class oppression as Durkheim, Foucault and Marxist analyses would respectively have it), but are also extended to the contradictory, or relations of non-correspondence, not only in terms of how ideas on the enterprising prisoner (Garland, 1997) might sit with the denial of volition in the penal philosophy of incapacitation (see O'Malley, 1999 on the incoherence of contemporary penality and Carrabine, Lee and South, 2000 for the implications of this argument) yet also the ways in which men can be imprisoned not only by their criminality, as conventionally understood, but also in their masculinity (for comments on the difference between conceptualising 'men as prisoners' and 'prisoners as men' see Sim, 1995). In what follows I want to provide something approximating an archaeological mapping of various discourses that are of some significance in understanding imprisonment. Subsequent chapters examine their genealogy at Strangeways, not least because I agree with Williams' (1999: 87) observation that discourse should be regarded as 'practice rather than a monolithic theoretical architecture'. I would go even further, and argue that those versions of discourse theory that dispense with concrete social analysis are missing the point.

Discourses and Imprisonment

An important text that recognises the significance of discourse is Adler and Longhurst's (1994a) examination of the Scottish Prison System, where they illustrate how it 'is the site of struggles between different social actors mobilising, constructing and reinterpreting particular discourses' (Adler and Longhurst, 1994a: 47). Although their characterisation of discourse is explicitly informed by Karl Mannheim's approach to the sociology of knowledge, their work remains highly suggestive and is clearly directed toward developing a fresh and theoretically informed study of imprisonment. Such a project can only be welcomed, but their text lacks a conceptual apparatus to explain how the general systems of thought they identify are translated by various actors into the practices operating in specific prisons in the Scottish penal estate.

Before I outline the structure of various discourses that are central to imprisonment I want to reiterate the point that I am using the term discourse in the sense of a system of thought that informs practice. It refers to both a framework of belief and a guide for appropriate conduct. As such, the various discourses serve to 'incorporate' the agencies of the powerful within the project of imprisonment – that is civil servants, governors, staff and so forth articulate these ideas and practices. Few prisoners readily submit to such formations, and neither the metaphors of consent nor coercion manage to convey adequately the dull compulsion that the routines of prison life represent for most of the incarcerated,[7] in which existence is largely made bearable through, to use Goffman's (1961: 187) memorable phrase, 'make-dos'. I return to the implications of this argument for conceptualising prison order in the following chapter but the point to emphasise here is that the extent to which the experience of imprisonment is felt as psychologically damaging, or otherwise, by prisoners is conditioned in significant ways by the discursive practices prevalent in a particular prison. For instance, certain rights, privileges, material standards and obligations are made possible or withheld according to the discursive principles in operation.

Six discourses that are of some significance in structuring the experience of imprisonment (this discussion develops and modifies Adler and Longhurst's, 1994a: 34–45 account; see also Carrabine, 1998, 2000 for further clarification) will be outlined for the purpose of identifying their conceptual structure. Each discourse has a distinctive history, with some older than others, and not every one appears with equal force in every prison but there are three discourses that relate to the *ends* of imprisonment (rehabilitation, normalisation and control) and three *means* discourses (bureaucracy, professionalism and authoritarianism) that are of particular significance.[8] Means discourses should be regarded as governmental technologies – methods of running prisons; whereas ends discourses correspond to political rationalities – the appropriate mentalities justifying what prisons are for. My claim is that there are dominant alignments operating within institutions and across societies at any given moment and that these alignments are continually produced and are open to contestation by actors in the penal system. Such a characterisation enables the analysis to comprehend what the prison is *for*, in a macrosociological sense, and reveals what the experience of imprisonment is *like*, in a microsociological sense, without promoting one level at the expense of the other.

To individually summarise each of the three ends discourses, the discourse of rehabilitation focuses on the 'deviant' individual, suffering from some form of maladjustment that can be treated though the correct programme in an institutional setting. Normalisation in many ways marks a point of departure from rehabilitation, in that it seeks to prevent the 'worse' effects of imprisonment. It has its roots in the 'just deserts' movement of the 1970s, which insisted that offenders should only be punished as severely as they deserve in reaction to the unfair excesses of rehabilitation, especially indeterminate sentencing. Consequently it contrasts sharply with rehabilitation, which maintains that a prisoner can get 'better' in prison, and instead it considers the prisoner to be a 'normal' individual who has committed a crime, and the prison sentence represents the punishment. This reflects the dictum that prisoners are sent to prison *as* punishment, rather than *for* punishment, or rehabilitation, but that opportunities should be available to facilitate change if this is the prisoner's wish. The normalisation discourse also advocates that prisoners should enjoy, as far as practicable, the same standards as individuals in the community, so that prison life is made as 'normal' as possible. Control discourse, on the other hand, stresses the importance of maintaining good order and discipline in the prison, and is not concerned with the rehabilitation of the individual, nor the normalisation of the prison. Instead, it places paramount importance on the conformity of the prisoner to whatever measures are considered to be appropriate for the smooth functioning of the institution. Consequently, it takes as its main focus the 'disruptive' individual prisoner who challenges the stability of the regime and regards such behaviour as pathological.

These three ends discourses are concerned with what prisons are for, and in this sense are political rationalities, as they both provide the moral justifications and define the subjects and objects of penal intervention. In each discourse subjects are positioned in particular ways. For instance, prisoners can be addressed as 'deviant', 'normal' or 'disruptive' according to the ways in which the subject is constructed in the discursive formation that occupies institutional hegemony. Of course, this can bear little relationship to the subjectivity that a prisoner, as a social agent, performs and feels. But it does have major implications if the conduct departs from subject positions associated with the dominant discourse alignment. The same also holds for other actors in the penal setting, including prison officers, governors, medical staff and so forth, who are all positioned according to the social topography of the discursive formation. For instance, in the discourse of rehabilitation medical staff will occupy a more elevated subject position in the 'treatment' of prisoners than uniformed officers on the wings and landings of a prison. These positions are practically reversed in the discourse of control, but this crucially does not automatically mean that the subjectivities of agents will follow the same trajectory, as examined in greater detail in subsequent chapters. Instead, what needs to be emphasised here is that each discursive formation will be composed of specific configurations of 'enunciative modalities' (Foucault, 1972), which broadly define who has the right to 'speak' and what can be 'said' within a discursively organised field of 'statements'[9] that constitute objects, position subjects and distribute values.

Means discourses are concerned with how prisons should be run, and are in turn explicitly concerned with technologies of governance and regulation. Three discourses concerned with the means of imprisonment (bureaucracy, professionalism and authoritarianism) can be identified. The bureaucratic discourse is that which is most frequently associated with, and articulated by, civil servants and tends to focus on the prison system as a whole. It seeks to achieve fairness, impartiality, uniformity and consistency in the application of rules and procedures across the penal system, whereas the professional discourse primarily finds expression in the sentiments of governors and tends to concentrate on an individual establishment. It emphasises 'leadership, experience and judgement as means of enhancing the institutional ethos' (Adler and Longhurst, 1994a: 45). The discourse of professionalism obtains its legitimacy from governors' knowledge claims that they understand prisons and prisoners through their experience, because they see them on a routine basis and as a result of their responsibility for running prisons, which demands skills grounded in practice. Authoritarianism is a third form of means discourse. A characteristic feature of the discourse is that it is based on militaristic lines of regulation and the sources of its legitimacy are firmly rooted in the traditions of the prison service. As concerns relations with prisoners this does not necessarily entail coercive and divisive 'us versus them' rationalities but can be manifest in 'firm but fair' codes of conduct.

Despite its limitations that I mentioned earlier, Giddens' theory of structuration provides a useful repertoire of concepts to understand how such discursive formations are mobilised by human agency and here I will comment on four. First, the assertion that human subjects have 'as an inherent aspect of what they do, the capacity to understand what they do while they do it' (Giddens, 1984: xxii) is a central contention. It implies that the subject is aware of their actions and is capable of exercising a degree of choice over them, for even in prisons, where the possibilities for such autonomy are severely curtailed, there are still opportunities for the assertion of individual identity. Indeed, as Sparks et al. (1996: 81) recognise, 'it is precisely the struggle to maintain a sense of personal agency in the face of overweening institutional constraint which motivates and sustains some of prisoners' most intractable contests with the system, long after they would seem to have "lost"'. However, this is not to argue that the actor should be understood as the centred author of social practice, but it instead enables a consideration of the diverse forms of knowledgeability exercised by prisoners and staff.

Second, the distinction that Giddens (1984: xxiii) draws between 'practical' and 'discursive' consciousness is highly suggestive. Practical consciousness 'consists of all the things which actors know tacitly about how to "go on" in the contexts of social life without being able to give them direct discursive expression' (Giddens, 1984: xxiii). The importance of this distinction is vital to understanding the connections between discursive power and human agency, for whilst I would emphasise that actors do not possess a fully mapped out conception of the structure of each discourse, they nevertheless mobilise and interpret the discursive formations of imprisonment that are described above and analysed later in the book.

Third, the importance of routines in managing day-to-day activity can hardly be understated in the context of imprisonment, particularly if Foucault's (1977) analysis of disciplinary power is recalled though the time-tables, files, repetition and classification that are central to his account. Yet, for Giddens (1984: xxiii) routines are 'vital to the psychological mechanisms whereby a sense of trust or ontological security is sustained in daily life' and they also provide the means by which the structured properties of social life are recreated and maintained by human agents. Two rather distinct dimensions of experience are invoked here. In the former, routines are held to be of some significance in assuaging the anxieties that unpredictability can render in daily encounters. Giddens could be accused here of implying that boredom is reassuring (see Cohen and Taylor, 1976, for an account of attempts to escape the 'nightmare of repetition') yet, as he demonstrates with reference to Garfinkel's (1963) seemingly trivial 'experiments with trust', slight departures from the taken-for-granted can provoke quite intense feelings of anxiety (Giddens, 1984: 23). The concentration camp represents the extreme case of such 'experiments' (see Giddens, 1984: 61–3, and more generally Levi, 1988, whilst Sofsky's, 1997, analysis of the social order based on terror at Dachau is perhaps the most meticulously detailed).

As concerns the role of routines in reproducing the structured properties of social life, Giddens here echoes Foucault (1977) in referring to the ways in which institutions seek to regulate the activities of their members through the precise control of time; the reinforcement of hierarchy through the designation of space; and the monitoring of achievements (or departures) through the surveillance of subordinates (Giddens, 1987: 157). The importance of routines in the prison context is that:

> Many infractions of prison discipline precisely arise when staff feel that the smooth running of the routine is in jeopardy, for example because prisoners are 'too slow' in going to work, or finishing showering, or leaving a television room. This is in part, clearly a matter of compliance and the need felt by office holders to have their authority acknowledged; but it also reflects upon the importance to the organization of the routine as such. Whether prisoners too have an interest in the reproduction of the routine (either for the sake of 'ontological security' or more pragmatically for the reliable delivery of services they value, like food and visits) is a moot point. We suspect that very often they do, and hence co-operate more or less willingly in the running of routines. (Sparks et al., 1996: 82)

As will be seen in subsequent chapters, it is the breakdown of such mechanisms of regulation that can be of immense importance in opening up discontent and undermining the ontological security of prisoners and staff.

Fourth, Giddens' suggestive notion of the 'dialectic of control' is implicitly concerned with the possibilities of resistance, for 'all forms of dependence offer some resources whereby those who are subordinate can influence the activities of their superiors' (Giddens, 1984: 16). It is here that he comes closest to an understanding of how global projects are ruptured by the ability to act and dislocate strategies of domination and transformation, issues which are central to the sociology of translation and the governmentality literature. Yet as Sparks et al. (1996: 79) recognise, 'Giddens's references to the dialectic of control are in the main rather brief', but as they argue it does clearly indicate that prisons are 'rendered complex and unpredictable by the human agency of both captives and custodians'. It is this complexity and unpredictability that will be explored in the second half of the book.

To summarise then, the argument is that the power of a state apparatus (in this instance, the penal system) to regulate (as in normalisation or control discourses) or transform (the discourse of rehabilitation) the confined results from the composition of actors, devices, and strategies, in relatively durable associations through discursive alignments to achieve particular ends. The mobilisation of relatively durable associations, or networks, is achieved through the translation of thought and action from 'centres of calculation'. Translation refers both to movement across time and space, and the enrolment of agency within particular projects. The composition of networks enables calculated action upon conduct in a diversity of locales through discursive formations.

Thus the penal system can be envisaged as an effect of such networks, with each member actively involved in the translation of systems of thought and conduct. This necessarily entails understanding it in terms of competing actors engaged in struggles, accommodations, alliances, and separations. For example, as Adler and Longhurst (1994a: 27) indicate, prisoners develop forms of culture that are relatively separate and autonomous from prison officers and administrators. Alliances may develop, for example, where prison officers collude with certain prisoners to ensure the brutalisation of sex offenders. Governors will also form alliances with particular officers who share their interpretations of the 'correct' way to run the prison, which is informed by and performed through a discursive framing of the situation. It is important to recognise that such associations, as the translation approach emphasises, only possess a relative durability. The pattern of alliances, accommodations and separations are always liable to shift and rupture since struggles over, and resistance to, power are permanent features of social life, as the book will demonstrate in subsequent chapters.

Notes

1   This debt is not only present in the preferred research strategies: case studies, in-depth interviews, participant observation, documentary materials, and a 'tell it like it is' approach to social investigation, but also in the 'appreciative', sympathetic understanding of the individual's response to harsh and competitive environments. This empathy for the underdog illustrates both the accomplishments and limitations of the school's sociology. A good illustration of this legacy in subsequent prison research is the discussion of prisoner argot that frequents most monographs on imprisonment. This tradition stems from the fascination the Chicagoans had with the language of delinquency (see Thrasher, 1927), and Gouldner's (1973: xiv, in Taylor et al.) claim that this type of sociology amounts to 'zoo-keeping' is illustrated perfectly in Sykes' (1958) depictions of 'gorillas', 'rats', and 'wolves' in the prisoner subculture at Trenton. The argument in this book shares Gouldner's view that the activities of the powerful are as relevant as the sufferings of the powerless in understanding social practice.

2   Mathiesen's (1965: 2) notion of 'individual censoriousness' (defined as 'criticisms of the ruler for his lack of adherence to his own norms') is a highly significant intervention, not least because the prisoners in his study of a Norwegian institution exhibited a profound lack of solidarity and expressed established, conventional norms particularly in their relationships with staff, as opposed to the subterranean values and beliefs which Sykes and others were finding in North America's 'Big Houses'. Mathiesen's (1965) is a key study and will be discussed at greater length at various points in the book.

3   I discuss the governmentality and translation literature at greater length in Carrabine (2000).

4   It is clear that many of the key authors now express reservations over the term 'actor network theory' (see Law and Hassard, 1999). But this demonstrates the analytical purchase of the concept of translation – one does not have the power to control meaning – or to put it simply, something is either lost or gained in translation. It is also the case that the Internet has changed, probably for ever, our understanding of what a network is, since it now implies a smooth, instant, transportation of information. This is almost certainly not what was meant by the term in the original formulations.

5   Good recent overviews include Fairclough (1992), Mills (1997), Torfing (1999), Williams (1999) and Howarth (2000).

6   These difficulties are underlined in Foucault's understanding of resistance, which I discuss in the next chapter. However, a number of commentators tend to draw a distinction between the archaeological method of his early work, 'which is essentially synchronic and revolves around the interrelationship of elements which are centred upon typological identities' and the subsequent genealogical method, which is 'essentially diachronic, beginning with the present in a search for historical continuities' (Williams, 1999: 77). The important point I would make is that the strict analysis of discourse (archaeology) cannot be separated from a consideration of the historical location of discursive formations (genealogy). This point of connection is crucial as it enables a comprehension of how discourses are 'produced' and 'lived'.

7   This is an extension of the central arguments in Abercrombie et al.'s (1980) critique of the dominant ideology thesis, where they argue that it is not the subordinate classes who are incorporated by the dominant ideology, but rather the dominant classes.

8   Others exist, and they would include reformation, legality and incapacitation, but the purpose here is to provide a mapping of those discourses that were particularly salient at Strangeways between 1965 and 1990.

9   This field is never settled, for any discursive formation, but what can be highlighted is the unifying practice of establishing a series of classifications and relations of dependence across and within a discourse over time and space. A good example, which Foucault (1972: 57) uses, is the case of Natural History in the Classical period in contrast to the sixteenth century and he argues that in 'the seventeenth and eighteenth centuries Natural History was not simply a form of knowledge that gave a new definition to concepts like "genus" or "character", and which introduced new concepts like that of "natural classification" or "mammal"; above all it was a set of rules for arranging statements in series, an obligatory set of schemata of dependence, of order, and of successions, in which the recurrent elements that may have values as concepts were distributed'. In other words, the point of a discourse is to establish relations of obligation and the distribution of value within a hierarchical system of coding.

Chapter 3

Thinking about Disorder:
For a Genealogy of Resistance

Introduction

Few examples of social practice demonstrate the inherently contested and
discursively constructed conditions of existence better than the thinking on
civil unrest. The often told story of King Louis XVI in France, captures this
most perfectly, for on seeing the protests in the streets of Paris in 1789, the
King turned in exasperation to his companion, the duc de La Rochefoucauld-
Liancourt, and cried out, 'My God! It's a revolt!' 'No, Sire,' La Rochefoucauld
is said to have replied. 'That is a revolution.' Whilst the duc's reply is rightly
renowned, as it exposed the king's inability to grasp what was going on
beneath his window (Kimmel, 1990: 1), it also serves to remind us of the
power of definition, in that situations will never have an objective reality but
are culturally constructed, historically relative and politically loaded. Violent
dissent can be (and frequently has been) regarded as the action of mindless
mobs that violates an otherwise tranquil harmony through desolating all that
is good and decent in society; whereas for other commentators rioting is the
only voice through which the dispossessed can make themselves heard, and
should therefore be embraced as a motor of change and catalyst for reform,
as Oscar Wilde put it, in *The Soul of Man Under Socialism*:

> Disobedience in the eyes of anyone who has read history, is man's original
> virtue. It is through disobedience that progress has been made, through
> disobedience and through rebellion. (Wilde, 1999 [1891]: 1176)

My point is that merely labelling the events at Strangeways prison in April 1990
as a 'riot' raises a whole series of important conceptual, ethical, methodological
and theoretical questions. For instance, what is the difference between mindless
violence and meaningful resistance? How should distinctions be made? What
are the regimes of truth? Whose side are you on?

No appeal to the evidence can mask the fundamentally political nature of
the answers. In other words, the definition of a 'riot', 'disturbance', or 'protest'

is the result of cultural, social and political processes, and not a reflection of an objective reality. These issues are central to understanding the two dominant theoretical perspectives on collective dissent, *disorganisation* and *deprivation*, that inform sociological analyses of prison unrest. The examples chosen for illustration here are the exemplars of their respective traditions, and have not been chosen as straw targets. Instead what I want to indicate are the limits of orthodox thinking on prison protest so that an alternative genealogical approach can be developed that is better equipped to deal with the lacunae in sociological treatments of disorder. So the argument is not that the existing literatures are fatally misguided or woefully inept, but rather that there are conceptual and theoretical difficulties raised in their respective formulations, and that recent attempts at synthesis through prioritising *legitimacy* continue to overlook these problems. This is one of the main reasons why an alternative genealogical analysis is developed, which takes as its starting point the impossibility of an objective reality. But this in no sense means that the resulting analysis will be an uncritical, relativist and trivial account of a significant moment in British penal history, as one of the central tasks is to disturb certainties so that it is possible to think differently and problematise existing approaches to social and political phenomena.

Although there are a number of different styles of genealogical analysis, which can encompass studies that emphasise the contingent singularity of events, exhibit profound distrust of Enlightenment ideals and reject Cartesian understandings of subjectivity, there is an important sense in which the perspective involves a commitment to exposing the limits of established systems of thought. Consequently the discussion begins with sociological accounts of prison disorder, so that their key concerns and limitations can be identified. An alternative genealogy of resistance is then outlined, which is informed by Nietzsche and Foucault, but also recognises the difficulties in the latter's conceptualisation of resistance. These are addressed through recent work in Cultural Studies that offers the notion of transgression (Stallybrass and White, 1986) as a more potent metaphor of counter conduct and one that attempts to overcome binary oppositions in social and cultural thought. The chapter concludes with a discussion of the problem of order, as it has been conceptualised in prison sociology, so that the distinctive contribution offered in this book can be further clarified.

Orthodox Explanations of Prison Unrest

Disorganisation

The roots of the disorganisation perspective can be traced back to nineteenth century aristocratic fears over the rise of democracy, urbanisation, nation-state formation and industrialisation which fractured the traditional, feudal bonds of conformity and the emergence of urban 'dangerous classes'. As is well known, Gustave Le Bon (1960: 32) gave voice to these anxieties through asserting that by 'the mere fact that he forms part of a crowd, a man descends several rungs in the ladder of civilisation'. For Le Bon, the crowd is synonymous with barbarism in which the disease of irrationality spreads through processes of contagion, suggestion and imitation. It would be difficult to underestimate the significance of Le Bon's intervention, as it provided scientific legitimacy to terms like 'degenerate mob', 'crowd mentality' and 'mass hysteria' that remain common currency. What is more, his theory of leadership, which centred on his contention that the masses desire domination, had a profound influence on politics to the extent that it is said that 'Roosevelt met him, de Gaulle cited him and Hitler was proud to admit that he took Le Bon as his teacher' (Lindholm, 1990: 39).

In American sociology, the crowd was replaced by the study of collective behaviour,[1] which is defined as the behaviour of individuals under the influence of a collective impulse that was fundamentally different from that which guided 'normal' behaviour.[2] Durkheim is a key figure, and his legacy can be traced through Parsons (1960) and reaches its fullest expression in Smelser (1962), as the central assumption in this perspective is that society functions through control mechanisms that check irrational behaviour and promote consensus. Such regulatory mechanisms include the family, religion and community ties, which socialise the individual into conformity. If disorder occurs it is seen as a result of a breakdown or disorganisation in the mechanisms that engender solidarity and prevent antisocial activity. This deflects attention away from the demands of the rioters on to defects in socialisation and the mechanisms of control (and how they can be improved), as the stress is on the integration of the individual into community life through shared values and customs.

Two examples of how the disorganisation perspective has been deployed in accounts of prison unrest can be identified. The first is Gresham Sykes' (1958) classic monograph on the Trenton maximum security prison, where he argued that the authorities maintained order through a system of power sharing with leaders of the society of captives. He argues that it was only as a result of the administration attempting to regain control of the institution, through curbing the abuse of official rules, cracking down on the illegal economy and tightening security that the prison experienced a spate of riots in 1952. This undermined *'the cohesive forces at work in the inmate population and it is these forces which play a critical part in keeping the society of the prison on an even keel'* (Sykes, 1958: 136, emphasis in original). The implication of Sykes' analysis is that order is achieved through illicit alliances with inmate leaders – the 'corruption of authority' – and that this exerts a restraining and conservative influence on the captive society. It should also be recognised that prisons achieve stability through the 'tacit consent' and 'active cooperation' of prisoners (Martin and Zimmerman, 1994: 316). A precarious balance of informal obligations and reciprocities structure the power relationships within the institution so that either reform *or* a tightening up of security can destroy this gossamer of accommodations between prisoners, staff and governors. If this internal reality is thrown into a state of disorganisation, the formal and informal mechanisms of social control are destabilised, which means that the possibilities for disorder are enhanced.

A more recent rendering of this perspective is advanced in Mark Colvin's (1992) analysis of the riot at the Penitentiary of New Mexico in 1980, in which 33 prisoners were killed and hundreds injured. His argument is that:

> from 1978 to 1980, the prison organisation and the corrections bureaucracy experienced a period of fragmentation. The confrontations of previous years gave way to administrative confusion and disorganisation. The feuding top officials in New Mexico corrections provided little direction or leadership as the prison drifted toward increasingly arbitrary, inconsistent, and coercive tactics of control, which further incited inmate rage. Inmate relations also fragmented as the organised protests of the earlier period gave way to infighting and violence among inmates. The riot that erupted in 1980 reflected the disorganised relations among both agents of the state and inmates. (Colvin, 1992: 7)

In essence, the riot was a result of organisational changes which lay in a move from a period of accommodation, in the late 1960s and early 1970s, to a period of confrontation and fragmentation. The introduction of coercive controls in the late 1970s followed allegations of corruption, which included inmates using community contact programmes to smuggle drugs into the prison. The new administration that came to power in 1975 set about ending rehabilitation programmes, cracking down on the drug economy and abolishing the inmate council. Taken together these changes effectively ended an era of consensual avenues of communication between staff and prisoners. In this interpretation order in prisons becomes more problematic when the accommodations between the authorities and prisoners become disrupted and control shifts toward a greater reliance on coercion, so that the 'inmates perceive they have nothing to lose by rebelling' (Colvin, 1992: 39).

The particular strength of his analysis is that it is an in-depth history of control strategies at a particular prison and it highlights chronic organisational breakdown as a decisive factor contributing to the worst prison riot to date in the United States. As regards the prisoners, the fragmentation of the inmate society is charted, from one that was characterised by solidarity to one that was disorganised, atomistic and predatory. This latter interpretation diverges considerably from how prison protest is conceptualised in deprivational approaches.

Deprivation

In contrast, those theories (including rising expectations, grievance dramatisation and relative deprivation) that can be broadly subsumed under the category of deprivation tend to emphasise that disorder occurs in a context of injustice and stresses that violent protest is rational and purposive action pursued by those excluded from the organisational and distributional benefits of modernity. To put the matter simply, 'people revolt when there is tyranny, poverty and oppression' (Useem and Kimball, 1989: 232). In response to the obvious criticism that deprivation is widespread, yet only some places at certain times experience protest, a number of theoretical responses have been advanced. *Absolute* levels of deprivation are generally discredited, since there is little direct correspondence between economic hardship and instances of public unrest. Instead of an objective notion of absolute deprivation a number of authors subscribe to the idea of *relative* deprivation. For instance, John Lea and Jock Young (1993), in their analysis of the English inner city riots in the 1980s, portray relative deprivation as a subjective interpretation of unjust inequalities, arising from the individual's exclusion from the 'glittering prizes' of society and marginalisation from legitimate channels of redress. The focus on subjective interpretation allows space for the innovative character of adaptations to deprivation to be articulated, in which rioting is one 'solution' amongst others.

What unites deprivation analyses is the implication that there is a relationship between a precipitating event and a reservoir of grievances. Such interpretations can range from the simplistic powder keg theory, applied to prisons, to the more sophisticated flashpoints model (see Waddington et al.,

1989; Waddington, 1992), in which reference is made to the 'sparks' which are the immediate precipitants, that trigger the 'tinder' – the underlying causes that provide the potential for urban disorder. In other words, widespread deprivation is one element that interacts with high unemployment, racial discrimination, political exclusion, ideological vilification and mistrust of the police. I address the conceptual and theoretical implications of this argument below, for I want to illustrate how this perspective has been deployed in the prison context.

The powder keg theory (Fox, 1971, 1973) maintains that inhuman conditions prime the prison into a time bomb waiting to explode that can be sparked by a relatively trivial incident. This has many similarities to the accounts advanced by some journalists and officials in the British context to explain prison riots. It points to such 'factors' as bad conditions, overcrowding, understaffing, poor security and the 'toxic mix' of inappropriate prisoners.[3] These factors interact in a mechanistic manner and 'trigger off' the periodic riots to which the prison system has become increasingly susceptible. The major flaw, though, in this account is that it does not tie in with where and when riots have happened. As Michael Cavadino and James Dignan (1992: 18) argue, if riots are caused by overcrowding, understaffing, bad physical conditions and poor security, then riots would only occur in local prisons and remand centres, where these 'factors' are particularly prevalent. Yet prior to the 1986 riots, major disorder was almost entirely in the province of the dispersal prisons – where security is at a maximum and they are not overcrowded or understaffed to the same extent as the locals. Since 1986 the pattern has been reversed, with most major disorders occurring in local prisons, remand centres and lower-security establishments. Again this account faces difficulties in explaining these incidents, because the institutions lack the 'toxic mix' of prisoners (lifers and the politically motivated) which are held to be important 'factors' propelling disorder.

Both the powder keg theory and the orthodox account subscribe to an objective notion of deprivation, which is underpinned by a simplistic positivist conception of social action and causation. In these accounts it is the absolute levels of deprivation that impel prisoners to riot against conditions. On the other hand, if the subjective interpretation of deprivation is considered, then more plausible explanations are possible – especially if attention is drawn to the ways in which grievances are dramatised in prisons (Ohlin, 1956; Cohen, 1976). The most sophisticated version of this is Phil Scraton, Joe Sim and Paula Skidmore's (1991) discussion of the protests at Peterhead prison in 1986 and 1987,[4] which provides a chilling, critical and thought-provoking account of the existential terror experienced by long-term prisoners unfortunate enough to have reached the 'end of the road'. Their analysis vividly demonstrates 'the alienation and boredom, the rigorous enforcement of petty rules, the psychological desolation through lack of outside contact and the fear and reality of violence' experienced by prisoners (Scraton et al., 1991: 132). Such feelings, derived from the cultural, environmental and material context of Peterhead, structured the meaning of protest for prisoners. The authors argue that the major unrest at long-term prisons over the last two decades can be understood as a rational 'response to both the arbitrary use of power which confronts them every day and the misanthropic smothering of what they regard as legitimate complaints about the system' (Scraton et al., 1991: 133). It is in this sense that their perspective can be defined as one which emphasises the deprivational approach through the dramatisation of deeply-held grievances and injustices.

For Scraton et al. (1991: 61) 'the authority imposed by the prison is not a consensual authority', it is fundamentally absolute and coercive. Whilst the authors provide extensive evidence for such an interpretation of Peterhead from prisoners, the difficulty with such an understanding is that the 'whole emphasis on the imposition of order by relentless force glosses over many important complexities of prison life and effaces some significant variations in the social organization of different prisons' (Sparks et al., 1996: 35). Additionally, as Colvin (1992), Jacobs (1977) and the subsequent analysis of Strangeways in this book will demonstrate, there are significant historical variations within particular prisons. It is unfortunate that Scraton et al. (1991) chose not to examine the shifting dynamics of such mechanisms of regulation as this could have strengthened their analysis of the problem of order, as this chapter will later suggest.

Toward Synthesis

It has been claimed that Bert Useem and Peter Kimball's (1989) *States of Siege: U.S. Prison Riots 1971–1986*, is the 'single most important book on prison riots published in the last 50 years' (DiIulio,1991b: 67).[5] The text is an examination of nine prison riots in the United States, in five states, which begins with Attica, 1971 and ends with a disturbance at West Virginia Penitentiary in 1986. The authors provide detailed case studies of these events through a five-stage model of the state's loss and subsequent reclamation of the institution. The fresh understanding their work brings to theorising prison disorder is that there is a fusion of disorganisation and deprivation approaches. Here the assumption of irrationality is discarded and the breakdown of social control mechanisms is kept from the disorganisation perspective and the issue of legitimacy is introduced to the deprivation approach. The first move is important because riots are held to be expressive, emotive outbursts in this tradition, which can be compared to the instrumental, rational protest associated with some versions of the deprivation position. However, they are aware that not all activities associated with a riot are a form of protest, since:

> if one supposes that the instrumental context of riots is limited to their role in bargaining with the state or dramatizing grievances to the outside world, and one notes that many riot participants do things poorly suited to those ends, like looting, raping, killing, and burning, one is tempted to conclude that those persons' actions were 'expressive'. But it is not 'irrational' to lack collective spirit. Nothing is so individualistically instrumental as theft and rape. Bearing this in mind, we conclude that there was little activity in the riots we studied which could not be called rational or instrumental. (Useem and Kimball, 1989: 202)

This is suggestive of a shift from a monolithic conception of riots, in which only one type of human action and motivation is said to be present, instead of the high level of differentiation and diversity of conduct that actually occurs.

For instance, they note the wide variation of activity in their analysis of nine riots (and, it should be added, within each) over a 15-year period.

> Some are mere racial brawls among inmates; in others, inmate leaders consciously promote racial harmony. Others have no leaders at all. Some are good natured looting sprees; others the rationally calculated tactics of gangs. Some are highly ideological rebellions; others serve largely as a chance for inmates to steal from each other – or murder each other. Inmates may take guards hostage and torture them – or treat them kindly – or take no hostages at all. In cost, in casualties, in organisation they span the spectrum. Is there any pattern to this? (Useem and Kimball, 1989: 4)

The answer to this question is that in 'all the riots under study there was a breakdown in the administrative control and operation of the prison' (Useem and Kimball, 1989: 218). This would include such features as poor communication systems, scandals, incoherent rules for inmates and guards, unstable chains of command, struggles between guards and administrators, and so forth. In effect it is the disorganisation of the state rather than the organisation of the prisoners that is the paramount precondition for a riot to occur.

As regards deprivation, they introduce the notion of legitimacy to structuring a stable prison:

Inmates are not propelled to riot merely because they are deprived of the amenities available outside of prison – for punishment is the purpose of prison – but because the prison violates the standards subscribed to concurrently or previously by the state or by significant groups outside of the prison. Well managed prisons, with adequate staffing and physical resources perpetuate a feeling among inmates that the system conforms to reasonable standards of imprisonment. When stability and uniformity are not present, inmates look to other standards to judge their conditions ... [W]here administrators and guards are powerful, unified and competent, the conditions of imprisonment themselves seem more legitimate; the captors are seen as authoritative rather than merely powerful. (Useem and Kimball, 1989: 219)

The stress here anticipates recent British academic commentary on the importance of legitimacy in creating an orderly prison and identifying circumstances in which prisoners consent to the authority of staff and regimes (see, for instance, Sparks, 1994; Bottoms and Sparks, 1995; Sparks et al., 1996) and the Woolf (Woolf and Tumim, 1991) emphasis on injustice as a major cause of the unrest in British prisons in April 1990.

Useem and Kimball's (1989) argument is that in well managed institutions with adequate resources most prisoners will subjectively perceive their surroundings and interactions to be within the confines of acceptable punishment. In stating that prison unrest is a consequence of a breakdown in administrative control, the effects of this are, first, it renders the practice of imprisonment illegitimate from the prisoners' perspective and thereby intensifies feelings of deprivation. The second consequence is that security arrangements become highly disorganised – which is an obvious precondition for protest to occur. Whilst their approach provides the most systematic framework with which to explain prison disorder, there are a number of problems that need to be addressed.[6]

First, their attempt at synthesis is to be welcomed as it involves a move from one- to two-dimensional thinking on disorder through discarding the more obviously untenable aspects of disorganisation and deprivation perspectives to provide a fuller picture of prison unrest. However, their central argument rests upon the assumption that those prisons which experience some form of collective disturbance depart from legitimate institutions to a pathological extent (Useem and Kimball, 1989: 218). The problem with such a characterisation is that it not only masks the degree to which 'normal' prisons are also governed by ambiguities, disagreements and incoherence but also routinely face legitimating deficits without erupting into riots.

Second, there is a related difficulty in that if their synthesis is accepted as correct then it ought to yield far more discord than there actually is. This point is similar to David Matza's (1964: 21–2) critique of positivist criminology's accounts of juvenile delinquency in that they offer an 'embarrassment of riches' as disorder ought to be more pervasive than is the case. As is well known, Matza (1964: 28) argues that juveniles drift into and out of delinquency 'casually, intermittently, and transiently'. Whilst Useem and Kimball (1989:209) note that Matza's (1964: 184–91) notion of 'preparation' is extremely useful in characterising the events preceding a riot (discussed in more detail here in Chapter 6) they do not consider the full implications of his argument as the concept of drift offers a more fluid, contingent and dynamic means of characterising disorder.

The third problem, which is shared by all the various perspectives discussed so far, concerns explaining how resistance is articulated[7] into collective dissent. There are a whole series of issues raised here and the following discussion is devoted to indicating the limits of orthodox thinking on disorder and proposes an alternative genealogical approach that recognises the complex diversity of institutions and conceptualises the extent to which the question of order is always a variable matter and one of degree in the final section.

For a Genealogy of Discontent

The Limits of Orthodoxy

In all the above deprivation accounts the key explanation is the relationship between a precipitating, or interactional, event that sets in motion the riot that may follow (depending on the reaction of the authorities). It is 'the action by prisoners which first crosses the line into open rebellion' (Useem and Kimball, 1989: 96) in the context of administrative failure that serves to promote beliefs that the system is unjust. Similarly, the 'flashpoints' model of public disorder (D. Waddington et al., 1989; D. Waddington, 1992) points to the importance of a 'spark' that sets off the 'fire', which may result from an uncompromising arrest or when crowd members throw bricks at a police line. It is important to recognise that in both accounts the social, cultural, and political contexts are described as the underlying causal mechanisms that 'trigger' the unrest and sets in motion the spirals of recrimination.

The similarities are drawn here as Peter Waddington's (1991, 1994, 2000) important objections against what he has defined as the 'critical consensus' on the British inner-city riots of the 1980s are a crucial intervention. He regards them as 'critical', in the sense that such accounts sought to distance themselves and critique the Establishment-conservative view that the riots were outbursts of irrational and criminal behaviour, 'consensual' in that they share the core belief that the riots were motivated by genuine grievances arising from deprivation, discrimination and police harassment. Yet the crux of the problem with such interpretations is that:

> it is one thing to observe that a disorderly or riotous group suffers injustices. It is quite another thing to assert that those injustices are perceived by the members of the group in the way that they are by the analyst, or indeed that they are perceived by the members of the group at all. It is yet a further step to say that it was perceived injustice that caused the disorder. (Waddington, 1991: 228)

This leads to an associated difficulty with the flashpoints model, in that it is tautological: 'if disorder occurred there must have been a flashpoint; if disorder was averted, a flashpoint could not have occurred' (Waddington, 1991: 232).

These two problems arise from what can be termed a retrospective fallacy in which actions and events are read off from *ex post facto* (after the fact) rationalisations and interpretations of situations, which tends to give rise to a sense of inevitability to the incidence of disorder. In response David Waddington (1998: 377, emphasis in original) has maintained that social deprivation is not '*always* a cause of public disorder but that it is a *predisposing factor* which becomes crucial dependent upon the precise combination of other mediating variables'. These include the ideological vilification of a group, repressive policing, media dramatisation, the nature and perception of the spatial setting. However, this amounts to saying little more than that 'disorder occurs within a context of injustice' (Waddington, 2000: 106f) and provides, at best, a picture of the climate in which the disorder took place.

This kind of analysis is a perfect example of what Foucault would describe as a 'descending' analysis, which begins with the identification of broad structural features and then proceeds to make a series of pronouncements on the extent to which they animate micro levels of social practice. The crucial issue is that one 'can always make this deduction, it is always easily done and that is precisely what I hold against it … I believe that anything can be deduced from the general phenomenon of the domination of the bourgeois class' (Foucault, 1980: 100). This, of course, is another way of stating the macro–micro issue, and the alternative method is to provide an 'ascending' analysis of power, that is best approached through genealogy, which I outline below. There is a further problem that Peter Waddington (2000: 96–7) raises, in that the crowd is treated as a homogenous entity, in a manner reminiscent of Le Bon's notion of a crowd mind, 'albeit one governed by the rational expression of grievances rather than liberated primordial passions'. This is closely related to the problem of selectivity, in that certain types of disorder are regarded as genuine articulations of grievance whereas others are dismissed or characterised as misguided attempts to deal with oppression.

Whilst Peter Waddington has raised some crucial conceptual and theoretical questions he provides no real attempt to answer them as his goal is one of demonstrating the political partisanship of critical commentators who use criminology as a vehicle to advocate liberal policies and restrict police powers. I do not share this project. Instead what is taken seriously here is the way in which he has revealed the limitations of orthodoxy in sociological thinking on riots. As regards resistance, Stevenson (1992: 4) also reminds us that 'one of the subtler forms of condescension in historical writing is to see all violence as 'protest' and all the participants in riots as sobersided and self-conscious proletarians'. The investment of meaning is always a hazardous endeavour, but the more fundamental point is that it has to be restored to its social context, rather than retrospectively imputed. Cohen (1980) makes a similar point with regard to a tendency in 1970s versions of subcultural theory (see Hall and Jefferson, 1976; Pearson, 1976) to read delinquent acts as rudimentary forms of political action, as symbolic resistance to oppression. In this school of thought, styles of dress and behaviour are seen as more, or less, successful forms of historically informed, political resistance against the hegemony of the dominant class. There is an open invitation to read, or deconstruct, the symbols for the underlying signification of opposition. In this manner, the fact that 'many riot participants do things poorly suited' to the dramatisation of grievance (Useem and Kimball, 1989: 202) could be understood in this context – as contradictory and elusive attempts at resolution, in the sense that the behaviour does not confront the real bases of oppression imposed by imprisonment or an unjust society.

There are two problems with such readings. First, they avoid confronting the complex issues of intent and consciousness, or a fuller understanding of human agency. Consequently, this appeal to history implies that a 'double leap of imagination' is required to grasp the political and economic significance of violence, for:

> it lies not in the kids' understanding of what it is they are resisting (they would probably say something like, 'When you get some long stick in your 'and and you are bashing some Paki's face in, you don't think about it') but in the fact that the machine smashers of 1826 would *also* not have been aware of the real political significance of their action. (Cohen, 1980: xiii, emphasis in original)

Second, they tend to operate with binary opposition between ideological incorporation and symbolic resistance, that in some sense challenges or, at least, negotiates the dominant order. In prisons this would imply that those who do not appear to challenge authority, are, instead, somehow incorporated or coerced into accepting the legitimacy of the institution. Such a belief would implicitly criticise those who perhaps seek only to avoid conflict (see also Carrabine and Bosworth, 2001). What is more, it would fail to do justice to the ways in which imprisonment is experienced as an external, brutal, social fact for the incarcerated, in which life is made bearable through making do.

Transgressing Resistance

It has become increasingly recognised in cultural theory at least, that simple metaphors which involve binary oppositions of inversion, reversal and substitution are unlikely to capture the complexity of social and symbolic practice. Peter Stallybrass and Allon White's (1986) landmark text, *The Politics and Poetics of Transgression*, has provided a metaphor of transformation (through transgression) that manages to convey the hybrid, impure and profane implications of the reversal of order. The book explores the persistent hierarchical mappings of 'high' and 'low' culture in Europe and 'the process through which the low troubles the high' (Stallybrass and White, 1986: 3). This process is transgression, and it is grounded in the work of the Russian literary theorist, Mikhail Bakhtin (1984), and his notion of 'carnival'. Carnival is a Rabelaisian metaphor for the temporary, licensed suspension and reversal of order – when the world is turned upside down and inside out, when the low becomes high and the high, low – on occasions of popular festivity at fairs, festivals and mardi gras. As Stuart Hall (1996b: 291) recognises, it is the 'sense of the overflowing of libidinal energy associated with the moment of "carnival" that makes it such a potent metaphor of social and symbolic transformation'. For, in Bahktin, the notion of carnival is not simply a metaphor of inversion, whereby the 'low' replaces the 'high', it is instead the purity of this binary distinction that is transgressed, blurred and made 'grotesque'.

It is this shift in the metaphors of transformation that Stallybrass and White (1986) expand on and explore in their work, as a means of overcoming binary thinking so that relations of antagonism can be defined in terms of both excess and absence that disrupt and transgress the hierarchical ordering of social formations. These are important arguments and they suggest a way of addressing the determinism and reductionism that can be found in the orthodox treatments of prison riots and public disorder. Foucault also sought to reject binary oppositions and the homogenisation of resistance through maintaining that:

> there is no single locus of great Refusal, no soul of revolt, source of all rebellions, or pure law of the revolutionary. Instead there is a plurality of resistances that are possible, necessary, improbable; others that are spontaneous, savage, solitary, concerted, rampant, or violent; still others that are quick to compromise, interested, or sacrificial; by definition they can only exist in the strategic field of power relations. But this does not mean they are only a reaction or rebound, forming with respect to the basic domination or underside that is in the end always passive, doomed to perpetual defeat. (Foucault, 1979: 95–6)

At one level, Foucault is drawing attention to the versatile range of actions that may be understood as resistance. On another, he is reasserting his insistence that power in modernity is not centralised in a single site, rather it is dispersed throughout the social totality.

Furthermore, such power relationships produce and provide the possibility for resistance – a claim that requires further clarification. Foucault (1979: 95) unequivocally states that 'where there is power there is resistance, and yet, or rather consequently, this resistance is never in a position of exteriority in relation to power'. However, there is little in his work that corresponds to an examination of concrete, historically grounded instances of resistance, which accounts for his difficulties in theorising the concept. For instance, in an interview Foucault was pushed on the issue of the 'ever silent target for apparatuses of power'; his response illuminates some of the difficulties:

> No doubt it would be mistaken to conceive the plebs as the permanent ground of history, the final objective of all subjections, the ever smouldering centre of all revolts. The plebs is no doubt not a real sociological entity. But there is indeed always something in the social body, in classes, groups and individuals themselves which in some sense escapes relations of power, something which is by no means a more or less docile or reactive primal matter, but rather a centrifugal movement, an inverse energy, a discharge. There is certainly no such thing as 'the' plebs; rather there is, as it were, a certain plebian quality or aspect … This measure of plebs is not so much what stands outside relations of power as their limit, their underside, their counter-stroke, that which responds to every advance of power by a movement of disengagement. (Foucault, 1980: 137–8)

In this passage Foucault resorts to explaining resistance as a form of plebian spirit or essence of refusal that manages to evade power relationships. This raises a profound inconsistency in his thinking, for his appeal to some privileged quality of the human spirit that lies outside history is entirely at odds with his entire intellectual project – a crusade against precisely this centring of the subject in social analysis! Likewise, Habermas (1987b: 284) has criticised Foucault for failing to convincingly answer the normative question of 'why fight?' – though it is debatable whether Habermas' own response is any more satisfying (see Conway, 1999).

The Precedence of Genealogy

What in fact is required is an extension of genealogical principles to an understanding of resistance. So rather than trying to locate some originating, ahistorical essence as the engine of resistance, the analysis should instead attempt to excavate the diverse ways in which such acts of resistance are made possible – how alternative meanings and practices are generated in imprecise networks of power relations. The genealogical method was initially propounded by Nietzsche (1996) in his celebrated history of ethics that exposed the Judaeo-Christian and liberal traditions of compassion, equality and justice as products of brutal and cruel processes of conditioning designed to tame the vitality of earlier cultures. As Smith (1996: ix) puts it, genealogy 'is less concerned with origins conceived as single punctual events (birth) and more with origins understood as the complex intersection of a number of different and competing forces (genealogy)'. Nietzsche is particularly scathing of notions of causality:

> Cause and effect: such a duality probably never occurs – in reality there stands before us a continuum of which we isolate a couple of pieces; just as we always perceive a moment only as isolated points, therefore do not really see it but infer it. The suddenness with which many events rise up leads us astray; but it happens suddenly only for us. There is an infinite host of occurrences in this sudden second which elude us. An intellect which saw cause and effect as a continuum and not, as we do, as a capricious division and fragmentation, which saw the flux of events – would reject the concept cause and effect and deny all conditionality. (Nietzsche, 1977: 62)

This passage is important as it insists that any search for origins is a deluded enterprise and masks continuities in practice that are obscured by the isolation of configurations of reality into a 'cause' and an 'effect', which is precisely the problem with even the most sophisticated analyses of prison riots and public disorder. Instead, the genealogist looks to the emergence of a field of struggles rather than an originating, foundational moment.[8] It seeks to historicise values, sentiments and actions in terms of their relationship to past events that have a complex bearing on whatever our present concerns might be. The 'present' for my purposes is the occupation of Strangeways prison in April 1990, but this requires a commitment to the past. But, I should emphasise that in genealogical method, 'there is no essence or original unity to be discovered. When genealogy looks to beginnings, it looks for accidents, chance, passion, petty malice, surprises, feverish agitation, unsteady victories and power' (Hoy, 1986: 224). As Chapter 6 will demonstrate, the concept of drift is particularly well suited to capturing the complexity of origins.

Foucault's (1984a) essay 'Nietzsche, Genealogy, History', which was originally published in 1971, offers a textual exegesis of Nietzsche's thinking that was to have a profound effect on Foucault's subsequent genealogies of punishment and sexuality that enabled him to elaborate his distinctive understanding of power, in terms of the 'history of the present'. I return to it here, as I want to argue that resistance should be afforded the same genealogical insights, so that the events at Strangeways can be understood in their messy detail as opposed to an inevitable march toward a fateful conclusion. Foucault (1984: 76) argues that genealogy is opposed to traditional historical methods, in that its aim is to 'record the singularity of events outside of any monotonous finality' so that an 'effective history' can be written. History only becomes 'effective' once discontinuity is introduced, since genealogy 'is not the erecting of foundations: on the contrary, it disturbs what was previously considered immobile; it fragments what was thought unified; it shows the heterogeneity of what was imagined consistent with itself' (Foucault, 1984a: 82).

Although Nietzsche was outraged by the historian's claim to objectivity (that hides subjective motivations) and pretence of standing outside of time, Foucault is rather more interested in the ways in which 'both scientific objectivity and subjective intentions emerge together in a space set up not by individuals but by social practices' (Dreyfus and Rabinow, 1983: 108). In other words, 'no one is responsible for an emergence; no one can glory in it, since it always occurs at the interstice' (Foucault, 1984a: 85). This is both a reassertion of the futility of the search for origins and a proclamation that there is no individual or collective subject moving history. Such a formulation insists that subjects:

> do not first preexist and later enter into combat or harmony. In genealogy subjects emerge on a field of battle and play their roles, there and there alone. The world is not a play which simply masks a truer reality that exists behind the scenes. It is as it appears. This is the profundity of the genealogist's insight. (Dreyfus and Rabinow, 1983: 109)

The battle is one of domination, but is not simply the relationship between rulers and the ruled, it is to be found throughout history 'in rituals, in meticulous procedures that impose rights and obligations' (Foucault, 1984a: 85). The painstaking excavation of rituals of power came to inform Foucault's later genealogies of punishment and sexuality (respectively in Bentham's Panopticon and the Christian confession). However, the concern here is with extending these insights to resistance, in all its impure and grotesque manifestations.

By drawing on the work on transgression it needs to be emphasised that the argument is not that the riot at Strangeways was a direct descendant of the 'carnival' and other popular festivities (though some of the activities were informed by a sense of the 'carnivalesque'). Nor will the analysis be involved in decrying the 'orgy of destruction' that journalists, politicians and officials were quick to condemn in April 1990. Instead, what needs to be acknowledged is that forms of counter conduct will be motivated as much by anger, rage and injustice as by pleasure, play and boredom. It is truly striking just how absent the sense of excitement, fear and urgency is from many accounts of riots and disorder, to the extent that it appears as if these events were never *lived*. Of course, suggesting that protest might be entertaining would be heresy to much of the radical Left, as it is all too clear that the conservative Establishment have the monopoly on decrying the 'mindless hedonism' of rioters, for obvious political reasons. Nevertheless, it is precisely the excesses of transgression that make it such a powerful metaphor of transformation, through its refusal to homogenise resistance into binary oppositions between earnest, noble protesters and mindless, irrational rioters, whilst bearing witness to the libidinal energy and sheer vitality that accompanies the inversion of order through counter conduct.

In other words, it enables an understanding of the sensual attractions of disruption. Likewise, Jack Katz (1988) and Mike Presdee (2000) have drawn attention to the exciting, pleasurable and emotional dynamics that are very much at the 'foreground' of criminal activity in an effort to critique the 'sentimental materialism' (as Katz, 1988: 313–17, terms it) of much liberal and radical criminology. Such work is important as it 'neither reduces emotions purely to the level of individual psychology (Katz should be credited for taking the emotions out of the realm of pathology) nor pre-locates the question of those emotions in the drama of state resistance and political rebellion' (Hayward, 2002: 83). Instead it suggests that not only is an account of human agency vital to capturing the experiential qualities of transgression but that some understanding of psychic complexity is necessary (Jefferson, 2002: 158) to grasp the motivations for wrongdoing.

To summarise, the genealogical method is attentive to history not in the sense of going back in time to indicate how the past continues to animate the present from some originating and decisive moment, but to 'cultivate the details and accidents that accompany every beginning' and to 'recognise the events of history, its jolts, its surprises, its unsteady victories and unpalatable defeats' (Foucault, 1984a: 80). This is one of the main reasons why the institutional culture of Strangeways is examined over a 25 year period, whereas Woolf's (1991) analysis begins only months before the riot. A number of consequences flow from this decision; not least, a failure to provide an adequate understanding of how a prison the size of Strangeways, with all its problems of overcrowding, chronic conditions and so forth was able to achieve a semblance of order for most of the time. But more importantly, his analysis insists that Strangeways had become by April 1990 a pathological prison, with chronic organisational failures that served to create serious legitimacy deficits. However, as will be seen in the second part of this book, the picture is considerably more complex than this, not least because there has been a long history of dissent at the prison and disorganised administration was in many ways a matter of routine across local prisons. Consequently, the genealogy here will emphasise the significance of the drift into and out of periods of heightened conflict and the importance of contingency in the second part of the book – for perhaps the key question that needs to be answered is: Why is it that prisons are mostly characterised by an uneasy peace rather than interminable discord? By way of answering the question the discussion now turns to how the problem of order has been posed in prison sociology.

The Problem of Order

The problem of order that preoccupies social and political theorists is largely one derived from the work of Talcott Parsons (1952) and his attempts to establish this issue as the central concern in sociological theory in the postwar period (Giddens, 1984; Lockwood, 1992; Wrong, 1994). Although he acknowledges Thomas Hobbes as the first to formulate the problem of order as a presocial 'state of nature' where life is 'solitary, poor, nasty, brutish and short' and characterised by universal conflict in the celebrated 'war of each against all', he rejects Hobbes' solution produced in the aftermath of the English Civil War, which emphasised the need for a coercive state apparatus to secure order through monopolising the use of force. In contrast, the Parsonian solution is resolutely normative as it prioritises the role of shared norms and values in maintaining social cohesion, without denying that self-interest might make some contribution to order. While it is therefore possible to identify at least three different solutions to the problem of order it is important to recognise that no single characterisation will capture the diversity of social practice, for as Wrong (1994: 9) succinctly puts it, whereas the typical 'error of sociologists, most notably of Durkheim and Parsons, has been to overemphasise consensus on norms and values as the solution, the Machiavellian-Hobbesian tradition in political thought has tended to exaggerate the role of force, and economists, including Marx, have notoriously overstressed economic interest'.

Clearly then the problem of order is multi-faceted and any account that relies on a singular solution to the neglect of others is unlikely to grasp the variable ways in which economic interest, political force and moral commitment might combine to sustain stable and orderly patterns of life. When the issue of order in prison has been considered, most commentators have been struck by the fact that the institution generates intrinsic and fundamental conflicts, not least since prisoners are confined against their will, with people they would normally not choose to be with, in circumstances they can do little to change and governed by custodians who police practically every aspect of their daily lives. Given these basic antagonisms it is perhaps not surprising that it is the Hobbesian solution to the problem of order that is most frequently drawn in sociological discussions of imprisonment. For instance, the critical criminologists that examined the Peterhead uprisings in the 1980s unequivocally stated that:

> All forms of incarceration imply the use of force. Regardless of the outward appearance of compliance few people taken into custody would accept their loss of liberty so willingly if the full potential of state coercion was not handcuffed to their wrists ... The authority imposed by the prison is not a consensual authority. (Scraton et al., 1991: 61)

Yet, as Sparks et al. (1996: 34) convincingly argue, such 'an account that places its whole emphasis on the imposition of order by relentless force glosses over many important complexities of prison life and effaces some significant variations in the social organization of different prisons'. Of course, they recognise that in the final analysis prisons are coercive institutions, but that first and foremost the power exercised in prisons is subject to problems of legitimacy. Nevertheless, it is important to emphasise that the *threat* of force is never far away, even if the actual use of force is only exercised intermittently. The significance of Sparks et al.'s (1996) account of order in prisons will be discussed below for it is important to acknowledge an earlier study that addresses the relationships between institutional power and social order in a suggestive fashion.

Colvin's (1992) analysis of the 1980 riot at the Penitentiary of New Mexico was used as an example of an especially nuanced representative of the disorganisation perspective as it highlighted both chronic administrative breakdown and the fragmentation of the inmate society through a detailed account of the history of control strategies at the prison. The model of organisational control used in the text is Etzioni's (1970) 'compliance theory' which identifies three types of power in organisations: normative, remunerative and coercive. Each of these tends to produce various types of commitment to the organisation by subordinates, with differing degrees of attachment. These types of power clearly echo the different solutions to the problem of order. However, Colvin (1992) argues that it is difficult to see a place for a normative compliance structure operating in prisons, since it assumes a voluntaristic, moral involvement on the part of subordinates to the organisational project. Consequently, power in prisons rests, in the main, with the manipulation of material rewards, which 'can include the chance of better living conditions, possibility of early release on parole, a better prison job, or entry into a desirable program' and the 'prisoner calculates the possible rewards to be gained through compliance with authorities and the possible privileges that can be lost for non-compliance' (Colvin, 1992: 35). Remunerative power involves subordinates acting in their own self-interests through calculating the advantages and disadvantages that acquiescence or defiance might bring.

Nevertheless, coercive control is the basic source of power available to authorities. During periods of stability it remains in the background, yet highly visible in the locks, walls, barbed wire, dogs, riot control gear and so forth. However, when 'the system of remunerative controls breaks down, coercion is relied on to a greater extent', which creates an 'alienative environment, or an intensely negative orientation, toward authorities by subordinates' (Colvin, 1992: 36). In essence, the riot was a result of organisational changes which lay in the move from a period of accommodation, based on remunerative controls, in the late 1960s and early 1970s, to a period of confrontation and fragmentation, rendered by a reliance on coercive controls in the late 1970s.[9] In this interpretation social order becomes more problematic when the inducements once offered by the authorities to buy out prisoners are withdrawn and control shifts toward a greater reliance on coercion, so that the 'inmates perceive they have nothing to lose by rebelling' (Colvin, 1992: 39).

Although there is a sense here of how order is negotiated, there remains the pervasive sociological assumption that power in prisons is non-legitimate and relies purely on corrective influence, of either a coercive or manipulative cast. At this point, some of the arguments from Chapter 2 on the question of power require revisiting to illustrate the limitations of such an understanding. It will be recalled that in Scott's (2001) discussion of the diverse accounts of social power he identifies four elementary forms: force, manipulation, signification and legitimation, which combine in different and variable ways so as to give rise to concrete patterns of domination and resistance. Consequently, the real strength of Sparks et al.'s (1996) account of order in prisons is that it develops the issue of legitimacy in a far more robust manner than has hitherto been attempted, through arguing that:

> one can identify a number of facets of legitimacy relevant to the maintenance of order and the incidence of disorder in prisons. Amongst these one would certainly have to include the centrality of fair procedures and ... consistent outcomes. A third component concerns the quality of behaviour of officials – regarded in some quite strong sense as *representing* the system. Fourthly it is possible that the basic regime of the institution – its accommodation, services, and activities – may itself be regarded as illegitimate in failing to meet commonly expected standards (cf. Woolf, 1991). Therefore one can envisage circumstances under which institutions meet some of these criteria but not others. A procedurally 'correct' and bureaucratically efficient regime might simply fail on grounds of impersonality and lack of humaneness (cf. Jacobs, 1977), perhaps helping to explain why prison disorders can occur in brand new, uncrowded, well resourced facilities. (Sparks et al., 1996: 89, emphasis in original)

Their particular definition of legitimacy builds primarily on the work of Beetham (1991) who argues that all systems of power relations seek legitimation and in his discussion he emphasises the normative dimension, since 'a given power relationship is not legitimate because people believe in its legitimacy, but because it can be *justified in terms* of their beliefs' (Beetham, 1991: 11, emphasis in original).

Beetham (1991: 16) states that, although the specific content of legitimating principles is historically variable, there is a common underlying structure, and he identifies three dimensions which provide the legitimate basis for the exercise of power:

(i) it *conforms* to established rules;
(ii) the rules can be justified through *beliefs shared* by both dominant and subordinate;
(iii) there is evidence of *consent* by the subordinate to the particular power relations that obtain.

The three dimensions are not alternatives, they all contribute to legitimacy and generate the moral basis for the subordinate to comply or cooperate with the powerful – the extent to which each component is realised in any given context will be one of degree. For Sparks et al. (1996: 87) the strength of Beetham's (1991) characterisation lies in the way it can highlight variations in prison regimes, and it highlights:

> the ways in which prisoners experience these variations, to what they want or expect from the prison and its staff, and to how the latter respond to these demands. Amongst the dimensions of prison life which this concern throws into sharp relief, we will argue, are questions of consistency and discretion in the application of rules, and prisoners' perceptions of the fairness or otherwise of disciplinary and grievance procedures. Moreover, we will suggest, the legitimacy of such arrangements is generally integral to the success or otherwise of a prison in sustaining order over time. (Sparks et al., 1996: 87)

Tyler's (1990) *Why People Obey the Law* is an equally important text in their account. His analysis is less a treatise on political theory and more an empirical investigation into the bases of legitimacy; as it is based on a panel study of Chicago's citizens that examines their experiences and attitudes to encounters with the police or courts, it appears to confirm that the key to securing compliance lies in people's experience of the fairness of procedures. Greater concern was expressed for equality of treatment and the manner of their treatment, rather than an overriding emphasis placed purely on the outcome of their case. This suggests that 'people are more likely to accept an adverse outcome whilst retaining intact their prior view of the legitimacy of the system as such if they feel that their case has been dealt with in a procedurally correct way and that they have been accorded respect by those in authority' (Sparks et al., 1996: 88). Furthermore, in prisons consistency of outcomes is particularly important due not only to the frequency of such encounters with authority, but also as knowledge of outcomes is likely to be widespread in a relatively short period of time, not least since such matters form substantive topics of prisoners' conversations.

Clearly Sparks et al. (1996) are emphasising, in contrast to Colvin (1992), the importance of normative compliance and the moral involvement of prisoners in their subordination. Additionally, they insist that their 'understanding that prisons embody some version of a normative order is not in any sense intended to imply consensualism' (Sparks, 1996: 303), yet it is at this point that their account of legitimacy faces difficulties. There is, as they are aware, a fine distinction 'between the "taken-for-granted" and the "accepted-as-legitimate"' (Sparks et al., 1996: 89). This distinction is crucial, for it could be argued that, in a number of ways, power in prisons represents an inevitable, 'external fact' for prisoners – in which the experience of confinement is endured without any reference to some version of legitimacy. It is unfortunate that Sparks et al. (1996) chose not to pursue the implications of this distinction, as it is vital to shedding light on how social order is possible, and it will be argued that the dull compulsion of prison rituals produces a fourth solution to the problem of order, through Durkheim's (1966) overlooked concept of fatalism (see Lockwood, 1992) that explains why crises of disorder are not more frequent even when penal power lacks legitimacy. Nevertheless, it is important to emphasise that social order is always 'a matter of degree' (Wrong, 1994: 9) and whilst it is possible to classify social relations according to whether they are predominantly coercive, remunerative, normative or fatalistic the overall point is that order in prisons is a messy process. It is this variable dynamic that much of the book will be attempting to capture.

The discussion over the last two chapters has primarily been concerned with defining the key concepts of power, discourse, resistance and genealogy in the context of reconciling micro and macro forms of sociological analysis. The next chapter is rather less preoccupied with conceptual development. Instead it attends to the state of imprisonment in England and Wales over the last few decades so that an indication of the severe problems to be found in prisons, penal policy and crime control can be sketched. This will enable an initial understanding of how changing modes of governance articulated at the level of the state are translated in a specific site that the remainder of the book will document.

Notes

1 Park and Burgess (1921) first defined the term (Miller, 1986: 5). See also Park's (1972) doctoral dissertation, *The Crowd and the Public*, originally published in 1904, which provides a fascinating discussion of the irrationality of crowd mentality and the democracy of the public sphere – a contradiction that has plagued twentieth-century thought.

2 Collective behaviour is a broad concept and covers a diverse range of phenomena – from panics, riots, crazes, disasters to UFOs. Yet underlying this diversity is the notion that each, in some sense, departs from the more routine and institutionalised aspects of social life (Skolnick, 1969: 331).

3 It should also be recognised that these 'factors' are ones which administrators claim to have little influence over, accounting for its popularity in official diagnoses of unrest.

4   The text itself arises from the Independent Inquiry conducted by the Gateway Exchange (1987), in which the authors formed part of the Committee of Inquiry. The Independent Inquiry arose in response to a series of protests in the Scottish prison system in the mid-1980s and sought to counter the selective, reductive accounts produced by the prison department, the Scottish Office, and the media (see also Sim, 1991, 1992).

5   Simon (2000) draws an important distinction in U.S. prison sociology between the 'golden era' of Clemmer (1958), Sykes (1958) and Jacobs (1977), texts which sought to provide a knowledge for the state to govern the social through inclusive strategies, and those more recent accounts like DiIulio (1987) and Useem and Kimball (1989), which represent a 'post-social' approach to governing through emphasising technocratic practices that 'work'. In other words, there is a reversal of priority from the prisoner community to prison management (and its failures) as the most efficient source of knowledge on prison disorder, and the more appropriate point of prevention. As should be clear, from the previous chapter, the principle of symmetry that I advocate insists that neither staff nor prisoners should be privileged in any analysis, for this only produces partial and selective accounts of prison life. Nevertheless, it is true that prison management had received scant attention in the literature, but this does not necessarily mean that their reintroduction to the analytical gaze automatically involves a commitment to technocratic solutions to the problem of order in prisons, as I will indicate in this book (see also Liebling, 2000, for another attempt to go beyond administrative penology).

6   Bert Useem has refined his position in collaboration with Jack Goldstone (Goldstone and Useem, 1999), in an attempt to bring the discussion of prison unrest into closer harmony with the sociological thinking on revolution. For instance, they extend Skocpol's (1979, 1994) argument that the origins of revolution are not to be found in the desires of revolutionaries to overthrow the state, but in the vulnerability of particular states to revolutionary conflicts. Clearly, this is an important development, but it does not serve to challenge his overall thesis that the activities of the powerful remain at the forefront of explanation, in relation to widespread grievances amongst the prisoner population, so that 'warden or staff actions, taken in response to expressions of grievance, that are seen as excessive, arbitrary, unjust, ineffective, or precluding peaceful reform, therefore turning efforts by aggrieved parties to seek remedy into attempts to create a prison riot' (Goldstone and Useem, 1999: 1003). Their more recent work illustrates how policy interventions can have a rapid and decisive impact on social order (Useem and Goldstone, 2002).

7   There is, of course, a 'resource mobilisation' school of thinking on collective action, in which civil disorder is characterised as an overtly political struggle with the powerful (influential statements include Tilly et al., 1975; Tilly, 1978; Gamson, 1975; Jenkins and Perrow, 1977; McAdam, 1982; McCarthy and Zald, 1977; Oberschall, 1973, 1978). It is, perhaps, not surprising that this approach has not been employed to inform an understanding of prison protest, as there is a tendency to concentrate on the emergence of well defined and organised social movements. Though it could be used to explain the uprising at Attica in 1971 and the organised sit-ins that occurred across British and French prisons in the early 1970s (in which there was clear evidence of prisoner solidarity and outside support for these political struggles against authority) it runs into crucial difficulties when accounting for the protests in the more recent past (such as at the Penitentiary of New Mexico in 1980 and Strangeways in 1990), which were characterised more by a fragmented, atomised and predatory set of responses to incarceration. In other words, the central explanatory features (an increase in prisoner solidarity and heightened political

awareness) of a resource mobilisation account of unrest are missing. It is equally the case that the concept of resistance is underdeveloped in this school of thought. For instance, one proponent insists that 'all forms of collective action, including violent ones [are] essentially purposeful, rational pursuit or defences of collective interests' (Oberschall, 1978: 298). The implications of this claim will be examined in what follows.

8   It is no coincidence that Nietzsche's (1961) Zarathustra is continually plagued by a monkey jumping along behind him and pulling on his coat-tails. The metaphor is a permanent reminder of humankind's 'lowly origins'.

9   Such controls included the introduction of the notorious 'snitch' system, which involved coercive (as opposed to voluntary) informing. Prisoners were forced to give up information on fellow prisoners; if they refused officers would deceitfully tell other inmates that the prisoner had informed anyway. In consequence inmate solidarity was corroded as mistrust fragmented prisoners into small cliques and generated an atmosphere of hate that would culminate in the murder of 33 prisoners and torture of a further 200 during the riot.

Chapter 4

Imprisonment in Context: 1965–90

Introduction

There is considerable consensus that the penal system in England and Wales has been in a state of ever deepening crisis since the 1960s – ranging from what Cavadino and Dignan (1992) describe as the orthodox account of Evans (1980), to the radical analysis of Fitzgerald and Sim (1982), the mainstream interpretation of Bottoms (1980), the liberal account of Woolf (1991) and the radical pluralism which Cavadino and Dignan themselves advocate. Whilst few would deny that the penal system has serious, if not irreversible problems, perhaps the key question is how is it able to maintain a semblance of order for most of the time in the face of grave and often intractable difficulties. Moreover, the term crisis implies a critical point in time, usually short-lived, when a situation either ends in catastrophe or the danger is averted. Yet the penal system has not yet totally collapsed nor has it or various governments of the day begun to seriously address the structural properties that give rise to the periodic symptoms of malaise (such as overcrowding, brutality, riots, strikes and so forth) to anything like the extent necessary to proclaim a dramatic improvement in the condition of the system. Instead it makes more sense to view the penal 'crisis' as an enduring feature of the last few decades, a crisis which is composed of several interweaving components that compromise not only the ability of the state to maintain order but also challenge moral sensibilities on what the purposes of imprisonment might, or ought to, be.

The task of this chapter is to indicate the substance of these problems, through focusing on the period 1965 to 1990. This time frame has been chosen for three reasons. First, it will situate the institutional portrait of Strangeways that follows in the context of the broader debates in penal policy that dominated the era. Second, it will give a sense of the shifting dynamics in the composition of the prison population across the penal estate. Third, the time period covers the significant transformation in modes of government based on the welfare state in the management of the economy and social problems, to neo-liberal strategies of rule, which combine free market philosophies, traditional conservative values and the increasing politicisation of crime and control. Nevertheless, it needs to be emphasised that whilst this chapter is primarily concerned with a macro characterisation of crises, change and politics, the picture at particular sites is rather different. This is not to say that the micro level of social interaction is intrinsically more complex than the macro scale of penal change, but rather that the tempo of institutional life is at once more dynamic *and* more static than a general history of penality will allow. However, interaction always occurs in a context, and in these opening remarks some of the major themes in crime and control that have contributed to the durability of the penal system's problems are outlined.

It is clear that stark comparisons can be drawn between the immediate postwar period, when only half a million indictable crimes were recorded each year and the prison population remained under 15,000 (Newburn, 1995: 15), and the relentless penal expansion and accompanying sixfold increase in recorded crime (Sparks, 1996: 207) over the last half of the twentieth century. Even if the usual injunctions against taking statistics at face value stand, the tale is one of increasing crime and control (albeit with short term fluctuations). Nevertheless, there was a widespread expectation at the end of the war that crime levels would remain stable, if not decrease, on account of the anticipated benefits to living standards that the end of hostilities would bring and the new dawning of the welfare state. Yet, in the early years of postwar austerity and reconstruction few could have predicted the enormity of cultural, economic and social change that began to gather pace in the early 1960s and which was to ultimately transform the world forever. As Hobsbawm (1995: 288, emphasis in original) puts it, for '80 per cent of humanity the Middle Ages ended suddenly in the 1950s; or perhaps better still, they were *felt* to end in the 1960s'. The key contradiction, which is still perplexing criminological thought, is that whilst increasing prosperity, security and certainty should have rendered crime a relic of the past in many Western countries the reverse happened as crime inexplicably and inexorably began to rise. For instance, in England and Wales between 1945 and 1955 the total number of recorded offences hovered under and around the half million mark, yet between 1955 and 1965 the total number of offences doubled to over a million in 1965, by 1975 the figure had surpassed two million, approached three and a half million in 1985 and reached five million in 1990 (Home Office, 1993: 8).

This remarkable increase in crime has had at least four consequences. First, it has profoundly challenged that branch of criminological theory which has concentrated on causation, and given rise to intense debate on the Left between neo-Marxist idealists and social-democratic realists, the return to biological positivism and folk demonism on the Right, whilst the bureaucratic branch of the state has been busy developing an 'administrative' criminology which has come to regard crime as a normal, if regrettable, outcome of everyday life. From a certain vantage point all of this makes postmodern sense, as the fragmentation of narratives is really a story of the collapse of deference, the embrace of difference, and the disguising of difficulty, which the cultural revolution of the 1960s instigated.

Second, crime in both the popular imagination and personal experience has become a central tenet of public concern and cultural consumption. Moreover, certain kinds of 'hidden' crime, such as domestic violence, child sex abuse and rape have become more visible, whilst forms of corporate, state and 'white collar' crime have periodically attracted sustained attention in ways that would have been unimaginable 30 years ago. Yet, it remains the case that crimes of the powerful and those committed in the home are under-represented in recorded crime figures, and as feminist research has consistently demonstrated, violence against women is widespread and exists throughout the class structure.

The third consequence of the increase in crime is the ways in which 'law and order' became politicised from the mid-1960s, was to prove a telling factor in the 1979 election and is now the very stuff of party politics. Downes and Morgan (1997: 90) have convincingly indicated that 1970 was the decisive election at which the Conservative Party turned the politics of law and order into a winning electoral formula that was to be further refined through the 1970s to the extent that in 1979 their priority was to restore the country to the 'rule of law'. By the 1980s it had become clear that no party could afford to remain silent on law and order, and it has taken Labour a substantial period of time to convince the electorate that it too can be 'tough on crime', whilst also being 'tough on the causes of crime'. However, the main target of Labour criticism in the mid-1990s concentrated on flaws in the criminal justice system under the Conservatives, in particular falling conviction rates, juvenile justice reforms and inconsistent sentencing.

The fourth consequence of the increase in crime is that there have been profound transformations in the criminal justice system over this period to the extent that the penal crisis, at a very basic level, can be regarded as simply too many offenders and too few prison places, which has given rise to overcrowding, understaffing, decrepit conditions and poor security. However, whilst the overall number of prisoners has increased sharply, the use of imprisonment as a proportion of all sentences has actually decreased since the war. As Young (1999: 44–6) points out, this has little to do with leniency but rather the rise of actuarial techniques of justice (Feeley and Simon, 1992, 1994) in which the bureaucratic management of problem populations through risk calculation has become paramount. The scale of these transformations cannot be underestimated and they have resonated throughout the criminal justice system, from the policing of streets, through to judges passing sentence, and encompass not only prison landings but also extend out into the 'community' from supervisory orders to shopping centres. What unites these otherwise diverse places is the anticipation, monitoring and distribution of potential trouble according to the principle of risk probability based on social classifications, such as being young, black, working class, male and so forth. In fact, some 25 years ago Bottoms (1977) identified a strategy of bifurcation operating in penal policy, which refers to the explicit attempts to distinguish between 'ordinary' and 'run of the mill' offenders from those regarded as 'serious' and 'dangerous', in which 'community penalties' are designed for the former, whilst imprisonment is reserved for the latter. This philosophy was made explicit in the Criminal Justice Act of 1991, though the introduction of parole in 1967 and subsequent developments in its use, particularly in the 1980s, are also informed by the logic of bifurcation, a point to which I return below. However, the more general point to be drawn is that whilst the range of sentences which encompasses fines and compensation orders through to various forms of supervision in the 'community', has expanded since the 1960s, imprisonment remains the organising principle of punishment.

Here is not the place to offer a detailed discussion of crime in postwar Britain (see Carrabine et al., 2002, for one interpretation). Instead what needs to be emphasised is that the increase in crime has had wide-ranging implications for criminological theory, relations in civil society, the politicisation of crime, and the management of control, to the extent that any discussion of the penal crisis must recognise the salience of the crisis in criminality that confronts Western societies. Of course, this is not simply a question of counting penal expansion, decrying prison overcrowding, condemning decrepit conditions and so forth, but is above all else a comment on social justice. For as Young (1999: 31) puts it, 'what sort of liberal democratic state is it, that is unable to protect its population from crime yet brings a wider and wider swathe of its population under penal supervision?' In other words, the various dimensions of the penal crisis that I now discuss cannot be divorced from the complex relationships that obtain between political economy, state power and punitive exclusion.

Although 1965 has been chosen as the starting point of this chapter (primarily to dovetail with the narrative in the following chapter), it should be clear that no single year can mark the point at which the English penal system began to deteriorate. Yet, a strong case can be made for insisting that the mid-1960s do mark something of a watershed in English penal history as the term crisis began to assume prescience. For up until this point, the death penalty had dominated public debate on punishment in the postwar era.[1] The decisive events were a series of spectacular, highly publicised and embarrassingly easy prison escapes by two of the 'Great Train Robbers' in 1964 and 1965, and the spy George Blake in 1966, who had served four years of his 42-year sentence for espionage. The latter's flight forced matters to a head, and the Home Secretary's response was to invite Lord Mountbatten (Home Office, 1966) to conduct an inquiry into the escape of Blake and prison security more generally, which was to have far reaching significance.

Classification, Security and Control

It is generally recognised that up until this point the issue of prison security assumed a fairly low priority in the minds of the prison authorities[2] and the debates that followed in the wake of Mountbatten's recommendations have done much, and continue, to shape the penal system of today. Two out of three of his major recommendations were immediately adopted. The first was the introduction of a new four-tier classification system to be applied to all prisoners on reception into prison. The categories are clearly predicated on their assumed security risk, and are: Category A prisoners, 'whose escape would be highly dangerous to the public or police or to the security of the state'; Category B are 'those who need less secure conditions but for whom escape must be made very difficult'; Category C are 'those who cannot be trusted in open conditions but who do not have the ability or resources to make a determined escape bid'; and Category D are 'those who could be trusted under open conditions' (Home Office, 1966: para. 217).

The second recommendation, again swiftly adopted, was that major improvements in the physical security of selected prisons should be implemented, including strengthening perimeter security, the introduction of television surveillance of key areas and the deployment of dog patrols. However, this 'upgrading' of security did not remain restricted to a handful of prisons, as Mountbatten advised, but quickly came to permeate throughout the system, and is captured well in Terence Morris's following observation that:

> when prisons like Pentonville, which by 1967 had been dedicated to holding recidivists serving less than 12 months, became be-decked with wire, closed-circuit TV cameras, dogs and all the other *impendimenta* of security, cynics

remarked that the inhabitants of Islington could sleep safe in their beds in the knowledge that the prison's pathetic collection of drunks and vagrants serving short sentences were safely contained within its walls. (Morris, 1989: 134, emphasis in original)

The third recommendation proved to be the most controversial and called for the 'concentration' of all Category A prisoners into one, new, single-purpose maximum security 'fortress'. The intention behind this policy was that it would not only ensure that 'high risk' prisoners were to be kept in secure surroundings on the Isle of Wight (a 'British Alcatraz' as it quickly became dubbed),[3] but that security could be relaxed in other regimes. This proposal was rejected by the Home Secretary and a subcommittee of the Advisory Council on the Penal System, chaired by Leon Radzinowicz, were asked to consider what type of regime would be the most appropriate for Category A prisoners.

When it reported back (Advisory Council on the Penal System, 1968) alarm was expressed at concentrating all high risk prisoners within a single fortress prison on the grounds that maintaining order and providing a constructive regime would be difficult, if not impossible, in a population composed almost exclusively of 'no-hopers'. Instead the sub-committee advocated what has become known as a policy of 'dispersal', in that maximum security prisoners should be spread around in three training prisons with up-graded perimeter security, and that since Category A prisoners would be a small minority in each 'dispersal' prison, they would therefore be able to be 'absorbed into the general population of those prisons', which would be mainly Category B prisoners (Sparks et al., 1996: 5). Initially, there were three 'dispersal' prisons, by 1970 there were five, by 1980 seven, and by 1990 eight. It is fair to say that whilst the dispersal policy might have solved the issue of perimeter security, it has intensified the problems of internal control; for within the dispersal prison the presence of a small number of maximum security prisoners affects the vast majority of other prisoners who are subjected to a much more custodial and restrictive regime. These problems were soon to surface and would become a major focus of prisoner protest in the 1970s.

For instance, Ryan (1983: 38–9) argues that the riot at Parkhurst prison in 1969 was a direct response to the withdrawal of a constructive regime and the tightening of security in the wake of Mountbatten's recommendations.[4] Out of a prison population of around 350, 50 were regularly Category A prisoners. As football matches were cancelled and working allotments gave way to barbed wire and dog patrols, the discontent resulted in over 150 prisoners barricading themselves in association rooms with a number of hostages. A petition signed by 120 prisoners against these restrictions and allegations of

Power, Discourse and Resistance

staff brutality was made public and the Home Secretary immediately ordered an inquiry. However, the report was never published and only a small number of staffing changes were implemented. Within months the prison erupted into the worst riot since the Dartmoor mutiny of 1932, in which 28 prisoners and 35 officers were injured.

The response of the prison authorities to the unrest was oppressive and included the introduction of tactical intervention squads, the segregation of prisoners under 'Rule 43', and the reallocation of prisoners deemed to be disruptive (Newburn, 1995: 21). In many respects the events at Parkhurst marked a new era of prisoner protest and an embittering of relationships. Within three years a national prisoners' rights movement was organised in the wake of unrest at Brixton in early 1972 and the rise of the civil rights movement more generally. The Preservation of the Rights of Prisoners (PROP) was formed by a small group of ex-prisoners who drew up a 'Prisoners' Charter', which called for a wide ranging set of demands. These included, amongst many others, the right to institute legal proceedings without the permission of the Home Office; the right to consult legal advisors in confidence; the right to legal representation at disciplinary hearings; the right to receive reasons from the Parole Board when applications were rejected; and the ending of censorship over correspondence. These demands were widely supported by prisoners and months later, in August 1972, a national sit-down demonstration was organised to publicise the demands, in which it is estimated that between 5,000 to 10,000 prisoners took part around the country (Ryan, 1983: 47–8).

It is, perhaps, not unsurprising that the disturbances brought an increasingly paramilitary response, in which the introduction of control units that operated on the principle of sensory deprivation is one instance of the security crack-down. Following the controversy surrounding their use, the units were suspended in 1975, and in 1983 the government's own Control Review Committee accepted that this approach to disorder was a dead end for the prison service (Cavadino and Dignan, 1992: 130). Equally importantly, the politicisation of the prisoners' movement inspired the increasing militancy of the prison officers themselves and the significant point is that the 1970s were characterised by problems of control. Following on from the largely peaceful demonstrations organised by PROP in 1972, major prison unrest was almost entirely conducted in the dispersal prisons (such as at Gartree and Albany in 1972, Hull in 1976, and Wormwood Scrubs in 1979), and was met by the paramilitary Minimum Use of Force Tactical Intervention squad (MUFTI). Yet, as Rutherford (1986: 82) argues at the end of the decade 'it was not prisoners but unionised custodial staff that posed the greatest challenge to the Home

Office control of the prison system'. For instance, in 1978 over 60 branches of the Prison Officers' Association (POA) were involved in over one hundred separate disputes (Ryan, 1983: 66). The industrial action centred on staffing levels, pay, conditions and overtime (Newburn, 1995: 25) and the threat of further strikes in the autumn of 1979 forced the government to announce an inquiry into the state of the prison system in November 1978, under the chairmanship of a High Court judge, Mr Justice May.

Whilst the May Report (Home Office, 1979) was an important examination of the prison system, it was published five months into the first Thatcher administration, and its insistence that the prison population should be reduced was greeted in 1982 by the biggest prison building programme the century had yet seen, in which 25 new prisons were to be built at an estimated cost of over £1,300 million (Newburn, 1995: 27). The various debates, implications and recommendations of the report are discussed in more detail below, for the Inquiry's verdict on the Mountbatten Report is worth quoting, as they found it:

> hard to evaluate just how much of a change in ethos the Mountbatten report did initiate, but there is certainly a widespread belief that it ushered in an era in which concern with security became, and has remained, central to large parts of the system. (Cited in Newburn, 1995: 20)

Although elements of this obsession with security have been documented, there are two important points to be drawn from this observation. First, the emphasis across the penal system became so centred on blanket security and technological control that they increasingly dominated managerial thinking and staff practice at the expense of other objectives, such as the development of constructive regimes, which will be discussed in more detail in the following chapter. The second, and related point, is that the system of classification maintains a sharp differentiation between dispersal, training and local prisons, to the extent that the latter have come to bear the brunt of the chronic overcrowding, squalid conditions and understaffing that characterise the various dimensions of the prison crisis, whilst the dispersal and training prisons have to a large extent been protected from these problems. It is important to recognise that the May Inquiry did not simply restrict itself to a consideration of staff unrest, but interpreted its terms of reference broadly – as an opportunity to assess the state of the prison system in the UK. For by the late 1970s the consequences of an expanding prison population were such that they could no longer be ignored, and it is to these matters that I now turn.

Expansion, Overcrowding and Conditions

In order to make sense of the expanding prison population it is helpful to begin with some discussion of longer-term trends. It is clear that since the 1950s the growth in the prison population has consistently kept pace with available space in penal institutions. This is in marked contrast to the inter-war era, when prisons were routinely half full. For instance, in 1928 there were only just over 11,000 prisoners in a system that could offer 20,000 cells, and by 1938 the number of prisoners remained around the 11,000 mark, but many prisons had been closed on the grounds that they were no longer required – reducing the number of places available by about 5,000 (Stern, 1993: 24). This was in spite of a considerable increase in recorded indictable crime, particularly in the 1930s. The main reason for this general reduction in the courts' proportionate use of imprisonment was the probation order, which had been introduced in 1907, and a prevailing sense of optimism about the achievements of probation had developed by the 1930s (Bottoms, 1987: 179). As should now be apparent this is in marked contrast to the postwar era, in which there was a fivefold increase in recorded crime (from 280,000 in 1938 to 1,334,000 in 1965). During this period the courts' proportionate use of imprisonment continued to decrease (but the fine had now replaced probation as the main form of sentence), yet the prison population practically tripled – from 11,100 in 1938 to 32,500 in 1968 (Bottoms, 1987: 181).

Again the mid-1960s mark something of a watershed for the penal system, in that the prison population was three times its pre-war level at a time when the courts were using imprisonment proportionately less than ever for indictable offences and employing a range of penalties originally conceived in 1907. In many respects this was a turning point in that the practical problems of running a prison system in these circumstances had become central to policy makers:

> one factor which was of obvious importance was the size of the prison population ... The population of the general local prisons exceeded their cellular capacity by about 40 per cent, and there were over 6,000 persons sleeping three in a cell. Even a cursory reading of the Parliamentary Debates which preceded the passing of the 1967 Criminal Justice act shows that this problem was clearly in the minds of both Government and Opposition. (Sparks, 1971: 384–5, cited in Bottoms, 1987: 181–2)

Since 1966, the general theme of reducing the prison population has been the mainstay of academic, reform group and Home Office debate, discussion and concern. The principal means by which criminal policy has attempted to discourage courts from sending people to prison has been through the creation of 'alternatives to custody', which include the suspended sentence, the community service order, and probation with special conditions (these are examined in detail by Bottoms, 1987).

Nevertheless, it is important to recognise that whilst the prison population had been rising fairly steadily since the war, the proportionate use of imprisonment had been decreasing. This long-term trend came to an end in the mid-1970s. For instance, in 1974 imprisonment had fallen as low as 15 per cent of all sentences imposed, yet by 1986 it represented 21 per cent (Hale, 1989: 334). However, the issue of prison numbers was clearly exercising ministerial minds, which was spelled out in a speech by the Home Secretary to NACRO in July 1975, where Roy Jenkins insisted that:

> The prison population now stands at over 40,500. It has never been higher. If it should rise to, say 42,000, conditions in the system would approach the intolerable and drastic action to relieve the position would be inescapable. We are perilously close to that position now. We must not just sit back and wait for it to happen. If we can prevent it, we must do so. (Quoted in Stern, 1993: 25)

It would seem that the Home Secretary was incapable of delivering 'drastic action', as the 'intolerable' figure was reached in October 1976. As Table 4.1 indicates, the prison population has consistently kept pace with the available accommodation throughout the 1980s, the implications of which I discuss below, but at this point it is worthwhile commenting on the recommendations of the May Inquiry (Home Office, 1979).

It is important to recall that the immediate context at the end of the 1970s was a spiralling prison population, industrial unrest and prisoner protest, combined with a profound sense of disillusionment that the fundamental objectives of the penal system, to reform and rehabilitate prisoners, were simply not working. Whilst the Inquiry had been set up by a Labour administration in November 1978, its Report did not appear until October 1979 at which point the Thatcher Government had been in power for some five months. Nevertheless, May's recommendations on pay and conditions were fully accepted in the hope that this would put an end to industrial action – yet quite the reverse happened. Disappointed with the settlement, industrial action escalated and for a period of time the army were called in to run two prisons (Ryan, 1983: 66), and intractable industrial relations were to be a persistent theme in the 1980s.

The lasting legacy of the report was the establishment of an inspectorate independent of the prison service, but directly accountable to the Home Secretary. This body continues to produce critical reports on particular prisons

Table 4.1   Prison overcrowding: 1966 to 1990

	Average daily population	Certified normal accommodation	Percentage occupied
1966	33,086	31,274	106
1968	32,461	32,474	100
1970	39,028	32,992	118
1972	38,328	36,236	106
1974	36,867	35,342	104
1976	41,443	36,675	113
1978	41,796	37,735	111
1980	43,109	38,472	112
1982	43,754	38,747	113
1984	43,349	39,033	111
1986	46,889	40,811	115
1988	49,949	44,149	113
1990	45,636	42,804	107

Source: Adapted from Home Office (1991: Table 6.1) and Stern (1993: Table 2).

and robust statements on aspects of penal policy. In addition, the report is significant as it articulated the ideological crisis of purpose that had become visible in the penal field, which was part of the broader economic, social and political transformations that were under way by the late 1970s and that are commented on in more detail below. All the same, the Committee maintained that imprisonment should be used as little as possible and supported policies to reduce prison numbers – a view that was shared by the new Home Secretary, William Whitelaw, who in a series of widely publicised speeches advocated a reduction in the use of imprisonment (see Stern, 1993: 142–4 for further commentary). In many respects, Whitelaw was adrift from the direction his party was taking and regularly received hostile receptions at Conservative conferences. He was succeeded in June 1983 by Leon Brittan and a new era of penal politics began.

Even though the Committee supported policies to reduce the prison population, they were realistic in their pessimistic assessment that these were unlikely to succeed and consequently recommended a massive prison building and refurbishment programme, which it was hoped would end overcrowding and 'slopping out' (King and McDermott, 1989: 109). However, the main failing of the May report in this regard was that it refused to confront the problems posed by the dispersal policy that had directly contributed to the impoverishment of penal regimes since the mid-1960s. As Table 4.1 indicates prison overcrowding has been a persistent problem over this period.

There are two important points to be made in relation to penal expansion and overcrowding. The first is that it is vital to make a distinction between the number of people in prison at any one time, which is the 'average daily population', and the number of people sent to prison in a given period, which are the 'receptions into custody'. In other words, it is important to distinguish between the stock and flow of the prison population, for most custodial experiences are surprisingly brief. As Morgan (1997: 1151–2) puts it, the overwhelming majority of prisoners 'are in prison for a matter of days, weeks, or months rather than years, even if, for some the experience is repeated'. Whilst this might sound counter-intuitive, it is important to recall that there has been a policy of bifurcation operating across criminal justice policy since at least the mid-1970s (Bottoms, 1977), which enables governments to pursue both 'soft' and 'tough' sentencing options simultaneously. For instance, on 30 June 1980, 22 per cent of prisoners were serving sentences of over four years, whereas 43 per cent were serving sentences of up to 16 months. By 1990 these figures had been practically reversed, with 42 per cent of prisoners serving sentences of over four years, whilst 24 per cent were serving sentences of up to 16 months (Home Office, 1992: Fig. 4a).

What is more, bifurcation is also present in executive release policy, and Morgan (1994: 904) suggests that the dividing point has been around the four year mark. Throughout the 1980s prisoners serving sentences of three years or less have gradually served proportionately less of their sentence, whereas those with sentences of more than five years have served proportionately more of their sentence, which has contributed to the expansion of the long-term prison population and reduction of the short-term population. These changes are partly explained by the introduction of parole in 1967 and subsequent developments in its use. Initially, parole was regarded as a privilege to be earnt by prisoners who had attained a 'recognisable peak in their training' (Home Office, 1965), yet following initiatives by two Home Secretaries, Roy Jenkins in 1974 and Leon Brittan in 1983, an increasing proportion of short and medium sentence prisoners received parole almost routinely (Morgan, 1997: 1154).

Although Jenkins encouraged the Parole Board to relax their policy in relation to minor property offenders, since they were unlikely to commit serious offences on licence, Brittan's package of controversial measures were designed not only to underline the 'law and order' credentials of the Conservative administration, but were also an attempt to rationalise a criminal justice system that was regarded as inadequate, prone to industrial dispute and simply not 'delivering'. Brittan's changes were far reaching and included the increase of maximum sentences for carrying firearms, introducing legislation to refer 'over-lenient' sentences back to the Court of Appeal and the highly contentious changes to the parole system. On the one hand, the threshold of eligibility for parole was reduced from 12 months to six months, which was a largely liberal measure, whilst on the other he introduced much tougher policies for long-term prisoners. It was this which generated controversy as it effectively meant that Ministers, and not the joint committee of Parole Board and Home Office officials, would now set a minimum tariff period to be served by life sentence prisoners; and that particular categories of lifer (those who had murdered police or prison officers, children, or who had killed in the course of terrorism or armed robbery) would not be released until they had served a minimum period of at least 20 years (Morgan, 1997: 1154). The consequences of these changes were profound, as it has meant a considerable increase in the size of the long-term prison population and generated significant discontent as the policy is widely regarded as unjust.[5]

The second point is that the degree of overcrowding is generally calculated with reference to what is termed the Certified Normal Accommodation (CNA). This is taken as the number of prisoners that the system can accommodate without overcrowding, which is one prisoner per cell. However, as Cavadino and Dignan (1992: 119) argue, the CNA should at best be regarded as a 'notional figure only', since not all accommodation said to be available is actually usable, some may be out of commission during refurbishment, whilst there is also a need to maintain spare capacity for receptions and transfers. More importantly, it does not provide an accurate account of where overcrowding is concentrated.[6] Table 4.2 indicates the extent of overcrowding in local prisons, which serve to confine the majority of short-term prisoners, those on remand, and to allocate or transfer prisoners to other institutions in the penal complex, such as dispersal or training prisons.

Even though their positions in this league table may vary, most of these local prisons have long lived with overcrowding, and one of the first books on imprisonment to mention the word crisis was explicitly concerned with the deteriorating conditions in the local prisons wrought by overcrowding (Sparks, 1971). The problem is partly explained by the inflexibility of prison space, which was compounded by the Mountbatten security classifications – for instance, a Category C training prison will not take higher security category prisoners (A and B). However, there have been and remain clear policy preferences to concentrate overcrowding in local prisons. For instance, the Prison Department Report for 1966 confidently asserted that:

Table 4.2   Most overcrowded prisons on 30 June 1989

Prison	Population	Certified normal accommodation	Percentage occupied
Leeds	1,291	642	201.1
Bedford	322	178	180.9
Leicester	368	204	175.5
Hull	653	386	169.2
Lewes	387	229	169.0
Chelmsford	400	242	165.3
Manchester	1,586	972	163.2
Reading	288	178	161.8
Oxford	205	127	161.4
Birmingham	950	592	160.5

Source: Home Office (personal communication).

> During the period since 1945 the local prisons have been increasingly overcrowded but the training prisons and borstals have been preserved from the effects of overcrowding so that progress with the treatment and training of offenders should continue. (Cited in Stern, 1993: 27)

This is a clear policy commitment to exclude the local prison population (and subsequently remand centres) from the 'treatment and training' mission, which is expressed less sanguinely 15 years later by the Chief Inspector of Prisons in 1981:

> Overcrowding is almost entirely restricted to local prisons. This is not a matter of coincidence but rather a result of deliberate Prison Department policy to optimize the regime in training prisons and make best use of the facilities available there. (Cited in Stern, 1993: 27–8)

The rationale behind this policy is the assumption that for prisoners serving short sentences there is too little time to achieve results, and as the following chapter will indicate, a number of the local prisons act as 'sin bins' for disruptive prisoners from the dispersal prisons under the guise of 'temporary transfers' in official rhetoric.

Table 4.3 indicates the extent to which the policy has been 'successful' in meeting these objectives of concentration and protection. As can be seen local prisons and remand centres bear the brunt of overcrowding, whilst the other institutions that comprise the penal estate are largely operating below capacity. The problem of numbers has to be located in the context of dilapidated physical conditions in which prisoners are contained, combined with poor sanitation, scarcely edible food, decaying cramped cells, clothing shortages and brief, inadequate family visits. Compounding this wretchedness in local prisons and remand centres is the severely restricted and oppressive regimes that are imposed since there is neither the space, facilities nor resources to provide prisoners with a range of training, work and educational opportunities when there are too many prisoners to cope with. The following chapters will document in more detail the conditions to be found at Strangeways, which functioned as both a local prison and remand centre, for a discussion of prisoners and staff is now necessary.

Table 4.3   Concentration of prison overcrowding, 1989

Type of institution	Population	Certified normal accommodation	Percentage occupied
Local prisons	17,354	12,247	141
Remand centres	3,079	2,809	110
Closed training prisons	16,543	17,086	97
All institutions for women	1,763	1,859	95
Open prisons	3,252	3,700	88
All Young Offender Institutions	6,509	7,626	85

Source: Home Office (1990: Table 1.6).

The Keepers and the Kept

In order to understand the nature of the staffing problems that have contributed to the crisis in prisons, it is worthwhile commenting on the nature of occupational culture of prison officers. Prior to the reorganisation of staffing in 1987 under the confident title of 'Fresh Start' the prison service staffing structure was formally organised on a paramilitary model with a 'lower ranks' force of prison officers up to the rank of Chief Officer, and an 'officer' class of managers composed of non-uniformed governor grades. As Michael Welch (1996: 132) observes, the paramilitary influence goes beyond the designation of titles, rank, uniforms, salutes and parades to encompass an organisational structure based on 'a strict hierarchy, an inflexible chain of command and vertical communication lines which are deliberately structured to enhance organizational performance'. In the early 1970s Thomas (1972: 6–7) could assert that the 'para-military structure ... and organisational culture, of the prison staff remains essentially the same as it was in 1877' (the date when the management of prisons came under centralised state control). Thomas (1972: 8–9) maintains that the justification for a paramilitary structure results from the 'primary task of containment and control' and that this should be read as a form of 'crisis-control' in which the paramilitary structure can be 'quickly mobilised to deal with threats to that control'. On this reading the militaristic structure is a requirement of the organisational needs that are essentially coercive in character and determine to exact obedience from *both* prisoners and staff.[7] The latter require clearly delineated roles to understand the extent and limit of their authority, in which the militaristic model is particularly well suited (Thomas and Pooley, 1980: 19).

More generally, the fact that, until recently, the majority of prison officers have been recruited from the armed services, usually as regulars rather than as national servicemen, has obviously contributed to the militaristic ethos of the service. For example, a study into staff attitudes in the early 1980s found that 51 per cent of Discipline Officers had experience of the armed services and most (78 per cent) of these were volunteer regulars (Marsh et al., 1985: 19). The authors of the study found that the officers were:

> a remarkably homogenous group of people. The great majority are middle-aged family men ... The majority share some kind of military background in an age where such a background is becoming increasingly rare. They have the kinds of educational and previous employment background usually associated with manual workers – but few other social characteristics that would place them as members of the working-class community. (Marsh et al., 1985: 22)

An important element of the occupational culture that emerges from the survey is that it provides a source of solidarity and support for a group of individuals who feel misunderstood, undervalued, pessimistic and insecure with social life beyond their immediate social relationships. Part of this remoteness from the working-class community arises from the strong likelihood that a prison officer can be moved on anywhere in the course of a career and, 'this must contribute to the prison officers' dependence on other prison officers for social and community life' (Stern, 1993: 65). Compounding this is the widely held belief among prison officers that outside society regards them as, at best, bullies. Hence a suspicious world view exists that is combined with views towards their job which were generally 'jaundiced ... a feeling that contains an odd mixture of bravado, cynicism, resentment and, it must be said, fear' (Marsh et al., 1985: 56). However, one commentator suggests that this picture has begun to change in recent years:

> Twenty years ago, virtually no prison officers had any education qualifications. Today the indelibly working class culture of the majority, shaped now by previous experience of manual or clerical work rather than military discipline, is blended with a sizeable minority of recruits with 'A' levels or a degree ... seeking advancement within an integrated career structure. (Morgan, 1994: 931)

The implications of these changes are examined in greater detail in the next chapter.

The relationships between governing staff and prison officers have been frequently portrayed in terms of mutual suspicion and resentment – exemplified in the fraught industrial relations between the Prison Officers Association (POA), the Home Office and local management. In spite of this antagonism it is important to recognise that there are a number of dimensions to the staffing crisis. It encompasses industrial action, relations between officers and both prisoners and governors, and understaffing. Fitzgerald and Sim (1982) have identified an additional 'crisis of authority'. This refers to the prison officers' belief that their positions have been undermined by the intrusion of welfare personnel and concerns over prisoners' rights entering into prisons. The most manifest component of the staffing crisis is the long history of industrial conflict. Industrial disputes have been a recurring theme since the 1970s. For instance, Stern (1993: 63) remarks that in 1976 there were 34 incidents of industrial action by POA branches; in 1977 there were 42 and in 1978 there were 119, with industrial unrest continuing unabated in the 1980s. The most serious of these occurred in April 1986 when prison officers imposed a work-to-rule over staffing levels. This led to major prisoner unrest and riots in eighteen prisons. The reorganisation of staffing in 1987 under Fresh Start was an attempt to unify the service on the model of the police force, in which endeavours were made to blur the distinctions between the management and the managed with only one point of entry, at the bottom, and the same career prospects for all who enter the service.

Whilst I deal in more detail with the implications of Fresh Start in the following chapter, it is fair to say that it has not alleviated the discontent. For instance, there was major industrial action at Wandsworth in 1989 and in July 1991 there were official disputes at 49 prisons (Cavadino and Dignan, 1992: 16). The issue of staff shortages is portrayed by the POA as one that can be dealt with through improved pay and enhanced status, whereas the Home Office views the question in terms of the arcane, restrictive and rigid practices developed by the POA.

The intractability of industrial relations is only one element of a wider prison staff crisis. Traditionally there has been a gulf between the uniformed officers and the governor grades, which partly relates to their differing class positions but also stems from feelings that their work is undervalued and that governors, and society more generally, care more for prisoners than officers. One of the reasons why the POA argued so vociferously for all levels of the service to wear a uniform at the time of Fresh Start (and were so embittered when the notion was rejected) can be understood in terms of the nature of authority, power, and status in the prison: it is the suit that possesses more of these attributes than the uniform.

A further source of resentment stems from the introduction of welfare specialists, such as probation officers, educational workers and psychologists since the 1960s. As Cavadino and Dignan (1992: 128) point out, not only are welfare personnel entitled to better standards of pay and conditions than basic grade prison officers, but they are also 'usurping a role to which the latter also aspire, however unsuited to it they might be by way of temperament, training or ideology'. The latter is important since it highlights a serious contradiction of roles. Nearly 75 per cent of prison officers thought they were the best people to look after prisoners' welfare (Marsh et al., 1985) – which is undoubtedly true since they are the group that has the most daily contact with prisoners. Yet this has to be tempered against the authoritarian attitudes that officers carry with them, not least since there are frequent calls for tighter prison regimes and greater discipline.

Concerning the characteristics of prisoners, the trend towards bifurcation has been explained – with an increase in long-term prisoners and decrease in short-term sentence prisoners, imprisonment remains numerically dominated by young adult men. For instance, in 1990, 60 per cent were under the age of 30, whilst women comprised 3.5 per cent of the average population in custody (Morgan, 1994: 908). A prison census, conducted in 1991, allows some general points to be made at the end of the historical period under consideration in this chapter. The survey (Walmsley et al., 1992) indicates that prisoners are disproportionately black (15 per cent of males and 23 per cent of females, as compared to less than 5 per cent of the population generally) and working class (83 per cent of male prisoners were from manual, partly skilled, or unskilled groups, compared to 55 per cent of the general population). Approximately two-thirds had left school by the age of 16, with a generally low level of qualifications and for those under 21 the figure was 38 per cent. Over a quarter, 26 per cent, of prisoners had been in local authority care below the age of 16 – the full significance of this indication of deprivation is revealed when it is compared to the figure of 2 per cent for the general population. The mentally disturbed comprise another characteristic element in the prison population – Morgan (1994: 911) estimates that 'approximately two-fifths of all males and two-thirds of all females have pronounced psychiatric or behavioural problems'.

The various agencies that comprise the Criminal Justice System in England and Wales are frequently compared (see Rutherford, 1986; Cavadino and Dignan, 1992; Hudson, 1993) to a series of filters that determine who gets enmeshed in the system and for how long. Though discussions can centre on the uniqueness of the situation in England and Wales, such as the power of discretion exercised by the various agencies under conditions of low visibility (for instance, the independence of the judiciary) – this tends to obscure the similarities in function shared with other criminal justice systems in the West. The various stages act to filter what may initially have been a heterogeneous population into one that is increasingly homogenous by the time it reaches prison. In essence the system selects, distributes, and classifies offences rather than reducing or controlling crime. For instance, the crimes reported to the police are only a proportion of those committed, those caught for committing a crime are only a proportion of offenders, and those sent to prisons are only a proportion of those caught. The situation is well demonstrated in the United States:

> very few of these acts come to the attention of the police ... only a small percentage (less than 20 per cent) results in an arrest. Even of those arrested, many are never charged with a crime ... As we proceed through the stages of the system, we see that the number of people involved become more and more alike in terms of age (younger), race (increasingly non-white), social class (increasing numbers of lower- and working-class people), offence (more and more 'index' offences) ... When we arrive at the last stage, we have the most homogenous grouping in which the vast majority are poor, unskilled, uneducated, and have had much more contact with the criminal (and juvenile) justice system. (Sheldon, 1982: 1–2)

It is important to recognise though that in this homogenous population there is a degree of diversity in the needs, problems and difficulties faced by this group of individuals, for instance the significant proportions of the prison population suffering from some form of mental distress.

Classic prison sociology literature in the United States has been directly concerned with the place of prisoner subcultures in power structures within institutions. However, more recent British sociological writing tends to emphasise the complexity of responses to confinement, which vary a great deal according to the category of prison, the quality of its regime, and the shifting patterns of stratification. As Sparks et al. (1996: 176–81) indicate, with reference to long-term dispersal prisons (where one might expect the presence of well developed subcultures), simple analogies based on class structures, with 'gangsters' portrayed as the 'ruling class' and 'nonces' as a 'lumpenproletariat' are seriously misleading. Instead, a rather more fluid pattern of competing groups (based on ethnic or regional affinities as much as on 'business' interests) was in evidence than the rigid separation of roles and group solidarity that was a defining characteristic of the classic subculture research.

As Rock (1996: 40) puts it, with reference to a women's prison, there is not one prisoner world 'but many'. This is an important point, and is one that has particular resonance for understanding a heterogeneous population in a local prison, whose membership is constantly in flux as new prisoners arrive to be allocated elsewhere, others are returning from dispersal prisons under 'transfers', yet more will be seeing out short-term sentences, whilst there will always be those deemed as 'unsuitable' for training prisons – the 'old lags' who have been imprisoned on many previous occasions. In other words, antagonisms, friendships and influence constantly have to be renegotiated amid the frantic pace of daily change and upheaval on the wings and landings of local prisons. As I will argue in the next chapter, it is the staff occupational culture that plays a pivotal role in conditioning the experience of place that a particular prison conveys, not least because prison officers spend a far greater proportion of their lives in an institution than either the prisoners or their managers.

Authority, Managerialism and Discourse

Up until the early 1970s the guiding principle justifying the use of imprisonment as a technique of crime control was the discourse of rehabilitation, which had become sanctified in 1964 as Prison Rule Number 1 – in that the 'purpose of the training and treatment of convicted prisoners shall be to encourage and assist them to lead a good and useful life'. The long history in which the religious reformation of offenders, advocated at the end of the eighteenth century, came to be replaced by the 'training and treatment' mission of rehabilitation, which emerged during the early twentieth century, has been charted elsewhere (Garland, 1985). Nevertheless, the important point is that the 'rehabilitative ideal' that came to form the orthodox ideology of experts and policy-makers for most of the twentieth century cannot be divorced from the emergence of the welfare state and its preference for the 'social' government of the economy and problem populations. Welfarism can be characterised as one of the great political compromises between organised labour and ruling elites to moderate the effects of unconstrained market forces through social and economic policies that provided safety nets for the poor and the weak, whilst promising a politics of inclusion (Stenson, 2001: 20). In the three decades following the end of the Second World War there was considerable political consensus that crime control was a business best left in the hands of informed professionals and social experts. In other words, these matters 'were seen as issues of routine government and administration rather than an occasion for the mayhem of public *politics*, in the sense of public forms of contest about how ... to conceptualise and manage crime' (Stenson, 2001: 20).

However, the important point is that no one could have predicted the collapse of rehabilitation in the 1970s (Garland, 2001: 53). Conventional accounts of this rupture tend to emphasise the significance of a series of critiques that questioned the effectiveness of treatment programmes (Brody, 1976; Lipton et al., 1975) and is captured in Martinson's (1974) widely popularised pessimism that 'nothing works'. The official disenchantment with rehabilitation was clearly articulated by the May Committee where they unequivocally stated that the 'rhetoric of "treatment and training" has had its day and should be replaced' (May, 1979: para. 4.27). In their evidence to the Inquiry, King and Morgan offered a wide-ranging critique of Prison Rule 1, in that:

> it had never squared with the reality of prison life. Rule 1 was so vague it had never been operationalized. It was inspired by aspirations incapable of fulfilment, something that prison staff had always known. Moreover, it quite arbitrarily excluded remand and trial prisoners from view. Far better, they argued, to try to turn the concept of 'humane containment' – the term coined by the Prison Department to describe the little they offered in local prisons – into a reality. (Morgan, 1997: 1146)

King and Morgan (1980: 31–7) went on to explain that 'humane containment' should be informed by three principles: the minimum use of custody; the minimum use of security; and, the normalisation of the prison. However, the Committee were not persuaded by the arguments on the grounds that '"humane containment" suffers from the fatal defect that it is a means without an end ... Prison staff cannot be asked to operate in a moral vacuum and the absence of real objectives can in the end lead only to the routine brutalization of all the participants' (May, 1979: paras 4.24 and 4.28). Instead, they formulated the notion of 'positive custody' to fill the void created by the scepticism over rehabilitation, which had even fewer supporters than 'humane containment'. In the end the proposed change to Rule 1 never materialised and as the 1980s progressed the question of the aims of imprisonment came subsumed under an increasing emphasis given to financial efficiency, effectiveness, management and performance.

To understand why questions relating to the ideological and material conditions of the prison system have shifted from broad concerns with moral purpose to what Rutherford (1993) terms 'expedient managerialism', where priority is given to narrowly defined performance measures and to short-term trouble-shooting over any articulation of purposes and values, we need to move beyond academic critiques of rehabilitation. For as Garland (2001: 64) forcefully argues, the 'notion that rehabilitation was abandoned because critics woke up one day and realized that it had dangerous possibilities and was prone to being abused is a modern version of the fairy story of Enlightenment reform'. In other words, the objections raised against rehabilitation were hardly new, yet what is important is that the 'institutional and cultural circumstances that gave these writings a contextual power that had not been present when previous writers had made the same criticisms' (Garland, 2001: 64). For Garland (2001) the coming of late modernity has transformed the social and political conditions on which the modern crime control field relied, whilst posing new problems of crime and insecurity, fresh challenges to welfare institutions, and the emergence of a politics that combines free market neo-liberalism and an authoritarian social conservatism.

A central part of Garland's (2001: 92–4) argument is that the welfare state was one of the key sites that helped shape late modernity through providing the conditions under which postwar capitalism could prosper and social democracy emerge. Yet the irony is that by the late 1970s the welfare state came under sustained attack in a political culture that was taking a reactionary stance towards late modernity and the social changes associated with it. In this context, it is difficult to underestimate the significance of the economic recession of the mid-1970s, which combined with widespread industrial unrest, rising crime and the failure of Keynesian economics to deal with unemployment provided the reinvigorated parties of the Right an opportunity to seize the moment. Nevertheless, it is important to recognise that what was truly striking about the election victories of Reagan and Thatcher at the end of the decade was that:

> they owed less to the appeal of their economic policies – which at that stage were conspicuously underdeveloped – than to their ability to articulate popular discontent. Hostility towards 'tax and spend' government, undeserving welfare recipients, 'soft on crime' policies, unelected trade unions who were running the country, the break-up of the family, the breakdown of law and order – these were focal points for a populist politics that commanded widespread support. Appealing to the social conservatism of 'hard working', 'respectable' (and largely white) middle classes, 'New Right' politicians blamed the shiftless poor for victimizing 'decent society' – for crime on the streets, welfare expenditure, high taxes, industrial militancy – and blamed liberal elites for licensing a permissive culture and the anti-social behaviour it encouraged. (Garland, 2001: 97)

The point of this brief discussion is to indicate that the collapse of the rehabilitative ideal as a legitimating principle for imprisonment is intimately connected to these broader changes in the ideological and material conditions of society. Under welfarism rehabilitation could operate as a force geared toward social reclamation in a consensual politics of inclusion, and whilst rehabilitation could be denounced by radical intellectuals as little more than a rhetorical sham that served to disguise the punitive functions of imprisonment, this does not explain its collapse nor what would happen in the 1980s. In other words, the disenchantment with rehabilitation must be located in changing cultural sensibilities that were coming to doubt the basic capacity or desirability of the state to promote welfare.

In many respects the failure of the May Committee to devise a coherent moral purpose for imprisonment in place of rehabilitation and the subsequent emergence of a managerialist agenda can be regarded as symptomatic of these broader historical transformations, from welfarist to neo-liberal forms of governance. However, this is to grant too much certainty and solidity to the neo-liberal project. Instead it is more accurate to view the development of the managerialist agenda as much as 'a reaction to political context and a sense of realpolitik, as an incompletely fleshed out political ideology' (McLaughlin and Murji, 2001: 108). The realpolitik that confronted Conservatives in the early

1980s was that their law and order strategy was not working, as the crime rate continued to soar and criminal justice agencies were condemned for 'failing to deliver'. In this context, a strategy developed that involved the redefinition of the ownership of the crime problem and the promotion of managerialist solutions (McLaughlin and Muncie, 1994: 117). The public now came to be told that the 'sources of crime and its control lie, first and foremost, in the actions of individual citizens and local communities' (McLaughlin and Muncie, 1994: 118), which effectively has led to a diminution of state responsibility for crime control. As Garland (1996) had argued in an earlier article, the *control* of crime has now come to be regarded as a matter that lies beyond the state that requires the institutions and individuals in civil society to manage, whilst the *punishment* of crime remains the business of the state and a significant symbol of state power.

It is important to recognise that alongside these broad transformations the administration of criminal justice fell subject to a series of managerial and legislative reviews that assessed cost-effectiveness and paved the way for reform, under the banner of monetarism. For instance, the prison system has been investigated by a combination of the Audit Commission, the National Audit Office and the Public Accounts Committee in 1985 and 1988 (Fowles, 1990) and it is clear that various criminal justice agencies have increasingly had to justify themselves in terms of 'market competitiveness, managerial resource control and certifiable cost effectiveness' (McLauglin and Muncie, 1994: 119). From the mid 1980s a major source of debate has been the issue of prison privatisation, which became a reality in the early 1990s, whilst the introduction of Fresh Start was justified on the grounds that it would herald a more efficient deployment of staff and resources. The overall point is that these changes and the increasing emphasis given to managerialism have had significant implications for working practices in core criminal justice agencies, not least 'because they necessitate the displacement of the old quasi-military model of administration' (McLaughlin and Muncie, 1994: 119).

The transformations documented in this chapter, as well as the enduring and intractable character of many of the problems outlined here, have a crucial significance in understanding the distinctive institutional history of Strangeways that now follows. It is instructive to conclude with the thoughts of two senior prison officials on this period:

> During the late 1970s and 1980s the prison system was quite clearly going through a long series of serious crises of different kinds, and it is extremely depressing to recall it. Its professed aspiration remained an idealistic mission

of industry and reform, as articulated in the system of training prisons for adult prisoners, and a considerable amount of new industrial plant had, in fact, been put in place during the 1970s. In reality, however, there had been an almost complete loss of confidence in rehabilitation, and the prison service was stumbling around unsuccessfully in a search for something to fill the vacuum. In the absence of anything else, sheer custodianship and security came close to appearing to be what it was all about. (Dunbar and Langdon, 1998: 22–3)

The next chapter begins by introducing the research, sources and methods used in the study. It is directed not only toward capturing something of the everyday life for prisoners, staff and governors in the prison over an extended period of time but also intends to demonstrate how these interactions are structured in important ways by penal discourses that enable certain kinds of conduct whilst constraining others to produce the institution's particular identity.

Notes

1   Legislation that would eventually lead to the abolition of capital punishment was introduced in 1965, which suspended rather than abolished the death penalty. After a free vote in parliament in 1969, the Commons decided by 343 votes to 185 that the Murder (Abolition of Death Penalty) Act 1965 should not expire (Windelsham, 1993: 91). It is fair to say that this was the central issue that mobilised penal reform campaigns and which commanded sustained public attention in the two decades following the end of the war, not least because of a series of cases (such as Derek Bentley, Timothy Evans, James Hanratty and Ruth Ellis) in the 1950s and early 1960s that challenged belief in the infallibility of the law and the appropriateness of the death penalty.

2   Although the Report is regarded as a crucial turning point in recent penal history, Fitzgerald and Sim (1982: 21) convincingly argue that 'the seeds of the security clampdown which followed, and the increasing classification and segregation of prisoners, were already sown'. For instance, special maximum security wings had already been introduced, the conditions in which Mountbatten condemned as such that no country 'with a record of civilized behaviour ought to tolerate any longer than is absolutely as a stop-gap measure' (cited in Fitzgerald and Sim, 1982: 21).

3   The prison was to be called 'Vectis', which was not only the Roman name for the island but also that of the local bus company, who were less than enthusiastic at the choice (Morris, 1989: 131–2). More seriously, Morris (1989: 132) contends that there was considerable opposition within the Prison Department to Mountbatten's proposal and his astute observations concerning the arcane practices of prison administration, one of which did lead to change. His suggestion that a new rank of senior officer should be created between the basic grade of prison officer and principal officer, was accepted without much controversy; whereas his insistence that there should be an Inspector General of Prisons, who would have direct access to the Home Secretary, was viewed as unacceptable by senior permanent officials – though such a post would be created in the 1980s.

4   Ryan's (1983) interpretation is a clear instance of deprivation reasoning and can be critiqued on the basis of the objections raised in Chapter 3. Nevertheless, it is important to emphasise that the security crackdown permeated the system.

5   Important changes to the parole system were introduced in the Criminal Justice Act 1991, which include automatic conditional release at the half-way point in sentences under four years; Parole Board responsibility for release decisions for prisoners serving sentences between four and seven years; the continued involvement of the Home Secretary in release decisions of sentences of seven years or more, whilst the Brittan rules have been abolished (Morgan, 1997: 1155).

6   A third caveat against the use of CNA is that the ideal of accommodating one prisoner per cell possesses little real meaning unless other features are taken into account, such as the desire of prisoners to share, cell size, and the amount of time spent in it (King and McDermott, 1989: 112).

7   A related reason why prison staff are organised in a structure which stresses obedience and supervision from above is to be found in the particular historical circumstances of staff abuses in the eighteenth and nineteenth centuries (Thomas and Pooley, 1980: 19–20).

Chapter 5

Strangeways in Context: 1965–90

Introducing the Research

So far I have argued that the concept of discourse offers a way of thinking that can connect how imprisonment is experienced at particular sites with broader rationalities justifying what prisons are for. This discussion primarily concentrated on a conceptual mapping of six discourses that are of some significance in structuring agency in the penal complex. In Chapter 3, I identified the limits of orthodox thinking on disorder and proposed that a genealogical understanding of resistance is best equipped to grasp the relations of antagonism, compromise and indifference that characterise social formations. There then followed a description of general developments and recurring themes in penal policy. The task in this chapter is to mobilise these theoretical arguments to provide a picture of the routine operation of Strangeways in the two and a half decades leading up to the most spectacular riot in British penal history, to convey the sense of place that the prison evoked with an attendant emphasis on the dynamics of organisational change. In other words, to understand why a prison 'explodes' requires a comprehension of how it 'works' over an extended period of time, for whilst major riots are comparatively rare events in an institution's history the maintenance of order is a precarious condition that needs to be accomplished anew each and every day. The particular focus in this chapter lies with the institutional identity of the prison over this period and the material used here is primarily drawn from oral narratives that are significant as much for their mythical and symbolic dimensions as their factual content, for the memories and reminiscences provide important insights into the individual and collective meanings that the organisation provoked.

In these opening remarks some comments on the methods, sources and purposes of this history are due. In Chapter 2 it was explained that the methodological approach advocated in the sociology of translation is a form of Machiavellian ethnography, which seeks to 'follow the actors' and describe with 'neither fear nor favour of what it is that actors do' (Callon et al., 1986: 5). An immediate, obvious impossibility is raised – I am not, nor was I, in a position to locate myself in Strangeways as a participant observer in the years and months before April 1990, examining and recording the various struggles, accommodations, alliances and conflicts between the actors. But this is to take the phrase too literally, and by way of illustration I will discuss a text that comes closest to the methods employed in the research, yet one that superficially seems to be many worlds removed from that which I will shortly be describing. However, there are many ways in which Diane Vaughan's (1996) analysis of the Challenger Space Shuttle tragedy, when the craft erupted into a fireball 73 seconds after launch on 28 January 1986, does bear important methodological and substantive similarities. Not least since she, like I, 'was not a participant observer inside the organization examining structure and process, but an outsider retrospectively reconstructing both, relying heavily on documents' (Vaughan, 1996: 461).

Her analysis challenges the conventional wisdom that the decision to launch the Shuttle, in the face of known design faults and some internal opposition, was taken on the basis of extraordinary production pressures to launch and a macho, 'can do' spirit of enterprise in NASA. This was the verdict of various Inquiries after the event, and the middle managers were particularly singled out for blame – in effect managerial misconduct is understood as white-collar deviance, rule violation and the 'wrong stuff'. Instead, she reconstructs the decision to launch from the documentary materials and interviews contained in the Inquiries, rendering the decision comprehensible when it is restored to its historical social context – it is seen as normal rather than deviant, and an outcome of following institutional rules rather than breaking them. She suggests that:

> once we relocate these controversial actions in the stream of actions of which they were a part, we see the native view: the meaning they had for participants when they occurred. Again we find the effects of cultural understandings on choice at NASA: actions that analysts defined as deviant after the disaster were acceptable and non-deviant within the NASA culture. (Vaughan, 1996: 120)

Her account is a form of Machiavellian ethnography through its careful adherence to following the actors *at the time* – thus avoiding the retrospective fallacy, highlighted in Chapter 3, which arises from *ex post facto* understandings and interpretations of actions and situations. Vaughan (1996: 393) puts this well when she argues that retrospection 'corrects history, altering the past to make it consistent with the present, implying that errors should have been anticipated'. Her alternative proposition is that action and meaning need to be restored to their local, social and cultural contexts. It is through this recovery that the macro–micro connection is made clear, demonstrating how discursive understandings of what prisons are for and how they should be run are translated in the particular setting of Strangeways. In this way, to use Clifford Geertz's (1973: 23) phrase, 'small facts speak to large issues' (see also Vaughan, 1996: 199). The kind of discourse analysis that is being developed in this book bears important similarities with Geertz's (1973) advocacy of 'thick description' in cultural anthropology. Howarth (2000: 128) has also noted the ways in which such an approach explores 'how, in what forms, and for what reasons social agents come to identify themselves with particular systems of meaning, as well as the constitution, functioning and transformation of systems of discursive practice'. I now turn to a discussion of the sources used in this reconstruction.

The research material that forms the basis of the analysis in the remaining chapters is drawn from a range of sources. The report of the Judicial Inquiry (Woolf and Tumim, 1991: 41–112) is the starting point for such a narrative as it provides a detailed, blow by blow account of the weeks prior to the dissent and the actions taken during the course of the riot. I restrict myself here to evaluating the strengths and weaknesses of using the Inquiry as a data source, since the Woolf diagnosis is critically assessed at various points in this book. In Chapter 1 I stated that a number of strategies were pursued in order to make the Inquiry open to the public and promote wide-scale consultation. These included public hearings and seminars, requests for submissions from individuals and organisations with expertise and experience of prisons, and visiting prisons in the United Kingdom and other countries. It also sought the views of prisoners and staff on what caused and happened during the riot and what action should be taken to prevent such disturbances happening again. This last strategy is to be particularly welcomed, but this evidence is presented in an annexed summary and attends to highlighting general reasons for prison unrest, rather than the specific causes within the individual prisons. This is a serious omission and needs consideration in explaining prison disorder, particularly when the Report stressed the significance of the perception of justice.

Yet here, the more fundamental point to make is that if this spirit of openness had not prevailed then much of the subsequent analysis undertaken in this book would not have been possible, as a substantial amount of material gathered for the Inquiry is archived at the Public Record Office (PRO) in Kew, London under the general listing HO 370. This material can be divided into three categories. The first (HO 370/2 to HO 370/29) contains the Manchester and Taunton public hearings, in which oral evidence from management, staff, probation officers and prisoners was given under cross-examination. The Manchester hearings concentrated on Strangeways while the Taunton sessions heard evidence about the events at the remaining prisons. All the individuals giving evidence were directly involved in the circumstances surrounding the disturbances at Strangeways, Glen Parva, Dartmoor, Cardiff, Bristol and Pucklechurch (HO 370/1 is the report itself, Woolf and Tumim, 1991). The verbatim transcripts from the proceedings at Manchester from 11 June 1990 to 29 June 1990 (HO 370/2 to HO 370/16) permit a detailed insight into the culture of Strangeways and the understandings that informed decisions and actions at the prison. Over this three-week period 64 individuals gave evidence and even if I had been in a position to trace and re-interview these people, the four to five year time period after the events would certainly have muddied their recollections. Consequently in what follows I tend to rely on these accounts for the detail in the events leading up to and during the riot. The convention I use here, when this evidence is cited in the text, is to give the PRO reference and page number as these testimonies are in the public domain and are open to consultation.

The second set of documents are the verbatim transcripts of the five public seminars on the tactical management of the prison population; active regimes; cooperation with the criminal justice system; the administration of the prison service; and justice in prisons (HO 370/30 to HO 370/34). These seminars, in which individuals were invited to speak in a personal capacity on these topics, provided part of the evidence for Part II of the Inquiry and were held in London in September and October 1990, together with one seminar in Lincoln prison. The third set of documents (HO 370/35 to HO 370/53) contain a wide range of evidence from liberal and radical prison reform groups, academics, the probation service, the Prison Governors Association, the Prison Officers Association and the Prison Service.

Notwithstanding the eight prisoners that gave evidence to the Inquiry, it was recognised from the start of the research that contacting prisoners involved in the protest would be a difficult task. To this end a number of strategies were pursued to try and gain access to the 1,730 letters from prisoners and prison staff written to the Inquiry. The Home Office refused access, stating that under 'the Public Records Acts, these papers will remain closed to the public for 30 years, and in view of their confidentiality may remain closed for 40 years in accordance with additional guidelines contained in the white paper on Open Government' (Home Office, personal communication). One, not uncommon, metaphor of the Woolf report, in its openness, and the reform agenda that arose briefly in its wake is to liken it to a 'Prague Spring' – the period in which this fieldwork was conducted, 1994 to 1996, felt like a very cold winter.

Whilst the obsessive secrecy in which the Home Office and Prison Service operate has been well documented (the classic is Cohen and Taylor, 1978) it would have been difficult to anticipate the extent to which this was the case in the mid-1990s. For instance, in response to a written request for access to Board of Visitors reports at Strangeways, I was informed that this would not be possible as the sort of research I was conducting needs to be officially sanctioned by the Home Office, yet if I applied for such authorisation this would not be, in any case, forthcoming. The fact that a number of prisons see fit to *publish* their Board of Visitors reports (see Leech, 1995) serves to underline this point.

I draw attention to these obstacles here not simply to illustrate the particular methodological difficulties involved in prison research but to thank those individuals who did willingly participate in the research and saw value in doing so, as some are still employed by the Home Office and the Prison Service. In total, 18 tape recorded interviews were conducted with former prisoners, members of staff, management and probation officers. These interviews began with a résumé of their career and typically covered such issues as their perceptions of Strangeways; how it compared to other prisons; management strategies; staff/prisoner relationships; staff/management relationships; changes and continuities in the years, months and weeks before the riot; events during it; the aftermath and the Woolf Inquiry. Although these were systematic topics, the interview style was predominantly open-ended, allowing for plenty of elaboration and discussion. Each interview normally took over an hour, but the range was from thirty minutes to three hours.

Vaughan makes the telling point, with reference to interviewing individuals who had been interviewed in Commission hearings on the Challenger tragedy that, perhaps:

> I would learn *more* (especially from whistle-blowers) but I was not likely to learn anything *different*. Only if I asked them different questions than the Commission had – questions that were grounded in my own independent analysis – would interviewing benefit me. (Vaughan, 1996: 59, emphasis in original)

The different questions I was posing in the interviews took a longer historical trajectory and were particularly concerned with the culture of Strangeways. Although the line of questioning followed by Woolf and various counsellors did not directly address these issues, they did arise (it would have been very surprising if they had not). The convention followed, when quoting from the interviews, is to put the transcript number in brackets and reference is made to the individual's relationship to the prison. I avoid naming individuals, unless the respondent intimated they were happy for this to happen. These interviews were supplemented by more informal discussions and conversations with ex-prisoners, prison officers, governors, reformers, academics, assessors and contributors to the Woolf Inquiry, which for a variety of reasons were not tape recorded, though field notes were made where necessary and written correspondence with some of the prisoners who remained on the roof was established.

Other sources consulted include HM Chief Inspector of Prisons reports on Strangeways, annual reports produced by the Inspectorate, television documentaries and various accounts and commentaries on the prison riot. In particular, Nicki Jameson and Eric Allison (1995) allowed me access to the material they had collected in their book *Strangeways 1990: A Serious Disturbance*. This account is an important collection of statements and testimonies by the men directly involved in the protest, some of which was gathered while the series of trials against 51 prisoners were continuing during 1992 and 1993. While the book is unashamedly partisan, their argument loses much of its force through characterising prison staff and management as, at best, vindictive bullies. This is not to imply that prisons are not brutal and oppressive places, but that the description of all social relations as naked tyranny is reductive, not least as it relies on the Hobbesian solution to the problem of order in its starkest and most coercive form. Despite these shortcomings their book is the one published text where prisoners' accounts can be found and for that reason alone it is an invaluable document of the riot and subsequent trials. Taken together, these diverse sources permit detailed insights into the culture of the prison, the discursive understandings that informed practice and the structures of domination in play at the institution.

In order to summarise the discussion that follows Figure 5.1 indicates the discursive formations that have sought institutional hegemony over a 25-year period. The matrix identifies three discourses on the *ends* of imprisonment (rehabilitation, normalisation and control) and three *means* discourses (bureaucracy, professionalism and authoritarianism) that are of particular significance in structuring the experience of imprisonment. As I argued in Chapter 2 means discourses are explicitly concerned with how prisons should be run, whereas ends discourses can be regarded as political rationalities that justify what prisons are for, and I outlined an archaeological mapping of their conceptual structure. In this chapter attention turns to the ways in which these general systems of thought are translated in a particular arena of

Means \ Ends	Rehabilitation	Normalisation	Control
Bureaucracy			1972–77
Professionalism		1986–90	
Authoritarianism			1965–72 1977–86

Figure 5.1   Strangeways discourse matrix: 1965 to 1990

Source: Carrabine (2000: 320).

social practice and consequently offers a more genealogical reading of the institution's history.

Gibson Burrell, in a wide-ranging discussion of Foucault's contribution to organisational theory, argues that:

> in Foucauldian analysis, the paradox arises when organizations are seen as totally contingent and particularly requiring patient, meticulous, documentary research of their individuality on the one hand, whilst on the other, they are viewed as manifestations of some underlying and generic Nietzschean 'will to knowledge'. Put simply … *They are all-unalike and all-alike at one and the same time.* They need to be studied both archaeologically and genealogically. (Burrell, 1998: 24–5, emphasis in original)

The discourse matrix is the means by which a genealogical attentiveness to the distinctive and unique qualities of particular institutions can be reconciled with a more abstract and systematic form of archaeological analysis. In other words, archaeology is essentially synchronic and revolves around the interrelationship of elements and is centred upon typologies whereas genealogy is typically diachronic and searches for historical ruptures and continuities. The important point I would make is that the strict analysis of discourse (archaeology) cannot be separated from a consideration of the historical deployment of discursive formations (genealogy). As I argued in Chapter 1, one of the aims of the book is the drawing together of ideographic procedures, which concentrate on particular places and times with a nomothetic method that identifies general processes in a more abstract fashion so that microsociological themes are situated in relation to macrosociological issues.

The reader unfamiliar with imprisonment in England may be surprised to find that the discourse of rehabilitation has not been a particularly strong rationality of governance at the prison over this 25-year period. But as the previous chapter emphasised the institutional function of being a 'local' prison means that such places have typically some of the worst conditions that the penal system can offer, despite the central importance of the discourse to the politics of law and order. For instance, throughout the 1970s and 1980s Strangeways routinely held more than 1,600 prisoners in conditions of severe overcrowding with two and not infrequently three prisoners confined in a cell designed for one. The local prison population is excluded from the 'treatment and training' mission for two reasons. First, for those serving short sentences there is an assumption that there is too little time to achieve rehabilitative results. Second, a number of the local prisons act as 'sin bins' for disruptive prisoners from dispersal prisons. As can be seen from Figure 5.1 the constellation of authoritarianism with the discourse of control has been particularly pronounced at Strangeways up to the mid-1980s and the discussion now turns to a closer examination of the implications of these ways of ruling the prison.

The Authoritarian Prison

One of the intentions when interviewing respondents was to probe for matters relating to the culture and tradition of Strangeways and thereby examine the extent to which these issues influenced daily practices in the institution. If respondents were drawn from reform groups or probation officers the prison was typically referred to as a 'POA prison', or as a 'screws' nick' by former prisoners. This argot signifies an institution run on strict militaristic lines, which rigidly enforced a minimum and basic regime with hardly any out-of-cell activities, such as education, work or recreation and instilled an 'us versus them' mentality between the keepers and the kept. In taking this further, respondents occasionally made unfavourable comparisons to Wandsworth – a local prison in London. Both were perceived as 'sin bins', as another part of their role as local prisons was to receive prisoners who were deemed to be disruptive from other prisons. This view is confirmed by a governor [04] who explained that, 'it was a dumping ground for difficult prisoners from the training prisons, who dumped their difficult prisoners back into Strangeways'. This governor, who had several periods of employment at the prison beginning in 1969, recalled that:

> Strangeways, when I first went there was one of the big, hard prisons. When I was there, as a young trainee officer, the staff were very much in control, the

prisoners did as they were told. It was a friendly enough place if things were going OK, but it certainly had a cutting edge.

Another former governor [02], who worked at the prison from 1971 to 1973, remarked that 'Wandsworth was the hard prison in the South and Manchester was the hard prison in the North, is the quick answer'. This echoes the sentiments expressed by reform groups and former prisoners, though the observation that this is 'the quick answer' is suggestive that this comparison requires some unpacking and will be returned to below, for the intention here is to provide a picture of the prison in the late 1960s and 1970s.

An insight into how prisoners perceived Strangeways is given by a former prisoner who has written that:

> In 1968 Strangeways, as a local prison, served mainly as a holding and allocation centre. Training and long-term prisons were established by now but the allocation system was such that up to and including four years sent you to a training prison; five years or over and it was off to a long-term nick. There was nothing for those in between! So the allocation board told me I could expect to spend at least the next two years in Strangeways. In the event I was to spend the best part of four years there ... The Governor at the time was a Captain Davies who did not like hearing applications from convicts; he didn't like convicts at all and made his dislike extremely plain. Strangeways then was a 'working' prison; everybody worked and it was a punishable offence not to. (Jameson and Allison, 1995: 78)

A number of significant inferences can be drawn from this passage. First, is that some prisoners were evidently spending considerably longer at the prison than they would have done in the more recent past due to limitations in the allocation system. Second, prisoners were expected, and forced, to work – which is in contrast to the situation from the mid-1970s to the mid-1980s. Third, the governor, Captain Davies, would not have been a popular figure among prisoners.

The view that Strangeways operated a strict, authoritarian regime at this time is not just restricted to former prisoners, it is suggested by a former assistant governor [04], who recalled that:

> There was a very high camaraderie there among officers who liked a formal, disciplined regime. They found it very satisfying, even down to the Night Patrols. They didn't like people who took the side of prisoners, but equally they didn't like officers who were viciously manipulative. They did love their

work and they did run it very strictly. There wasn't any training. There was no pretence of training at all, but they managed to make it work. And they got people to work. There was a routine which gave prisoners very little joy, but the prisoners by and large respected it.

Importantly this observation highlights the close connection between the local occupational culture and the regime of the prison. In other words, prison officers play a crucial role in structuring prison life through what Giddens (1984: xxiii) defines as the 'routinisation' of conduct. This is a fundamental concept in his structuration theory and refers to the ways in which 'practical consciousness' – the shored-up conventions of how to act – provides a vital mechanism whereby 'ontological security is sustained in the daily activities of social life' (Giddens, 1984: xxiii). A probation officer [10] similarly remarked that:

> Captain Davies' method of dealing with prisoners was based on a military one. This meant that the prison was very strong on discipline. It was noticeable, and the prisoners knew exactly where they stood. The governor was almost held in awe and the officers themselves were always military preoccupied. Let me explain, I can remember in the '60s and '70s there was a parade every morning – a whistle and stick parade, and they had to show their truncheons and whistles. Now over the years, I left in 1973 and didn't come back until 1986, officers seemed to be more relaxed, they weren't quite as hung up on having neatly pressed uniforms. I think they made an attempt to communicate more effectively, there were also other things I noticed, such as, formerly you never saw an inmate wandering around the prison, I don't mean between buildings, but inmates tended to wander from wing to wing, whereas at one time that would have been highly unusual – they would have been down the block for that. Now I did notice when I went back that inmates were wandering around, and even as a probation officer, I wasn't sure whether that was to the inmates' advantage.

The feeling that the governor was held in 'awe' is suggestive of the charismatic qualities Davies possessed, yet crucially what this passage highlights is some of the ambiguities, inconsistencies and dilemmas posed in the shift from a rigid, authoritarian regime to one which would be considered more liberal and relaxed and a question is posed over whether this was entirely to every prisoner's 'advantage'. It is important to recognise this as a dilemma rather than as a straightforward, progressive movement from repression to care as the different types of means discourse can affect rather different power relationships in the maintenance of order, and these issues will be returned to subsequently.

On the subject of the significance of the prison subculture one former prisoner [07], who had served a number of sentences at Strangeways and elsewhere from 1965 to 1990, recalled that:

> Strangeways was a local prison, the only people there who were doing long sentences were people who were either just starting their sentences and waiting to be allocated or people like [gives name of a prisoner who played a major role in the events of April 1990] who were doing long sentences and were sent there for a 'lie down' [moved from a dispersal to local prison – often regarded by prisoners as an 'informal' punishment]. Because of that there is no solidarity, it's a real moving population, so you don't get chances to get solid and organise resistance in any shape or form. That's why it [April 1990] was so unusual because you don't get the time, there's a lot of guys in there doing three months, six weeks, and they don't want to get involved. You know, guys who are going on to a better gaol the next day or next week, and they don't want to get involved. Whereas in the dispersals you've got people who are in there for a long time. The regime was better at Parkhurst, all long-term prisons have better regimes. I went from Liverpool to Hull in the '70s and, seriously, it was like being released.

This sense of movement in the prison population is a theme that persistently appeared in the interviews, and it certainly would have had a limiting effect on the development of a prisoner subculture whilst further demonstrating the impoverishment of local prison regimes, in comparison to the dispersal prisons documented in the previous chapter.

When the former prisoner was asked how the prison was perceived his response is worth quoting at length for he explained that:

> It was one of the worst prisons in the country, it was a screws' nick. They run the prison, it had always been in the top three or four for dogs – bullies strutting round, in big groups and slashed caps, terrible attitudes, severe beatings in the block over the years. But not so much that, as the general attitude – the everyday attitude amongst this hardcore of bullies and their fellow travellers. Looking for trouble. You're in gaol, you don't want to be there, but most prisoners they want to get in, do their time, and get out. But then you get a situation, like where you go along the landing in the morning, and you ask for something in a reasonable manner and you get told to, 'Fuck off' by some bully who's been on the beer the night before. It's a serious request that you're making ... There's always been a succession of dogs. We used to run daft competitions like dog of the month, dog of the week, dog of the year. There has always been a top dog, a real bastard. As they get older they pass it on to other people, I mean, that culture is there and it always has been there. Attitude, that's what causes

the problems. I did a small sentence in a place called Dorchester, I didn't even fucking know the gaol existed, I got nicked in Bournemouth. I went down there to do a cigarette warehouse and came unstuck, and got remanded in custody and went to Dorchester, a little, tiny nick, only holds about 300. A local prison, slopping out, piss pots in cells. The food was marginally better, but food has never been an issue for me. You can't complain about food in gaol, you're fucking in gaol, what do you expect. But the attitude was totally different, and I did about 8 months there. The day before I came out I went to see a governor, and the guy looked at my rail warrant, and said, 'Manchester, you're a long way from home' and I said, 'I came down here to do a bit of work and got nicked' sort of thing. So he said, 'What do you think of the prison?' and I said, 'Well as a yardstick, the fact you don't know me. I make my presence known if it's a bad gaol, so you run a good gaol'. I still had been locked up but the fact that I came out not hating the bastards meant that the attitude was different. It certainly wasn't Butlins. I only had one row with one screw all the time I was there.

This passage vividly highlights the significant variations in the ways in which imprisonment is experienced in different prisons and illustrates the antagonistic relationships between Strangeways staff and this prisoner in the late 1960s and early 1970s. It also crucially indicates how prisoners are not simply coerced or passively accept the institutional arrangements in which they find themselves. In fact, most prisoners 'want to get in, do their time, and get out' and as I will argue later this key dimension of prison life has largely been ignored in sociological accounts of imprisonment – with major consequences for how social order has been characterised. It also captures what Giddens (1984) terms the 'dialectic of control', which refers to the ability of human agency to subvert and undermine authority. Here the oppressive and heavy handed staff culture is mocked through 'top dog' competitions, which serve to take the edge off an aggressive atmosphere. Humour and other 'weapons of the weak' (Scott, 1985) such as foot-dragging, sabotage and wind-ups constitute everyday resistances to institutional hegemony so that an uneasy social order is achieved – often while maintaining a front of acquiescence (though clearly not in this particular prisoner's case). Nevertheless, such activities do contribute to the dialectic of *control* as they dilute open confrontation.

Captain Davies was succeeded by Arthur Moreton in 1972, who represented a very different style of management, which is captured in the following description by a governor [02]:

He wouldn't have that military experience [of Captain Davies], though he would have had National Service, and he was highly educated. He was very able, but an administrator. He was probably more of a civil servant than the civil servants. Everything had to have a checklist, you know, 'Have you checked the files?' He was a perfectionist, I like Arthur. When he arrived at Manchester people were very wary of him. He didn't often go in the mess.

Evidently, Arthur Moreton's source of authority lay firmly in bureaucratic discourse, though what is significant here is that staff were 'very wary of him' and that his arrival coincided with a period of remand prisoner unrest. This governor [02] subsequently recalled that:

> There was a transition of governors at that time and there was also a lot of prisoner unrest at Strangeways. We couldn't stop remand prisoner unrest – it was meant to be something that went on at Brixton and silly places in the south. It was shortly after a very strict governor had left and the staff felt that the new governor was far too influenced by a number of ideas that had come up from the south. So the fact that he said, 'The prisoners are demonstrating and the government's policy is not to intervene, then there is no point in putting ourselves at risk. There are an awful lot of prisoners out there and I'm not prepared to risk the staff'. Whereas the previous governor would have said, 'Get them in' and he wouldn't have had any qualms about it. So there was quite serious unrest in 1972 and some of that unrest focused on the chapel.

There are a number of important issues raised in this passage. First, there is a strong indication that the staff were not exactly enamoured with the new 'ideas' Moreton was trying to bring in to the prison. Second, the unrest itself was regarded as a new phenomenon and as the previous chapter indicated it would have been a part of the increasing politicisation of the prisoners' movement. Third, the differing discursive rationalities are highlighted in their respective views on how to handle the protests. Whilst this issue was to resurface in April 1990, what is of importance here is that the new 'ideas' were replaced in 1977 with the appointment of Norman Brown, who represented a return to the 'traditional' practices of Strangeways.

This sense of return was recollected by a governor [04] who knew Brown and his relationship with the staff and asserted that,

> He was very much one of the lads, he liked drinking with them. Brendan [O'Friel] would have been quite a surprise after Norman. Norman was very like Captain Davies, who was the boss when I was there and from his army experience [Brown had been a tank commander in World War II] he was used to having a whole regiment in front of him saying, 'Right, jump up and down'. So he had experience of getting his voice across to a large body of men and they did what he said and that was very popular at Manchester. Very popular.

This reveals the widespread support among staff for his particular style of governing, and significantly points again to the differences, this time with reference to Brendan O'Friel, who became the governor in 1986. More critically, one former officer [06] who had been in Strangeways from 1975 to 1985, stated that:

> it was a hard line regime, and it had traditionally been a hard line regime. Strangeways was considered to be the Prisons Service's ultimate deterrent, it was the end of the line. All the bad boys ended up down the block at Strangeways. There were a number of other prisons of a similar kind of nature, places like Wandsworth, Armley and Wormwood Scrubs. But generally speaking Strangeways was considered to be a screws' nick. There was also a clique at Strangeways of hard line attitude staff and there was an ethos of they got pissed at dinner time, they got pissed at night and when they were in the prison they behaved in a manner that indicated they were in charge and the prisoners would have to do exactly what the staff told them. And generally they did.

Before moving on to the significant changes which Brendan O'Friel introduced, it is worthwhile here to point out that many prison officers take an enormous pride from having worked at Strangeways. For example, one prison officer respondent [05], recalling his training at the prison in the early 1980s, remarked that it was:

> an excellent place to get your grounding in. Any local prison in my opinion is. In fact it is my belief that every single officer, after his initial training, should spend time in a local prison.

The range and diversity of experiences that working in a large, local prison engendered on a daily basis, are clearly an important part of the learning process since:

> every inmate of all types comes there and then our job is to allocate and move people to places suitable for them to serve their sentence ... So at Strangeways you can have remands, trial, Category A prisoners, prisoners on the Escape list, you can have what we used to call Rule 43 prisoners – prisoners under protection for one reason or another. You can have people in just for a few days, you know for not paying maintenance. So you can have every category of prisoner in there. You're very busy of course. There wasn't much that went on at Strangeways as regards association and things like that, because it's a moving prison – people are coming in and you're getting them out as fast as you can. At that time we were also serving the courts. So a lot of your time was

spent at court. Very, very interesting work and a very good grounding. I mean, it was so diverse. I would say an officer in a big local prison like that, and it's not only Strangeways there are places like Birmingham, Brixton, Liverpool – wherever, would get a very good grounding.

This officer was at Strangeways from 1981 to 1992 and the passage manages to capture the pace and movement of the regime over this period.

To summarise the period from the late 1960s to the mid-1980s it is clear that the combination of authoritarianism and control discourses was particularly pronounced. Nevertheless attempts were made, in the early 1970s, to establish a bureaucratic regime which did not meet with much success and subsequently came to be replaced by a return to traditional practices of authoritarian regulation. However, Strangeways could not remain aloof from broader changes in political culture and the rise of what has become known as new managerialism (McLaughlin and Muncie, 1994) in the 1980s and 1990s and the source of significant struggles between bureaucratically informed career civil servants in the Home Office and the more professionally orientated practices of prison service officials in particular prisons. The origins of new managerialism are diverse (see McLaughlin and Murji, 2001) but it represents a means through which the public sector becomes performance orientated in the interests of increased efficiency, less 'big government' and more enterprise. With specific reference to imprisonment this has meant the introduction of privatisation, agency status, key performance indicators and so forth. The following discussion will indicate how there was a shift to systems of regulation based on the discourses of professionalism and normalisation to create an 'active' regime for prisoners. However, it is important to recognise that this was not simply a purely benign and progressive move but is part of this process that involves the discrediting and displacement of older forms of public administration. Revealing that this process was neither smooth nor uniform will be an important theme in what follows.

The Active Regime

In 1986 there were significant changes in management at the prison which ushered in different control strategies. The new governor, Brendan O'Friel, brought a fresh philosophy with an emphasis on education programmes and employment for the prisoners to create an active regime, which he [01] summarised as:

I think I have got a fairly consistent management strategy, which I have used for years. Since I reached a reasonably senior position as Deputy Governor, really. It is only then that you can start to have a real influence on the place. It tends to be a learning process, well it's always a learning process, but it's more of a learning process in the early days. My consistent management policy is to try and produce a very active day for prisoners and make sure that staff are used to their greatest ability. Those were the sort of things I was trying to develop. Because when I arrived at Strangeways the prison had an awful lot of prisoners doing absolutely nothing. We got a lot of them back to work. In the period immediately before the riot we introduced a huge increase in education and we had a lot more time out of cell on association for prisoners. So your average prisoner would say that overall the regime at Strangeways had improved a great deal.

These changes were informed by the discourses of professionalism, as throughout the interview a recurring theme was the need for a governor 'to walk around and sniff the ground', and normalisation since 'we regard the deprivation of liberty as the punishment and that is the tradition of the Prison Service, going right back to Alexander Paterson'. An interesting insight into his technique is illustrated in response to a question posed about the regularity of disruptive behaviour in the prison.

You've got to distinguish between rowdy behaviour, if you have a large group of prisoners anywhere, there would be occasions when they'd be a bit football crowdish. I used to spend a lot of time walking around. Meal times were a very good time. You would see a lot of prisoners and you saw what was going on. We used to feed them under the Centre and we used to have quite a lot of the prisoners milling around, going up and down the stairs, all around the place. With half a dozen staff walking around, serving food, and generally supervising. If you stood there and thought, 'What the hell am I doing in the middle of all this lot' well that would suggest things weren't as they should be. In a rational way it wasn't very sensible, but it is what you need to do as a governor. In most establishments if you can't actually walk around on your own and get a reasonable response from prisoners, then how the hell can you expect the staff to do it? So I'd be in the middle of them and yes you would get moments when things got a bit rowdy.

From this passage it can be seen there was a heavy emphasis placed on 'walking around' and the recognition that this was not perhaps the most 'rational' use of his time but it was a practice which was seen as inspiring staff and prisoners. In fact one of the most striking aspects of the discourse of professionalism, as espoused by governors, is that the knowledge claims can verge on the mystical in that an almost prophetic ability to sense the prison's atmosphere is not infrequently articulated.

These changes in philosophy were warmly endorsed by the Chief Inspector of Prisons following an inspection in 1989:

> There was a feeling in Manchester that in the last three years the prison had emerged from the doldrums. This was confirmed by all that we saw. Management are to be congratulated for providing the successful impetus for this. The Governor had put in place a management structure which worked for Manchester and he had used it strongly to promote efficient use of staff and the beginnings of a reasonable regime for inmates. (HMCIP, 1990a: para. 4.0, 185)

In terms of using staff to their greatest ability, the Inspectorate noted that the 'degree of ownership demonstrated by all managers was outstanding', yet it was observed that with 'such a directive approach it was not surprising to hear some (unsubstantiated) feelings of disgruntlement from staff' (HMCIP: 1990a, paras 3.02 and 3.04, 33–4). These changes in regime also coincided with the implementation of Fresh Start. This was an attempt by the government to manage its fraught industrial relations with the Prison Officers Association (POA).

The next section analyses Fresh Start in greater detail, as there is considerable evidence indicating that struggles over the appropriate ends and means of imprisonment in the institution were commonplace. One former assistant governor [02], who had been involved in the 1989 inspection, remarked that

> Brendan had tried to get more people out doing activities, but he was finding it hard work because of the very strong culture which the more strict governors had set in place by saying, 'If they are in their cells then there won't be any trouble.' I can't say that it was in any way markedly different, but I think Brendan had brought a number of improvements. There were some people saying, 'OK it is a different place and we like it'. There was more tension between the old school and the new school. When I was there [1971–73] it was a very mechanistic regime, but everybody went to work – so they all trooped over to the workshops.

The view that there were strong tensions is confirmed by a probation officer [13], who stated that:

there were some that wished for the old days of Mr Brown, because he supported them through thick and thin. He had been ex-military and he certainly was of a completely different calibre than O'Friel. I mean they used to brag about how Mr. Brown used to be drunk most nights and play cards. They were always encouraged to drink, it was renowned that they would spend two hours in the club at lunch time. A lot of the older officers, or the ones that had been in the Service a few years, it was their life. I mean quite literally, their whole life revolved around the prison, including their social life. Prior to the Fresh Start agreement, they were spending hours upon hours in the place, and yes a lot of them were hard drinkers. And that was the culture. At lunch time they would be closed up by quarter to 12 and it was supposed to be opened up again by about 1 o'clock, and people spent lunch time in the club. He [O'Friel] didn't join them in the club whereas Brown would have done. So he wasn't that popular in some areas, they didn't really want change. The system had gone on for a long, long time. I mean, it is understandable, people get very frightened of change – they had got used to a system and there were a lot of officers there who didn't treat prisoners in a humane way because they were doing a job on behalf of the victim anyway so they could justify that behaviour. I think there was a mixed feeling about Brendan O'Friel.

It is significant that this passage highlights a particular culture of masculinity, in which many male prison officers enjoyed associating with each other to the exclusion of women (and certain kinds of men) – the defining characteristic of a fratriarchy (Remy, 1990). The term fratriarchy is used to describe social arrangements based on the self interest served by the association of men. This can range from the informal setting of the pub (Hey, 1986) to organisations (Rogers, 1988) like prisons where it is more structured. An important element of most forms of fratriarchy are unwritten codes which preserve and promote a sense of group solidarity. This is particularly important for prison officers who are remote from, and suspicious, of working class communities – even though they themselves often have working class roots. At Strangeways there was a strong canteen culture, actively supported and enjoyed by the former governor and manifest in the celebration of hard drinking and the associated ethic of hard men doing a hard job (see Carrabine and Longhurst, 1998, for a further account of the importance of understanding prisons as gendered organisations).

Nevertheless, the changes in regime are supported by the Inspectorate, who observed that from 'a moribund, cell-centred system, a developing regime for prisoners was now being encouraged' (HMCIP, 1990a: para. 3.18, 40) and that the 'imaginative education programmes and the increased use of workshops are examples of the improvements for inmates' (HMCIP, 1990a: 1). However, another probation officer [09] drew out the ambiguities involved in these changes:

Power, Discourse and Resistance

The one thing everybody used to say, both the prison officers and the older prisoners, was that when you were in Strangeways it was tough but you got what you were entitled to. If the prison rules said you got four blankets, then you got four blankets – the bloody sunlight could have been splitting the rocks and you only needed one but you were entitled to four and you got four. You were entitled to a change of underwear, you got it. The rest of the time it was tough, but you got what you were entitled to, and older cons in the prison would openly say that. Now it's a fact that the prison was ludicrously short of critical things like shoes that fit, sufficient underwear to go round, shower facilities to keep clean. So that business of it being fair had clearly moved on because a lot of the things that they would describe as the fair element – you got what you were entitled to; they weren't getting what they were entitled to, so to some extent the prison had moved anyway, but in terms of developments over the years both sides would see the gaol, in its widest sense, had gone soft. So if you talk to older prisoners you get the response, 'No wonder it happened. The bloody place was soft, it wouldn't have happened when I was younger because you were treated fairly but hardly.' I think that kind of thing had weakened. I think you also look to changes in attitudes towards the ethos of relationships – you move away from a kind of disciplinarian, essentially militaristic regime to one where there is more of an attempt to understand the individual, which always seems to have implicit the notion that you go soft. When you try to understand somebody that somehow means soft touch. So the overall ethic was one towards understanding more, and I think somehow on the back of that came the weakening in the direct power relationship between con and prison officer.

There are a number of important observations in this passage. First, under the former authoritarian regime there was a widespread feeling that the prison was procedurally precise in the distribution of resources, in contrast to the situation in the late 1980s, and the Inspectorate also point out that:

there were indications everywhere in the main prison that control of inmate clothing was a constant source of dissatisfaction for both prisoners and staff. Inmates told us that for several months they had not had full kits, being forced to wash their shirts and socks. No proper washing facilities existed in the wings. More seriously, it emerged that there was an ongoing shortage of underpants. We believe that all inmates should be supplied each week with their full clothing entitlement. Management was fully aware of the problems and was trying to resolve them ... It was evident that ... these initiatives had produced some improvement but had not solved the problem as too many items of kit were still being lost. (HMCIP, 1990a: para. 3.21, 41)

Second, this shift from control to normalisation was perceived to involve a process of going 'soft', and third, this led to a weakening of the power relationships between prisoners and prison officers.

A further indication of the shifts, with increased education and work programmes, is provided by one prison officer [05] who recalled that:

> When Mr O'Friel became the Governor we worked hard to get things in there that had never been believed in there before, you know things like better education facilities. We actually had a rota going for the work, instead of only half the prison working, what they did was half the prison worked in the morning, and the other half worked in the afternoon. So we were almost getting up to the stage where there was 100 per cent employment, Physical Education, things like that. Classes were rearranged and there were a lot of extra facilities coming in, but if anything the inmates had more at the time of the riot than what they'd had previously.

It is instructive to note that such things 'had never been believed in there before', and one probation officer [09] endorses this:

> when I was there [1987–90] they were really keen to look at anything which would bridge the gap between the prison and the community. And that, for Strangeways, was a significant move forward. I wouldn't take anything away from Brendan O'Friel in setting a standard, a kind of attitude, which allowed staff permission to look at this kind of innovative approach. I think he set the tone, that we are willing to try.

The important point to be gleaned from this discussion is that during the late 1980s Strangeways was the site of significant struggles over the most appropriate way to manage the prison. Conceptualising these struggles at the level of discursive practices enables penal power to be understood as diverse ways of thinking and acting that can provoke intense disagreement over the appropriate means of governing the confined.

Given that these differences will always, to some extent, be present, it is important to point out that they become particularly pronounced during periods of change as the final outcome is by no means certain, which affords strategic opportunities for dominant groups to battle over institutional hegemony.

Nevertheless, it is highly revealing to compare these changes at Strangeways with the situation, as depicted by the Inspectorate, at Wandsworth at the end of the 1980s:

Wandsworth was in many ways an enigma. For years as well as being an allocation centre it had also been the dumping ground for inmates who had 'failed' in the training and dispersal system. In addition, G, H and K wings were almost completely filled with Rule 43 (own request) inmates. Wandsworth has carried out these functions without an escape from inside and without major disturbance for over 20 years: yet it has done so by imposing a most basic, restrictive regime ... It has a reputation of being the cheapest prison in the country to run ... and from the numbers held, and the paucity of the regime, we could well believe it ... Wandsworth has a traditional 'nothing is given to prisoners' attitude and staff operated a thoroughly institutionalising routine by imposing many simple basic rules. Staff morale in carrying through this routine was very high but there was little contact between prisoners and staff except about the mechanics of the routine. Most prisoners acquiesced with what they found at Wandsworth; indeed to some extent they might enjoy the notoriety of being there and the restrictions that go with it ... We concluded that for prisoners, life at Wandsworth was a deadening experience broken only by conversation about routines or a future life of crime ... The staff culture was far more influential in what happened to inmates than any decisions taken by managers. Such a strong sub-culture has played its part in the history of unhappy industrial relations, culminating in serious industrial action by a large number of discipline staff early in 1989. (HMCIP, 1990b: paras 4.01–04: 81–2)

In a number of respects this passage could accurately describe the situation at Strangeways for most of the late 1970s and up to the mid-1980s – demonstrating how each prison has a specific constellation of discourses structuring action – and it calls into question over-generalising accounts in the sociology of imprisonment that assume all prisons are basically the same.

Perhaps one of the most striking features of this discussion is the high degree to which the various sources consulted not only agreed over the basic periodisation of the changes but also on the extent to which the tenor of institutional life was affected by the particular management style of a governor. The fact that there was such consensus over this demands some attention. Although I do not wish to advocate a 'Great Man' version of historical change nor imply a strictly top-down understanding of power, it does need to be emphasised that governors do exercise a great deal of control over the individual. For instance, prisoners 'can be segregated; transferred; confined to their cells; strip searched; refused physical contact with their families; sentenced to "additional days" and released temporarily by the Governor' (Bryans, 2000: 15). What is more, as much of this chapter indicates, they can do much to affect the ethos and shape the regime of a prison, due to the particular structures of authority inherent in the organisation. As a recent review of imprisonment by the Prison Service in 1997 recognises, 'Prisons remain very hierarchical and almost feudal. There is a strong dependency on the role and person of the Governor' (cited in Bryans, 2000: 14).

These points were not lost on the early sociologies of imprisonment. For instance, Thomas Mathiesen (1965) argued that prisons are very similar to traditional patriarchal or early modern monarchical regimes and he demonstrated how the Norwegian governors in his study exercised 'a mixture of personal and bureaucratic rule and decree many of the practices of their institution, that they control armed force to maintain order, and that a well-articulated hierarchy ... determines status and power' (Goldstone and Useem, 1999: 987).

Another example is Jacobs' (1977) account of the transformation of Stateville prison from a patriarchal organisation driven by charismatic authority and personal domination to a bureaucratic institution based on rational-legal authority over a 50-year period (1925–75). He was also attentive to the limits that a purely corporate bureaucratic model of confinement could achieve in the face of potential conflict from within (by prisoners, staff and management) and external opposition from the media, interest groups and politicians. His account is clearly indebted to Weber's (1968a, 1968b) characterisation of charismatic, traditional and bureaucratic structures of authority. Although Weber was primarily concerned with identifying the key elements of each type of authority in their ideal form, he nevertheless insisted that:

> 'ruling organizations' which belong only to one or another of these pure types are very exceptional ... Groups approximating the purely traditional type have certainly existed. But they have never been indefinitely and, as is also true of bureaucratic authority, have seldom been without a head who had a personally charismatic status by heredity or office. (Weber, 1968a: 262–3)

What is more he argued that 'the three basic types of domination cannot be placed into a simple evolutionary line: they in fact appear together in the most diverse combinations' (Weber, 1968b: 1133). This is undoubtedly the case, but what is perhaps more important is that by drawing attention to qualities of charisma he is emphasising the salience of face-to-face encounters in understanding power relations. As Scott (2001: 148) argues, 'domination is always realised in and through interpersonal relations'. In other words, the authority of a governor is not simply due to the formal powers attached to the office but is also embodied in personal characteristics, emotional resources and persuasive abilities. Recognising these formal and informal dimensions of power goes some way to explaining why it is that many are drawn to periodising an institution's history in terms of particular governors. Attention now turns to a significant restructuring of staff working practices in 1987, known as 'Fresh Start', as this serves to further demonstrate some of the significant struggles in play at the prison.

Fresh Start

Fresh Start was an attempt by the government to manage its historically fraught industrial relations with the POA. The reorganisation of staffing in 1987 under the optimistic title Fresh Start was an effort aimed at unifying the service on the model of the police force. There was an attempt to blur the distinctions between management and staff with only one level of entry, at the bottom, and the same career prospects for all who entered the service. Strangeways was in the vanguard of implementing this reorganisation, as Brendan O'Friel [01] confirmed:

> I had done some work on the run up to Fresh Start as Deputy Director in the Midlands, because one of my special responsibilities then was staffing. At the time we were trying to get a grip on the overtime budget which was not well controlled. I put Strangeways under Fresh Start in June 1987. We were the first major establishment to go under Fresh Start. Four establishments went under Fresh Start, it was Strangeways and three minnows – I think there was a detention centre, that sort of thing. So eyes were rather on us. Fresh Start went very well there. Very well.

King and McDermott (1995: 37) also observe that Brendan O'Friel gave an 'upbeat account of the positive opportunities that Fresh Start gave, especially for the impoverished regimes of local prisons' in September 1989 at the annual Perrie Lectures.

However, King and McDermott's (1995: 32–3) research findings qualify this as they found that most officers 'were nearly unanimous that, whilst they greatly enjoyed the improved pay and conditions, they had lost interest and satisfaction in the job' following the introduction of Fresh Start. Three main reasons are advanced to explain this displeasure. First, at the 'basic level' the question of manning levels remained unresolved since Fresh Start was introduced without the appropriate staff complements for each prison having been agreed. Second, at the 'symbolic level' the original intention of uniting the prison service through governors wearing uniform was never carried through. Third, and most importantly, the scheme was introduced without any serious analysis of the professional content of prison officers' work since the overriding concerns of 'security, control, and tactical management of the system' replaced the vocabulary of professionalism.

Moreover, there was a clear sense in which staff morale suffered through the leadership loss of the 'Chief Officer' role, who was typically an older prison officer with considerable experience. As one prison officer [05] reminisced when asked to describe staff/management relationships in the late 1980s:

> The relationships were very good. You had different POs [Principal Officers], different sorts of people. You had some POs who were very quiet and supportive about getting the job done and you made sure you got the job done right for them because you didn't want a bad report and you didn't want to fail. But you had other POs who were quite militarised and then of course you had the Chief Officer, which was the highest uniformed rank. The Chief Officer was God. The Chief Officer's job was to run the uniform staff and advise the Governor. If the governor wanted something doing by a uniformed staff he would pass that down through the Chief Officer. Going back to those early days, that was a real good thing looking back now. It was one of the changes that came about through Fresh Start. It was one of the changes that I don't agree with now, but I didn't realise at the time. But now you look back and think that is a big thing that is missing out of the Service, that was where the morale came from. The Chief Officer was very disciplined and made sure that everything was disciplined because he was answerable to the Governor. I do honestly think that the Chief Officer was a bad thing to go out of the Service.

This is supported by a probation officer [11] who remarked that:

> the uniform staff had a great, almost forces-like corporate identity and you'll know about the old grade of Chief Officer which is much missed by them, you know things like, 'Oh, when we had a Chief Officer' and so on, and these Chief Officers were like regimental sergeant majors – big, portly men and people were frightened of them. So it's almost like the boys and the headmaster really. They really miss that and they wish it was still the case.

Whilst the passing of the post of Chief Officer was widely mourned by uniformed staff it is important to locate this loss in relation to the discourse of control, which takes as its primary aim the maintenance of order and discipline in the prison (as opposed to the rehabilitation of prisoners or the normalisation of the institution), and as such played a significant role in structuring the subjectivities of uniformed staff.

The overall argument is that discourses provide both a framework of belief and a guide for conduct. As such they ideologically incorporate the agencies of the powerful into a dominant value system and it needs to be emphasised that prisoners rarely submit to these rationalities. In other words, powerful actors like civil servants, governor grades and uniformed staff firmly believe that their respective discourses are the correct way of running prisons whereas prisoners tend to experience these discourses through the dull compulsion of rituals that are endured as external constraints. The powerful on the other hand often articulate the various ideas and practices associated with competing discourses in terms of an internal conviction based on strong beliefs. In developing this characterisation Durkheim's (1964) discussion of the elementary forms of religious life is useful. In this book he drew a contrast between the external constraints of ritual in ancient religions and the internal constraints of conviction in modern religions. Of course, the distinction is overstated but it does draw attention to the different ways in which ritual and belief are experienced by the powerful (as inner conviction) and subordinate (as outer constraint). As I will argue, this has significant consequences for how social order is possible in prisons (see Lockwood, 1992 for a more general discussion).

It is also important to recognise that this period, the late 1980s, was a time of considerable transformations in the running of the prison. One probation officer [09] stated quite unequivocally that:

> management were stretched. I think main grade were, well my feeling was, at minimum level. Certainly after Fresh Start, you had the feeling that there just didn't seem to be enough around quite frankly. A combination of those kinds of features, you know, if you're stretched you are less likely to pick up that the population is changing. So much energy has to go into keeping the prison machine running that the subtleties and the nuances of the changing prisoner population in a key area probably went unnoticed.

This comes through very strongly in the evidence given to the Woolf Inquiry and one senior prison officer went so far as to say that:

> basically prior to Fresh Start when we had the Chief Officer rank, I think this whole incident or the lead-up to the incident [the riot in April 1990] would have been dealt with by the Chief Officer. It would have not got basically as far as the governors because the Chief would have done his little council of war and basically sorted it out. This is a level of command that has fell down with Fresh Start. (HO 370/13: 54)

The question of whether the Chief Officer would have been able to prevent the riot is highly debatable, yet the symbolic loss is clear enough. That certain members of the 'old school' were finding difficulties with the changes in the regime is captured in another prison officer's evidence:

> *Q* Now, throughout your evidence you have been referred to as perhaps an old style officer. There have always been young officers coming into the service?
>
> *A* Yes.
>
> *Q* Is there anything you wish to identify changing the recent status?
>
> *A* You see I was a young officer once. I was 25 when I joined my job and I was taught at the officers training school that once we got to my first job, I should find an older officer, an experienced officer and to maybe latch on to him and find out how he works and handles situations, which I did and it did me no harm at all. You know, I can do my job. I am quite good at my job, but these days the officers seem to come from the OTS [Officer Training School] with 10 years' experience. I don't know whether that is a personal opinion or speculation at all. You know, that's my feeling. They are taught body language, space, no eye contact. I mean, me, if I was to deal with a situation I would look the inmate in the eye – whether you call that eye contact, intimidation, whatever you want to call it – I would look him in the eye and tell him: 'No'. Now they seem to have to keep it out of the vocabulary, the word 'No' out of the OTS vocabulary. They can't use the word 'No'. I think it's 'maybe' or 'perhaps', but not 'no' and they daren't look at them when they say it. (HO 370/3: 165–6)

This passage also illustrates the preference for a firm, rigid, almost provocative style of interaction amongst this group of officers with prisoners, which was at some odds with that practised by the newer recruits to the service.

In his evidence to the Woolf Inquiry, Brendan O'Friel was asked whether he was aware of complaints from prisoners about staff attitudes, to which he replied:

> throughout my service you get this, and there were certainly examples of this from time to time at Strangeways, but I do stress that it's actually very difficult to disentangle the extent to which we're talking about personality conflicts and the extent to which we're talking about real attitudinal problems, but certainly there is always scope for improving the perceptions of some staff about their job and about the handling of prisoners, and to give you an example, you have heard from one member of staff during the Inquiry, about the difference in training for prison officers nowadays, and the sort of training a young officer

gets at training school today is very different from what, say somebody like
Mr Fagin got 25 years ago, and bringing the older staff up to date with some
of the new thinking is quite a substantial training task. Let me make it clear.
I'm not saying that all the old staff need retraining; far from it. But there will
always be an element of the older staff who need to be brought up to date, and
that's quite a sophisticated training requirement. (HO 370/14: 24)

Here a clear distinction between the 'old' and the 'new' school of officers is
drawn and the difficulties involved in addressing such issues. Yet, perhaps,
the fairest depiction of these officers is provided by one of the assessors [17]
to the Woolf Inquiry who recalled that:

my impression is of the prison officers, and I come from Manchester myself,
is that they were just straightforward, unimaginative, slightly right-wing,
working-class guys but not actually natural Gestapo members. Do you know
what I mean, they weren't great, they were looking at things for their own
interests but they loved Strangeways, they really loved Strangeways. And
they loved their group, but it's always the same – prisons are either run for
the prison officers or for the prisoners. And one was left with the feeling that
Strangeways was run for the prison officers.

Nevertheless the picture of the staff culture that emerges is one where there
were fraught conflicts between the 'old' and the 'new' school; a degree of
resentment to the changes introduced by Fresh Start and the attempts to
liberalise the regime; a firm and rigid approach to dealing with prisoners; a
strong sense of camaraderie and a deep attachment to the prison.

   The contention that power is translated is particularly important in
making sense of the conflicts between the 'old' and 'new' school of prison
officers. The 'old' school officers formed an alliance that was discursively
grounded in their knowledge of how to interact with prisoners. They were
not amenable to the changes, as they represented a 'softening' of approach,
which did not correspond with their interpretation of how a prison should be
run. Such interpretations gained legitimacy from the fact that the constellation
of authoritarian and control discourse had been the dominant alignment in
the prison. This slice of discursive action demonstrates how governmental
rationalities are deployed in practice, and illustrates how general systems
of domination and transformation are translated in and through discursively
structured local arenas of action. Elsewhere, I have argued (Carrabine, 2000:
323–5) that discursive formations also impact on gender relations to the extent
that the practices associated with both the new governors and staff represented

the antithesis of the hitherto hegemonic form of masculinity practised in the prison.

On one level the oppositions mounted by the 'old' school could be understood as a rejection or dismissal of a feminised Other. For instance, one probation officer [11] tellingly remarked that prison officers who became friendly with prisoners were regarded as 'care-bears or sissies' by other officers, implying that such action was considered unmanly or effeminate. Yet it would be quite mistaken to view professionalism and bureaucratic means of governance as discourses that constitute feminine practice. For example, the discourse of bureaucracy is explicitly concerned with instrumental reason, objective knowledge and solid impartiality. Such qualities are not unproblematic for as Seidler (1989) argues, ever 'since the Enlightenment men have sought to silence the voice of others in the name of reason'. In contrast, the discourse of professionalism is grounded in knowledge claims that prioritise experience, skill and responsibility in the business of administration with the crucial assumption that such virtues can only be acquired through an extended engagement with the public domain. This is not to suggest that the public sphere is exclusively male and the private purely female, rather it is to argue that gender divisions are organised along such understandings. As Tosh (1991) has highlighted, even when the notion of separate spheres was approaching its height in Victorian England, important connections between manliness and domesticity as the wielding of authority over dependants in the home provided a firm basis for men's public life. The overall argument is that while it might be fairly straightforward to equate a particular kind of aggressive, domineering and rugged masculinity with the discourse of authoritarianism, the other means of governance articulate different forms of masculinity that are of some significance in understanding the nature of the antagonisms between 'old' and 'new' school officers.

Conclusion

The intention of this chapter has been to chart the various organisational changes that occurred in Strangeways from the late 1960s up to the end of the 1980s. This is not only to illustrate the importance of discursive alliances and struggles between various actors but also to provide the sense of place that Strangeways evoked for respondents. As is clear it was understood to be 'hard line' arising from its role as 'sin bin' – a reputation which staff derived some satisfaction from, emphasising as it did the fratriarchal arrangements that the prison, as a gendered organisation, provided. Similarly there is evidence that staff interactions with prisoners were informed by an aggressive culture of masculinity – though there was far from a total reliance on the imposition of force and violence. The shift from being an authoritarian prison to one which sought to provide a more active regime for prisoners was compromised, in part, by a strong staff culture grounded in the 'old' school of officers.

I now want to turn to what these 'small facts' say about 'large issues' – that is the social and political contexts in which they are embedded. Of course, by following Geertz (1973: 21–3) here, the argument is that some locality cannot be regarded as 'the world in a teacup' or 'heaven in a grain of sand'; yet nevertheless these 'actions are comments on more than themselves'. In Britain and the United States the mid-1970s mark a watershed in state responses to the management of marginal groups. It will be recalled from Chapter 2, that Colvin (1992) draws attention to the shift from consensus and integration to coercion and repression in state policies. In prisons, this is associated with the collapse of the rehabilitative ideal and the movement toward more coercive tactics of control. Similarly, the law and order crusades associated with the politics of Thatcherism can be both understood as the regulation of peripheral populations and as the orchestration of consent in civil society through authoritarian programmes which have broad symbolic appeal (see Scraton et al., 1991 and *inter alia* Hall, 1988 and Sim et al., 1987). The increases in prison populations over this period charted in the last chapter, are indicative of such strategies of 'regressive modernisation'.

However, the 'small facts' at Strangeways speak of a movement from authoritarian, rigid structures of control to one that attempted to instil a more active day for prisoners. I have argued that this is not to be understood as a purely benign, progressive change – for, amongst other things, the former regime was perceived to be more procedurally precise in the distribution of valued resources (e.g., clothing), there were increased opportunities for victimisation between prisoners, and there were some oppositions from staff to this movement. On the face of it, this would appear to contradict the 'large issues' contained in the authoritarian drift thesis. The problems arise, not least, from viewing the period before the mid-1970s as an idealised and nostalgic era of consensus and integration to which the successive Thatcher administrations mark a decisive rupture. For as Gilroy and Sim (1987: 79) argue, such coercive tendencies have a much longer history 'in which the socialist movement has been deeply implicated'. An important example of this, in the prison setting, is the increasing emphasis on security and control as a result of the Mountbatten and Radzinowicz committees in the late 1960s, under Wilson's first term of government. Moreover, what these 'small facts' from Strangeways demonstrate is how the 'large issues' are translated in particular locales, which accounts for the contradictory and compromised nature of global projects in specific places.

Chapter 6

The Drift to Dissent

Introduction

In adopting the term 'drift' to describe the events leading up to the near month-long siege of Strangeways in April 1990, the intention is to avoid some of the problems identified in previous chapters. In particular, it is an attempt to move beyond simple metaphors which involve binary oppositions between consensus and conflict, for as Wrong (1994: 13) argues social order 'is always a matter of degree' and whilst 'prisons sometimes provoke rebellions and riots, so do they also (and more often) generate their own peculiar yet "ordinary" and "mundane" form of life' (Sparks, 1996: 36–7). The previous chapter can be read as an attempt to provide an indication of how the prison 'worked' to surmount the problems of institutional pathology, over-predicting disorder and historical retrospection that are implicit in even the most sophisticated sociological understandings of prison riots.

One of the tasks of genealogy is to restore action, meaning and sentiments to their social contexts rather than imputing them retrospectively, which involves locating the origins of disorder in a complex diversity of competing forces rather than being born of a singular convulsive event that punctures an otherwise stable patterning of daily life. Of course, this is not to insist that prisoner angst or managerial incompetence are irrelevant, but rather that these factors need to be understood in their detail as opposed to driving an inevitable march toward a fateful conclusion so that issues of specificity and continuity can be addressed rather than masked. For as I argued in the preceding chapter, the genealogical attentiveness to the distinctive and unique qualities of particular institutions needs to be combined with a more abstract and systematic form of archaeological analysis so that key similarities across social practices can be identified that are obscured by isolating configurations of reality into a 'cause' and an 'effect', which is precisely the problem with analyses of prison riots and public disorders that rely on some notion of a precipitating event to set in motion the unrest that follows. In contrast, the notion of drift offers a means by which the more fluid, contingent and dynamic aspects of disorder can be grasped.

Although there are important problems in Useem and Kimball's (1989: 5) analysis their approach does provide the most coherent framework with which to organise the narrative that follows, as they identify five stages that mark the passing of time before, during and after a prison riot. The first, not unsurprisingly, is the *pre-riot* stage 'during which prisoners and the forces of the state develop those material and cognitive resources that will determine the course of the riot event'. There then follows *initiation*, defined as 'the action by prisoners which first crosses the line into open rebellion; and the initial response by the state', whilst *expansion* refers to the period in which prisoners attempt to 'take control of as many human, material and spatial resources as possible against the resistance or non-resistance of the state'. The *state of siege* is when 'the prisoners control some territory in the institution, the state assembles its forces and concentrates its options for recapture options' whilst negotiations may take place between the state, prisoners and other parties. The final stage is *termination* or *recapture* and can result in three different endings: the state forcibly retaking the prison; resolution through negotiations; or conclusion simply because the prisoners are exhausted and do not want to continue further (Useem and Kimball, 1989: 215). This chapter provides an account of the pre-riot and initiation stages.

The discussion of the pre-riot stage begins here with a description of the prison and an account of the conditions in the prison in the weeks and months before the riot, which Woolf (Woolf and Tumim, 1991: para. 3.9:42) accurately describes as 'intolerable' (yet they have never been far from being anything else). Furthermore, Woolf also viewed the 'combination of errors' (Woolf and Tumim, 1991: para. 3.7:42) by staff and management at the prison and Headquarters of the Prison Service (in London) as a central contributing factor to the riot. Of course, these two features are rather pure statements of deprivation and disorganisation perspectives. Nevertheless, he argues that a 'substantial cause of the disturbance lies in the failures of the past' (Woolf and Tumim, 1991: para. 3.8:42) of successive governments 'to provide the resources to the Prison Service which were needed to enable the Service to provide for an increased prison population in a humane manner' (Woolf and Tumim, 1991: para. 3.432(5), 105). As can be seen from Chapter 4, this arises in the main from ploughing resources into dispersal and training institutions at the expense of local prisons and remand centres. The intention here is to locate such features as overcrowding, poor physical and material conditions, and an improving regime for prisoners in the context of how they were experienced at the time, and to demonstrate that there was a drift toward the events of April 1990. However, it is important to provide in this chapter a more detailed description of the actual prison layout to assist the reader in following the action that will shortly be described.

The prison, opened in 1868 as a local prison to replace a smaller gaol, the New Bailey, was intended to house 744 men and 315 women. The imposing Victorian gothic structure[1] followed the radial design principles of the model prison at Pentonville, built in 1840. From a central rotunda (known as the Centre) emanate six wings, four storeys high (see Figures 6.1 and 6.2). A to E wings contain cells. F Wing differs from the other wings in that the upper floor contains the Church of England chapel and, at the time of the riot, the lower floor contained administrative offices. The floor of the chapel slopes upwards to the Centre. This means that access to the chapel is gained from the Centre at the fourth landing level through two separate entrances. There are also two entrances at the lower end of the chapel, which is on the same level as the second landing in the wings.

A recent Inspectorate report (HMCIP, 1996: 7) remarks that from '1900 the spare space within the walls was progressively filled with a number of poor quality buildings in contrast to the original well planned and constructed jail'. These included the cruciform remand prison, with four wings: G, H, I and K of varying length, linked to the main prison through a kitchen and workshops. A hospital and communications room are adjacent to E wing, the longest of the wings. In addition, the area to the north of the original site, which is connected to the main complex by a high level bridge, is known as 'The Croft' and contains a number of workshops, stores and a laundry.

In 1963 women prisoners were transferred to Styal prison and the separate women's prison became a Borstal Allocation Centre for young offenders. Remand and trial prisoners were transferred to Risley Remand Centre in 1965. However, this function returned to Strangeways in 1980 and continues to the present day. This responsibility arose as a result of overcrowding at Risley, and produced serious effects on the regime at Strangeways (HMCIP, 1982: 4–5). At the time of the disturbance, in the main prison, convicted adult prisoners were accommodated in A, B, C, and D wings. Convicted young offenders were held in E wing, which was physically divided from the main prison at the Centre end of the wing by gates. The convicted prisoners held under Rule 43 (a) (own protection) were on C1 and C2 landings. The remand prisoners who were on Rule 43 (a) were held on the fourth landing of E wing.

HMP Manchester
(Redevelopment Plan)

1   Empire Street
2   Remand Wings
3   Hospital
4   Tower
5   Dog handlers
6   Future demolition
7   Chapel
8   Stores
9   Main building
10 Southall Street
11 Exercise area
12 Works Department
13 Laundry
14 Kitchen
15 Entry building

16 Industries and
    inmate training
17 Physical recreation
    centre
18 Workshops
19 Proposed road
    bridge
20 Sherborne Street
21 Services block
    below
22 Staff complex
23 Visitors Reception
    Centre
24 Great Ducie Street

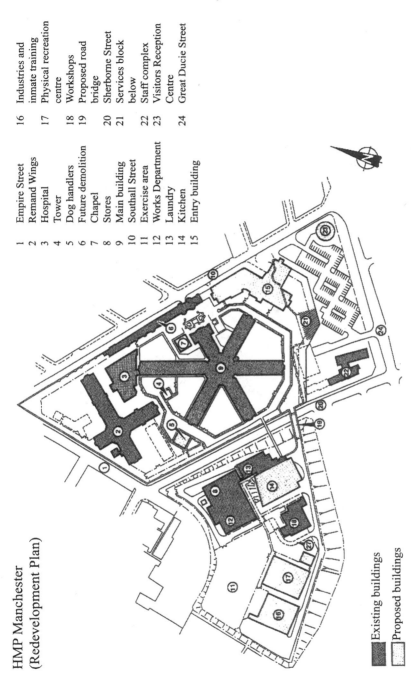

■ Existing buildings
▢ Proposed buildings

Figure 6.1   Layout of prison

Source: Woolf and Tumim (1991).

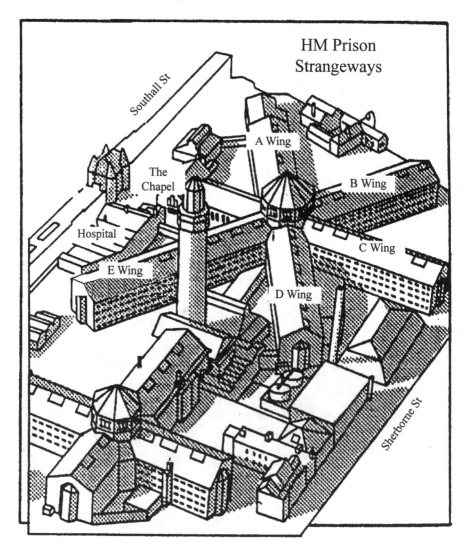

Figure 6.2   Schematic depiction of the prison

Source: *The Times*, 5 April 1990.

The Pre-riot Stage

'Intolerable' Conditions

Prisoners who begin their carceral career, as most do, in a local prison will typically find themselves in the midst of the worst conditions that the penal system can inflict, to the extent that it is difficult to convey exactly how miserable the conditions at Strangeways were. In common with many other local prisons overcrowding has been a daily feature of life within the institution for over two decades. Table 6.1 illustrates the enduring presence of overcrowding in the prison throughout the 1980s.[2] The problem of numbers has to be located in the debilitating context of dilapidated physical conditions in which prisoners are contained, combined with poor sanitation, clothing shortages and brief, inadequate family visits. Whilst the pervasive stench of urine, lack of washing facilities, scarcely edible food, decaying cramped cells and sheer degrading squalor of local prisons have been roundly damned in successive reports by the Chief Inspector of Prisons and widely reported in the national press, it is important to recognise that compounding this wretchedness was the severely restricted and oppressive regimes that these prisons imposed – with many prisoners routinely locked up for as much as 23 hours of the day.

Table 6.1   Prison population at Strangeways, 30 June 1980 to 1989

	Population	Certified normal accommodation	Percentage occupied
1980	1,437	873	164.6
1981	1,515	876	172.9
1982	1,468	876	167.6
1983	1,491	1,024	145.6
1984	1,412	1,024	145.6
1985	1,776	1,024	137.9
1986	1,454	927	156.9
1987	1,773	969	183.0
1988	1,784	970	183.9
1989	1,586	972	163.2

Source: Home Office, personal communication.

Though the previous chapter indicated there had been attempts to liberalise the regime at Strangeways in the late 1980s, it is important to recall that the generally appalling conditions in local prisons have long been justified on the administrative grounds that there is a high turnover of prisoners on short to medium sentences (from a few days to a few months) in which it is claimed that there is too little time to achieve rehabilitative results, whilst there is also an operational requirement for 'sin bins' to discipline disruptive long-term prisoners from dispersal prisons. The reasons why such abject conditions have not provoked wide-scale public outrage and shame are undoubtedly complex but part of the explanation lies in the resurgence of the Victorian penal doctrine of 'less eligibility'[3] which maintained that the criminal and the destitute should be subject to institutional regimes that were harsh, humiliating and punitive to not only instil dread but also to distinguish between the respectable poor and the dangerous rough classes. The forceful reappearance of less-eligibility principles from the mid-1970s can be related to the authoritarian politics of law and order then in ascendancy and the associated mobilisation of popular resentment directed toward 'soft' penal measures combined with widespread perceptions of urban lawlessness, social decay and economic decline.

Of course, overcrowding and unpleasant conditions are conventionally regarded as amongst the prime causes of prison unrest, though as I indicated in Chapter 3 this is ultimately misleading for these are persistent features that exist across a number of local prisons and in many respects it is clear that life at Strangeways had been improving in the years before the riot, whereas the European Committee for the Prevention of Torture (1991) would come to condemn the overcrowding, insanitary facilities and impoverished regimes found at three Victorian local prisons (Brixton, Wandsworth and Leeds) as inhuman and degrading treatment later in 1990. Nevertheless, it would be equally erroneous to claim that crowding has no effect on exacerbating tension and frustration. Rather, the key issue is how the organisation copes with the extra pressures placed on maintaining routines, ensuring security and distributing scarce resources – all of which contribute to sustaining the acquiescence of the confined.

I have argued that one of the tasks of genealogical analysis is the restoration of action, meaning and sentiments to their social contexts and the following passage conveys Brendan O'Friel's [01] recollection of the months before April 1990:

> Quite a lot of Strangeways was surviving day-to-day, you know, 'How do we get through today' pressures. During the winter of 1989/90 we had run

at between 1500 and 1600, and still the biggest prison in the country, but the population generally seemed down a little bit. We got even more back to work ... Then, for reasons that I don't think the Woolf report ever properly analysed, the population at Strangeways started to run at about 100 more than it had. This occurred in February and I think it was connected with some management changes, not within the prison but across the Service, that were made to LIDS [local inmate database system] and we did not seem to be getting them out at quite the same rate we were. And suddenly we found ourselves a 100 more than we had previously. That figure of between 1,640 and 1,650, the riot number, meant that there wasn't just 100 extra prisoners but that we had to double or treble more prisoners up. So it affected about 300 of them. So there were a significant bunch of people who said, 'It's getting worse'. I distinctly remember that in February and March. I had muttered about that on a number of occasions to various people, including the Deputy Director at the PGA [Prison Governors' Association] meeting we had. It's on record there that I said, 'there were population pressures again'. We were saying that at Strangeways, and nobody else was and nobody did anything about it. It wasn't taken sufficiently seriously. There was this belief at the time that big prisons will be alright, they'll get through.

There are a number of important issues raised here in relation to a population increase during February and March 1990 as the assertion is that it led to widespread feelings that conditions were deteriorating, an administrative belief that the large prisons muddle through these difficulties, and a criticism that the causes of the increase have not been sufficiently analysed.

There were three significant changes to the population. First, there was an exchange of Liverpool-based prisoners for a group of Manchester prisoners segregated under Rule 43 for their own protection. In fact 135 of the 801 sentenced prisoners on 1 April were from Liverpool, and given the longstanding rivalries between the two cities, the possibilities for mutual antagonisms were greatly enhanced. Second, in the six months before 1 April between 26 and 52 prisoners were returned to Strangeways per month from various training prisons. The figure would normally have been in the 30s. As Woolf (Woolf and Tumim, 1991: para. 3.40, 46) recognises such prisoners feel aggrieved, since as 'a result of being returned and the manner of that return they often harbour deep feelings of resentment'. Included in this group were ten prisoners from dispersal prisons who were sent to Strangeways for a six-month period.[4] Third, there had been a marked increase in Category C prisoners who were regarded as unsuited for dormitory accommodation and in Woolf's view were 'an extremely large group of potentially difficult inmates for a local prison to handle' (Woolf and Tumim, 1991: para. 3.41, 46).

In a revealing passage Woolf contends that this particular mix of prisoners and the general increase in numbers from January 1990 were:

> regarded by local management and staff as a possible cause of disruption, but no steps had been taken to deal specifically with this possibility in the handling or location of inmates. Mr. O'Friel, the governing Governor, was concerned that he did not have the resources to make a proper assessment of the problem. His request for a psychologist had not been met and without a psychologist he felt he was unable to adopt a more sophisticated approach to population management – a conclusion that I do not consider to be entirely justified. (Woolf and Tumim, 1991: para. 3.42, 46)

Whilst this judgment is a direct criticism of the administrative failure to respond to the potential problems posed by this particular increase in prisoners, an important question mark lies over just how unique the situation would have been but perhaps the most significant consequence of such population increases are the effects they have on routines, which was recognised by one governor:

> any large number of men being held together in a finite amount of capacity does have an effect and I think a significant effect on the prison regime because the more difficult it is or the more long-winded it is to carry out certain standard routines, I would mean things like feeding prisoners, bathing prisoners and getting them into employment. (HO 370/10: 90)

This passage is particularly salient for it illustrates how the routines, which are central to maintaining order, become compromised and less predictable through the stresses and strains associated with an increase in population.

It is, as Chapter 2 argued, highly debatable whether prisoners feel 'ontologically secure' through adhering to prison routines, yet nevertheless they do have a very real interest in the provision of such basic matters as eating and washing. If the regime is not seen to be providing such fundamental features of existence then this contributes to a perception of the authorities as lazy, incompetent and heartless, and the system itself as unjust and not in correspondence with the principles it espouses. Here Mathiesen's (1965: 23) notion of censoriousness is particularly important, which is defined as 'criticism of those in power for not following, in their behaviour, principles that are established as correct within the social system'. Consequently, the rupture of routines, engendered by this increase in the population, can be understood as promoting particularly intense feelings of censoriousness.

Disruption and Drift

It is, however, important to recognise that one of Mathiesen's (1965: 122–36) key arguments is that prisons are far more 'disrupted' institutions than conventionally understood, not least because the prisoners in his study did not develop a strongly organised prisoner subculture to counter the pains of imprisonment (as in the classic North American studies of the institution). Rather, prisoners are in a much weaker and more alienated situation as they are extremely dependent on the ways in which staff allocate food, clothing, visits and so on to the extent that the notion of 'peer solidarity is a norm more honoured in the breach than in the observance' (Sparks et al., 1996: 46). In other words, the 'inmate code' offers little practical compensation against the deprivations of confinement and instead promotes censoriousness 'on the part of isolated individuals, whereby the ruler is made to appear and feel as the real deviant, seeming to mitigate many of the pains of imprisonment that, according to other writers, are alleviated by peer solidarity' (Mathiesen, 1965: 12).

These are significant, though often overlooked, insights and they chime especially well with life in local prisons, for whilst prison staff and management tended to point to the problems associated with the rise in the prison population from January 1990 as an important contributing factor to the unrest, prisoners stressed the unjust grievance procedures that severely undermined the legitimacy of the institution. For instance, Woolf states that:

> Mr. O'Friel had delegated the handling of prisoners' grievances to the subordinate manager best placed to deal with the issues raised. This was not understood by the inmates, many of whom felt they had been deprived of their entitlement to have their complaints dealt with by the Governor. There was a lack of confidence in the system of justice within the prison. A number of prisoners attributed the riot which took place to the fact that no-one appeared to be taking any notice of their complaints. (Woolf and Tumim, 1991: para. 3.85, 52)

The vocabulary of justice indicates a certain level of consensus, between keepers and kept, over basic principles of fairness and the perception that no-one was listening served to foster a sense of righteous resentment against the regime. Furthermore, a probation officer [12] subsequently explained that:

> just prior to the riot you noticed that there was this feeling that staff didn't have the communication with management, they didn't feel that things filtered through to them and oddly enough the parallel to that was that prisoners also

were expressing the same feeling that information wasn't always filtering through ... There was general dissatisfaction, prison staff felt that they'd made reports that weren't being acted on, or what they had to say was being ignored. Similarly prisoners would feel either that they had not been told the outcome of something that they might have asked about or had been waiting for information from the wing office on whether something had been done or not and they'd be told that enquiries had been made and then they'd hear nothing. So there was this general feeling, which is difficult to put into words, but you picked up that neither prison staff nor prisoners were entirely happy.

The sense of confusion is palpable here and highlights severe communication problems between management, staff and prisoners that were rendering daily life arbitrary, unpredictable and divisive.

This particular state of affairs recalls what Mathiesen (1965: 100) has termed 'illegitimate patriarchalism' in that penal power often leaves prisoners in a situation much like that of a child perceiving the father to be carrying out what seems to be his personal, arbitrary and crushing domination and the only way to contest such oppression is through reference to some generalised expectation of fairness. As Sparks et al. (1996: 46) put it, the 'power of guards is both very great and rather unstable because it melds both personal and bureaucratic elements' and what is more when personal power becomes dominant 'this is viewed by inmates as a failure of bureaucratic rationality'. Clearly, the distribution of benefits and burdens in Strangeways was becoming highly individualised along arbitrary, discretionary and inconsistent lines that provoked prisoner censure, as the institution was seen to be failing to deliver justice and efficiency whilst departing from generally recognised rules and principles.

Of course these features are not enough to account for the riot as it is clear that 'illegitimate patriarchalism', as Mathiesen (1965: 100) defines it, is a normal rather than a pathological dynamic of prison life: officers and governors who insist on rigidly enforcing rules and regulations would be regarded as petty bureaucrats, whilst those who operate in a more discretionary way leave themselves open to accusations of unfairness, consequently typical penal social relations are characteristically 'disrupted' not only horizontally (between alienated censorious prisoners) but also hierarchically (in that staff and management frequently feel powerless when caught in this double bind). In overcoming such seemingly irreconcilable difficulties, Mathiesen (1965: 54) argues that the major goals of the organisation become reduced to the quest for a 'smooth administration of benefits of burdens' to ward off potential censorious challenges. Yet as this and the previous chapter have demonstrated such an organisational tranquillity has never existed, not least since struggles over how to govern are endemic features of institutional life, and it is perhaps no coincidence that Mathiesen (1974, 1990) subsequently would develop an abolitionist policy on the controversial grounds that a legitimate distribution of power is impossible in prison.

On one level, Mathiesen's (1965) *Defences of the Weak* offers a particularly nuanced account of how institutional life is persistently 'disrupted' that avoids characterising prisons as pathological, yet on another level it ought to predict more disorder than there actually is. Why there is not is due to his characterisation of individual prisoners as defensively censorious in a critique of functional prison sociology's preoccupation with collective prisoner subcultural solidarity. There is, as Sparks et al. (1996: 49) suggest, something of a false dichotomy here between solidarity and censoriousness, 'when some fluid combination of each (plus some other alternatives) may equally be imaginable', yet this still does not overcome the problem of over prediction, especially once prisoners' and staff's diverse understandings of and variable responses to their predicaments are taken into account. It is here that the notion of drift offers a means by which the fluid, contingent and dynamic aspects of disorder can be grasped.

During the second half of March 1990 there were a number of incidents that suggested tension was mounting in the prison. It is important to understand these incidents in the context of drift as advanced by Matza (1964) in his analysis of juvenile gang delinquency in which deviancy is regarded as a flexible affair. As I argued in Chapter 3 Useem and Kimball's (1989: 209) analysis does acknowledge that Matza's (1964) account of 'preparation' is of significance in the pre-riot stage, and they use it to refer to a heightened period of conflict between staff and prisoners in which the 'rebellious side won some sort of battle demonstrating the vulnerability of its opponents'. For, if the prisoners are successful in their exertions this highlights weaknesses in the administration, staff and buildings and gives an indication of their potential ability and prowess. Yet, if an act of resistance fails it can alert prisoners that the prison is secure, the staff vigilant, and it would be unwise to engage in future action.

So, importantly, the concept of drift does allow some insight into why prisons are not in a permanent state of turmoil, even when there are conditions of intense deprivation, for the events that initiate or deflect the motion to collective unrest are so numerous as to defy systematic identification. Moreover, they are more often than not accidental and unpredictable in the first instance so that the task is rather one of specifying the conditions that make 'drift possible and probable' (Matza, 1964: 29). Whilst I will return to the concept of drift below the following indicates the escalation of disorder in Strangeways.

March 15:   An incident in which two prisoners had to be restrained using control and restraint (C&R) techniques.

March 17:   One prisoner started a fire in his cell, while another prisoner threatened a governor that he would start a riot unless he was transferred to another prison.

March 26:   Two prisoners gained access to the roof via scaffolding which had been erected during refurbishment in the centre of the Main prison. It was almost 20 hours before two prison officers brought them down using a route through the chapel roof (Woolf and Tumim, 1991: para. 3.91, 53).

It is highly significant that the prisoners involved in these incidents were to play prominent roles in the disturbance; the two prisoners that were involved in the rooftop protest had just returned from the punishment block and it has been suggested that this action was intended as a protest against brutality in the segregation unit and initially 20 prisoners had agreed to participate (Jameson and Allison, 1995: 29). It is also clear that the scaffolding itself contributed to the tension in the prison, as one probation officer [13] recalled that:

> the big problem that arose was that they had put up scaffolding at the centre, and that had a dramatic effect on you when you walked in that prison. I don't think people realised it when they actually did it, but it did create an awful feeling, it was terribly depressing. We, at the time, thought it [the riot] was to do with the scaffolding, because there was a feeling around the place, it's difficult to explain, but there was a certain feeling around the place that something wasn't right. It made it dark in there, as that was where the light came from, so it darkened the place and what precious little space you had, went. A lot of us put it down to that, because there was such a depressing feeling in the place.

As for the prison staff, some 'spoke of a period leading up to the disturbance when they had been aware of heightened tension between staff and inmates, [but] this was not confirmed by others who should have been in a position to know' (Woolf and Tumim, 1991: para. 3.90, 53). As I will demonstrate in the next section there are a number of reasons why such warnings were not taken seriously, yet as regards prisoners Woolf asserts that:

those who played a prominent role in the riot indicated that, for differing reasons, they were labouring under an intense sense of grievance. These inmates encouraged others to become involved in the riot which started on 1 April. This encouragement no doubt explains why the majority of the inmates who gave evidence had been aware that there could well be an incident on that date and were confident that staff were aware of this as well. (Woolf and Tumim, 1991: para. 3.92, 54)

Yet 'an intense sense of grievance' is not enough to explain why the riot happened and here Matza's (1964: 188–91) account of drift is crucial, as it highlights the significance of 'desperation' that arises from a 'mood of fatalism', which provokes the will to commit 'new infractions' to provide a 'dramatic reassurance that he can still make things happen'. In other words, desperation refers to a crushing sense of hopelessness that in turn prompts a feeling that there is nothing left to lose.

It is important to recognise that Matza is not describing an inevitable process but rather explaining the existential motivations that can lead some delinquents to commit fresh crimes, which are crucially highly gendered. As he puts it:

> The mood of fatalism is the negation of the sense of active mastery over one's environment. It is likely to culminate in a sense of desperation among persons who place profound stress on the capacity to control the surroundings. Such a stress is implicit in customary precepts that celebrate the virtues of manliness. A man is above all one who will not allow himself to be 'pushed around' ... In any setting in which manliness is stressed, celebrated and regularly probed or sounded, the mood of fatalism will yield something approximating a sense of desperation. (Matza, 1964: 189)

There are few social situations that so routinely reinforce a culture of masculinity that idealises physical domination, intimidation, humiliation and violence as prison life (see Scraton et al., 1991; Carrabine and Longhurst, 1998; Bosworth and Carrabine, 2001 for further commentary on masculinity and imprisonment) and it is not too difficult to find an especially profound mood of fatalism hanging over Strangeways during February and March 1990 – the implications of fatalism as a solution to the problem of order will be drawn out in the final chapter.

Moreover, it is important to emphasise that everyday violence plays a significant role in structuring prison life (Edgar et al., 2003), as is vividly captured in the following observations:

> All male prisons house men who settle their arguments through fear, intimidation
> and fighting ... Protection rackets, dealing, settling scores and victimisation
> are the ingredients of the institutionalisation of male violence. The culture
> of masculinity which pervades male prisons is all-inclusive and reinforces
> hierarchies based on physical dominance ... Harsh regimes damage the minds
> and bodies of some people more than others but the oppressive climate which
> they establish and reproduce and the neglect or brutality experienced by certain
> prisoners contribute to depression, illness and death. The acts of violent men
> in prison, sustained by a culture of masculinity which idealises and equates
> personal power with physical dominance can be total, with nowhere to hide
> from the bullying of other prisoners. It is concentrated within a totality of
> masculinity, the ground-rules heavily underlined by official male authority.
> (Scraton et al., 1991: 66–7)

This passage highlights why it is important to understand prisons as gendered
organisations rather than simply arguing that prisoners suffer from some form
of troublesome masculinity, as this avoids confronting how the institution
itself reinforces aggressive cultures of masculinity.

Desperation, combined with those episodes of preparation outlined above,
played an important role in setting in motion the drift toward making something
new and dramatic happen in the prison on 1 April 1990. Nevertheless, it needs
to be emphasised that I am not simply arguing for a slightly more sophisticated
understanding of deprivation, as this ultimately offers a condescending
characterisation of prisoners-as-victims (of state oppression), but rather
that attention should also be drawn to the immediate, foreground, sensual
attractions of disorder. In other words, the drift to discontent offered increasing
opportunities for what Lyng (1990) has termed 'edgework', by which he means
the intense moments of pleasure and excitement that accompany the risk,
danger and skills associated with transgression. That the seductive qualities of
transgression are gendered is a matter that will be returned to in the following
chapter, but for now it is enough to stress that forms of transgression are
attempts to achieve a sense of control in 'ontologically insecure social worlds'
(Hayward, 2002: 86) and provide an attractive source of 'entertainment in a
bleak environment' (Carrabine et al., 2002: 76).

Initiation

Warnings and Organisation

In the days running up to the disturbance numerous warnings were given to staff that there could be trouble in the chapel during the Church of England service on the morning of Sunday 1 April 1990. Yet, it is also clear that warnings and rumours of trouble were not unusual in Strangeways; for example, one probation officer [09] commented that: 'I would guess that the truth is that every week, every weekend, you would find a reference to the fact that it was going to go up this weekend.' In fact, during 1989 there were 25 notes written, warning that trouble would occur in the Chapel on the Sunday (HO 370/2: 23). Nevertheless, what is of importance is the scale and source of the knowledge – whether it is an anonymous note or one from a prisoner known to provide reliable information. An example of the latter was given on the Saturday afternoon when a member of the Church choir told the officer who was in charge of A Wing, that he was not going to Chapel in the morning because it was 'going up'; when the officer said there were always these sort of rumours the prisoner replied, 'This is it', and he said that there were notes originating from Category A prisoners in the D1 cells circulating the prison urging prisoners 'to arouse the Scouser, to smash the chapel and take the roof off the place'. This information was passed on to the officers in charge of the Control Room (Woolf and Tumim, 1991: para. 3.95, 54).

One of the two Principal Officers responsible for security at the prison was called to the control room as a result of this information and there was some discussion over whether to cancel the service, or at the very least not allow Category A prisoners into the chapel. One of the officers, who had had seven years' experience in the main prison, eventually decided against this as he knew that 'there was frequently information to the effect that there might be trouble in the Chapel on Sunday' (Woolf and Tumin, 1991: para. 3.98,55). Significantly, no Security Information Report (SIR) was filled in, though it appears that this was far from unusual as 'action was "preferred to writing"', indicating that security information tended to be dealt with informally and that the coordination of security information was far from adequate (Woolf and Tumim, 1991: para. 3.98, 55), and further illustrating that social relations were running along individualistic, as opposed to bureaucratic, lines.

This was, perhaps, the most serious of the warnings which should have been acted on. Now it could be argued that as this Principal Officer only had five weeks' experience of being responsible for security matters, and he was 'learning on the job'. He agreed that the coordination of security information was inadequate and 'practices were lax' (HO 370/6: 102) which resulted in the warning not being given the attention it deserved. Yet, what is equally troubling is the fact that the officer had some 28 years' experience in the Prison Service, including seven years in the main prison, where such warnings were commonplace. An additional reason why these warnings were not taken seriously is that signals:

> of potential danger tend to lose their salience because they are interjected into a daily routine full of established signals with taken-for-granted meanings that represent the well-being of the relationship. (Vaughan, 1996: 414)

The argument is highly significant for understanding why the warnings were not given the attention they deserved, which an outsider to the prison's culture would have difficulties reconciling. This is almost certainly the case with Woolf, who seems to have been swayed by the evidence given by the other Principal Officer responsible for security. This officer had three years' experience and claimed that if the warning had been passed on to him he would not only have filled in an SIR but would have pursued the matter further:

> I would have said to Tony, 'Get yourself up the wing. Get a VO[5] and bring him out for a visit.' There was good value in that information ... I get the information and the source and where else, any other information, any other prisoners that I could perhaps lean on, call up, see. That is how we managed to avert a very serious disturbance last year. We had information a bit sooner then and during the course of the week we put a lot of pressure on a lot of people. We shipped a few out which means transferring them to other prisons. We recovered a lot of weapons and other gear. You have got to follow up information. Never ignore information.
> *Q* If you had been on duty, if you had followed the procedure that you had indicated, you felt that you would have been satisfied that was reliable information that should be acted on?
> *A* Yes. May I just elaborate on it, sir? We have at Manchester prison a first class pastoral service. They do superb work. They manage to get probably 200 to 300 prisoners out in the week for night classes and they believe they all go for their Christian views. I know by speaking to them that they go for the coffee and the Penguin [biscuits] but the choir boys are the ones who always attend the service. If a choir boy told me he was not going to service he would have made the hair on the back of the neck stand up. That is the significant

part in that. One of the choir boys. They are the ones who do have some faith and some feeling. The rest of the lads go to get an hour out of the cell and I don't criticise them for it. I would do exactly the same. (HO 370/10: 66–8)

Furthermore, he states that he would have contacted O'Friel (who was not normally on duty at weekends) and advised him that nobody from the punishment block should go to chapel and that there should be 'ad hoc rubdowns' given to prisoners going to chapel. Woolf goes so far to say that if 'Mr. Rutson had been on duty the riot in the Chapel may well not have started' (Woolf and Tumim, 1991: para. 3.97, 55).

At one level this illustrates the contingency of social life, as it is entirely feasible to suppose that events could have taken a different path if this officer had been on duty. Yet on another level it does not do full justice to the ways in which the other Principal Officer was interpreting and defining the situation, as his reading was based on his experience of the main prison, where such warnings were not unusual and served to confirm 'well-being'. It is in this sense that the meanings given to actions have to be restored to their social and cultural context. This is not to deny that individuals make mistakes, but that this decision which retrospectively was viewed as a calamitous error of judgement, becomes less so when it is restored to the world view of the actor, in which such warnings became neutralised because of their frequency. In other words, mistakes are systematic, socially organised and built into an institutional culture through the neutralisation of symbols of potential danger where risky situations are commonplace.

It is also the case that other warnings were passed on to Governor Morrison, who was responsible for the main prison. Before he went off duty on 31 March he left a message for Principal Officer Zegveldt, who would be in charge of C Wing on 1 April, to draw up contingency plans for the chapel service – at that time all he 'had in mind was the possibility of a sit-in next day' (Woolf and Tumim, 1991: para. 3.101, 55) – and as will become clear, this was also a reasonable decision as there had been a long history of such protests in the chapel. During that evening at least three other officers were given information that there would be trouble the next morning, but due to the informal lines of communication the full significance of these warnings was not appreciated and because of the regularity of such warnings their seriousness lost their immediacy.

That Saturday afternoon D Wing prisoners went to a film show in the chapel, and once it was over a number of prisoners refused to leave for half an hour as a sit-in protest, during which one of the prisoners made a speech.

The officers 'promised to listen to their grievances and make improvements, so they returned to their cells' (Jameson and Allison, 1995: 30–31). It has been confirmed that the prisoner who made the speech had been talking

> to other prisoners about the constant oppression and what to do about it. Together a few of them agreed it would be a good idea to stage a 'sit-in protest'. Rumours that such an event was to take place had already been circulating and they decided that they would make the rumours come true. They then talked to other prisoners in the punishment wing who agreed that: 'certainly something should be done in respect of bringing the governor to realise that there were real tensions that could not be ignored any further as they had been on so many occasions in the past'. (Jameson and Allison, 1995: 30)

It is also reported that later in the 'evening a black prisoner ... was beaten in the corridor in full view of other prisoners and injected with the "liquid cosh"' as a result of which the 'prisoners were sickened by this and decided to go ahead with a protest in the chapel the following day' (Jameson and Allison, 1995: 31).

On the morning of Sunday 1 April the staff that had come on duty were called together in the Centre at 07.50 and were addressed by Principal Officer Zegveldt. He told the staff of the events of the previous evening, as far as he was aware of them, though he had not checked with the Centre Senior Officer or any governor to gauge recent developments. He instructed staff to be careful in the way they unlocked prisoners for breakfast. The Senior Officers on A, B, C, and D Wing were told to put an extra officer in the chapel and that the officers there should move in pairs, not become isolated, and if there was any trouble they should evacuate the chapel. Zegveldt thought that if there was to be any trouble in the chapel it would take the form of sit-down protest with the possibility of a hostage-taking, consequently he did not wish staff to become isolated and he thought there was a greater possibility of trouble from D Wing prisoners that afternoon during exercise (Woolf and Tumim, 1991: para. 3.115, 57).

At 08.30 there was a meeting between governors and Principal Officers, where it was decided to advise C Wing Rule 43 prisoners, segregated for their own protection, not to attend the service and additional staff were sent to the vestry of the chapel under instruction that if there was any trouble they should make sure staff and clergy were evacuated. In Woolf's view:

> it is clear that there was a lack of co-ordinated organisation that Sunday morning. Although there was a meeting of Governor grades and Principal Officers there was no attempt to co-ordinate the information which was available or the action

which should be taken. The Governors and Principal Officers on duty appear to have been acting on their own individual assessment of the situation and on their own initiative. (Woolf and Tumim, 1991: para. 3.123, 59)

Three hundred and nine prisoners attended the 10 o'clock service, which was about the normal number, yet none of the Rule 43 prisoners went. Even though there was an extra staff presence on the landing, few prisoners were subjected to 'rub-down' searches. Instead of the usual eight, 14 officers supervised the chapel. There were an additional seven officers outside on the vestry. The officers that had been sent to supervise the prisoners going to the service left once they entered the chapel.

The Chapel of Unrest

At this point it is important to recognise that the chapel has a long history as a place for concerted dissent in the prison. As one respondent [02] recalled from his experience of Remand prisoner unrest in the early 1970s:

> as a junior governor grade who worked alternate weekends one of my jobs was to attend church services. So I used to go to the Church of England service and a lot of the prisoners used to go to the chapel services on Sunday morning, about 300 in one go. It is a large area, rather like an amphitheatre, which focuses down and you can easily get 300 prisoners in there. But I can remember occasions when tension was high, when the staff were on duty (perhaps ten staff in the chapel), they would all leave their keys with a senior member of staff before they went into the chapel in case there was unrest. So it was known that the chapel was a place where incidents could happen. On one occasion it very nearly did, when there was tension the chapel was an area where everybody knew the prisoners had a right to go there, but gosh they wished they hadn't. When the disturbance happened in April 1990, it was not the first time that the chapel was the focus of anxiety.

What is important here is not only the fact that the chapel has had a long history as 'focus of anxiety' but that staff used to leave their keys with a senior staff member in case there was trouble – this was not the case in 1990.

It is also important to acknowledge that the threat of disorder and actual prison unrest were fairly ubiquitous features of prison life in Strangeways (and not all of it centring on the chapel). As Brendan O'Friel [01] commented,

> If you look back over the last ten to 15 years at Strangeways there had been a series of warnings about misbehaviour at the weekends. Some of it centred

on the chapel, though not all of it. None of which, well only the odd thing, materialised. We had a disturbance on my first weekend there. It was a film in the afternoon, it was the remand prisoners who were down there. Partly as a result of that disturbance, not that disturbance actually, it was as the result of another disturbance that we broke up the numbers going into the film into smaller numbers. We did a whole variety of things to reduce the numbers of people around. We had a disturbance in the yard in 1987, maybe '88, and we broke up the numbers on exercise after that. The C of E chapel service was actually the only big service left. To be honest we hadn't got round to looking at it. We felt that it had worked for the last 30 years, the last 100 years even.

It will also be recalled that just under a year before, in May 1989, a protest had been averted. For the governor in charge of the prison that weekend:

> there is always a danger then of precipitating danger by overkill. The mere fact that you have put a lot of staff inside might indicate that there is going to be trouble and it might lead to it. The precautions were taken to have staff ready in case there was trouble but to keep the numbers actually in the chapel, although to boost them a little, to keep them within reason so that if nothing did occur then everything was okay, but in the event of something happening the staff were readily available to assist. (HO 370/12: 55)

This indicates the highly precarious nature of maintaining order, as an overzealous staff presence could have inspired the prisoners into action at the sight of a heavy-handed approach. However, the force of seven extra officers was hardly a crack outfit – two officers had angina and another suffered from back pain.

To return to the service, the first five rows from the front of the chapel, at the lower level, were occupied by about 90 young prisoners. There was then a gap of two rows and from the seventh row upward, adult prisoners were seated. The Category A prisoners and prisoners from the prison segregation unit arrived late and their 'arrival clearly caused a stir among the inmates who were already in the congregation' (Woolf and Tumim, 1991: para. 3.127, 59). There was obviously a tense atmosphere in the service for one prisoner, in his evidence to the Inquiry, said that although he had not heard of any rumours before the Sunday, he was told that morning:

> to take a stick with me to the chapel, but I just thought it would be, because like, this is the sort of thing that happens every Sunday. The inmates they have a slight sit-in. Like, this is something that happens on a Sunday, so, I thought it would be the same thing as usual going about, but obviously it wasn't.

Q Just help us. In other words, you are saying that it was quite frequent that messages went round saying that something was going to happen.

A Previous there had been sit-ins on Sunday that last about 10 minutes, when they stay in and they don't get up and they are asked to leave. This is the normal thing that seems to happen. (HO 370/4: 43–4)

Again, this passage illustrates the frequency with which the chapel served as a place for dissent. Another prisoner said that it 'was a known fact that for over a week that this particular sit-in was gonna take place' (Prisoner 0, HO 370/15: 120).

Reverend Proctor began the service with a warning that they were in God's house and should behave accordingly, no doubt as he too was aware of the rumours and the especially tense atmosphere, with some prisoners refusing to stand during hymns and clapping once they finished. The sermon attracted catcalls, at which point:

> as Mr. Proctor rose to announce the final hymn, an inmate came down from the centre aisle and took the microphone from a position in front of the choir. He began to address the congregation, talking about the hardness of the prison system. A tape recording was made of this part of the service ... This gives the best indication of what was happening. It makes it clear that pandemonium broke out. It is not surprising therefore that the accounts given by witnesses of precisely what happened differ. (Woolf and Tumim, 1991: para. 3.131, 60)

The service was being recorded for distribution to a prayer group and the transcript is as follows:

> *Noel Proctor*: After that remarkable message that has ...
>
> *A Prisoner*: I would like to say, right, that this man has just talked about blessing of the heart and a hardened heart can be delivered. No it cannot, not with resentment, anger and bitterness and hatred being instilled in people.
>
> [*General noise, over which*]:
>
> *A Prisoner*: Fuck your system, fuck your rules.
>
> [*Applause*]
>
> *Proctor*: Right lads, sit down.
>
> [*More noise*]
>
> *Proctor*: Right lads, down. Down. Come on, this is no way to carry on in God's house.
>
> [*More noise*]
>
> *A Prisoner*: Fuck your system.
>
> [*More noise*]

Proctor: Right lads, sit down. This is completely out of order. Sit down.
A Prisoner: Why is it? It's been waiting to happen forever. It will never change.
Proctor: This is terrible.
[*More noise; banging, shouting, cheering*]
All of you who want to go back to your cells go to the back of the church please.
A Prisoner: What? You're a fucking hypocrite, you.
Proctor: I'm trying to help you, to keep you.
A Prisoner: Leave it, mate.
[*More noise until microphone goes dead*] (Jamieson and Allison, 1995: 18–19)

While Reverend Proctor was appealing for order, a prisoner among those who had arrived late shouted out words to the effect that 'You've heard enough, let's do it, get the bastards' and brandished two sticks. This brought the lull to an end. Other prisoners waved weapons and put on masks. Some of the prisoners pressed towards the back of the chapel where most of the prison officers were. Those prison officers, following the orders given by Principal Officer Zegveldt, then started to leave (Woolf and Tumim, 1991: para. 3.132, 60).

A number of prisoners started to attack prison officers with fire extinguishers, table legs and fire buckets. One officer had his keys torn from him. In the meantime the seven officers who had been in the vestry were struggling to get into the chapel at the same time as a number of prisoners were trying to get out. Once in the chapel these officers were also attacked by some prisoners, and another officer lost his keys to a prisoner. Other prisoners helped injured officers and Reverend Proctor to the vestry. It seems clear that the prisoners were only interested in getting keys from prison officers and not taking them hostage, as there would have been ample opportunity to do so.

Nevertheless, there were some intense skirmishes between officers and prisoners and it is also clear that not every prisoner was involved in the conflict. For instance one prisoner recollected that,

Mr. Proctor hurriedly went over to him and wrestled the microphone from his hand and he got hit in the eye with the microphone. By then, all hell had broken loose. Inmates at the back of the congregation were hooded, chairs were being thrown, pews were being ripped off the floor and windows were being broken.
Q Can you help us as to what the prison officers were doing during that period?
A Well, when I looked, after I got my wits about me, I looked round. I looked to the top of the church because I fully expected to see an army of officers

coming in to break up the disturbance; I could not see any officer at all. The only officer I did see came to the front of the church and stood with his arms raised, trying to control things, but to no avail. (Prisoner A, HO 370/4: 32)

This prisoner then describes how he 'walked to the side of the chapel behind the curtains where there was not much activity going on' (Prisoner A, HO 370/4: 33).

The consequences of the prison officers' retreat will be discussed below, for it is important to recognise that at the time the incident occurred, which was at about 11.00, a governor was returning to the chapel by the spiral staircase between the second and third landings in A Wing when he first heard the disturbance. He arrived at the chapel on the fourth landing just as the gates to the chapel were being closed. There were about 15 officers standing around the gates. The governor decided to leave as he thought he could be of more use in preventing a possible escape from the other end of the chapel. However, he should have given 'orders to the staff to try and contain the prisoners in the chapel and prevent them getting in to the Centre' (Woolf and Tumim, 1991: para. 3.139, 61). Principal Officer Zegveldt arrived shortly after the Governor five had left, at which point there was only one officer left; precisely why 'they had left is not clear because they had not been ordered to do so and the prisoners initially made no attempt to leave the Chapel' (Woolf and Tumim, 1991: para. 3.140, 62). In fact the prisoners were busy barricading the doors into the Chapel as they thought the officers would try to regain control.

In charge of the Centre that morning was Acting Senior Officer Johnson, in effect a basic grade officer. The situation emerging was one he was quite unprepared for, had no training in and only limited experience as controller in the Centre. Those in the Centre were in a difficult position from which to view the higher levels because of the planks on the scaffolding. Johnson was under the mistaken impression that he saw, through the planks, prisoners streaming out of the chapel. As a result he informed staff on C1 and D1 of the incident, and later, when he heard that the prisoners had keys, told them, and staff on A1, that they should evacuate the prison. Governor Morrison, who was responsible for the main prison, was also present and did not intervene with these instructions. There were approximately 20–30 officers in the Centre[6] and it seems clear that:

those in the Centre were under the impression that a number of prisoners were on the landings in the Centre and elsewhere. But it is more likely that they were confused by the noise which Mr. Morrison accurately described as horrendous. In the early stages it is probable that only isolated inmates were out of the Chapel, and they were not on the Centre at the higher levels or on the scaffolding, but initially in A Wing on the fourth landing. Even if they were on the scaffolding having got on at the top of the rotunda, they could not have got from there into the Centre because of the protective mesh around the scaffolding which was never at any time penetrated. (Woolf and Tumim, 1991: para. 3.143, 62)

In spite of this Governor Morrison came to the conclusion that the Centre should be evacuated, without taking any measures to ascertain whether prisoners were on the Centre. He 'assumed they were because of the "tidal wave" of noise and the information he had been given that keys had been taken' (Woolf and Tumim, 1991: para. 3.144, 62). The staff evacuated the Centre at 11.13, though if a check had been made it would have been clear that the Centre was under no immediate threat. According to Woolf, up to this point:

Mr. Morrison had been required to act only as administrator and manager, a role which he performed well. On that Sunday morning he was suddenly required to act as an operational commander without previous experience or training. In the few minutes before he ordered the withdrawal from the Centre he was not in a position to provide the sort of leadership which was needed if the staff who were present were to become an effective force. (Woolf and Tumim, 1991: para. 3.149, 63)

In his evidence to the Inquiry, Morrison said his paramount concern was staff safety, and withdrawal would ensure this. Yet as Woolf (Woolf and Tumim, 1991: para. 3.150, 63) asserts, he had a number of other responsibilities which, not least, included the safety of the prisoners left in the main prison.

It is important to recognise that at this stage the prisoners were busy building barricades or otherwise trying to keep a distance from the events. A number of prisoners were terrified. Only a few were trying to make their way on to the roof at this point, though a good number would shortly follow them, when it became clear that the expected attack on the chapel would not materialise. At this moment, then, the planned sit-in protest had, perhaps, gone a little beyond what was intended, yet nevertheless the disturbance was at this stage primarily confined to the chapel. That it was able to spread and came to symbolise the crisis in British prisons is described in the next chapter, for at this stage it was far from taking on these properties.

Notes

1   The building was designed by the architect Alfred Waterhouse, whose other neo-gothic creations included the Town Hall in Manchester and the Natural History Museum in London.

2   The certified normal accommodation (CNA) of the prison was 970. On 1 April 1990 the total population was 1,647. In the past, though, this figure had been larger: in March 1988 the prison population reached 1,803. Nevertheless, what did have an effect on conditions was the population increase from January 1990, when it was 1,417, to a peak on 27 March, when the figure reached 1,658. The full significance of this increase is discussed in the text.

3   See Pratt (2002: 61–72) for an informed discussion of how the less-eligibility principle became the guiding imperative of social policy during the nineteenth century, which effectively meant that those who became dependent on the state would have to endure a less favourable existence than the poorest free citizens.

4   The two main methods of dealing with disruptive prisoners are segregation and transfer (see King and McDermott, 1989 on the social construction of what constitutes a disruptive prisoner – and the variability this entails) and they both contribute to a source of grievance stemming from the arbitrary and oppressive power exercised over prisoners. Segregation under Rule 43, which entails solitary confinement, is intended as an administrative procedure, but it is perceived by those on the receiving end as a punishment, and it has been used for many years as a means of isolating 'troublemakers' rather than investigating the grievances that may have led to the disruption. The temporary transfer, under the Circular Instruction 10/74, whilst also being an administrative procedure, was frequently used for disciplinary purposes in conjunction with segregation and is one of the most resented actions that the Prison Service can take (which Woolf explicitly acknowledged and which subsequently led to a revision of procedures for managing disruptive prisoners); since there are no rights of appeal nor any reasons usually given for either segregation or transfer, this can engender deeply held resentments.

5   A Visiting Order, which would have been a subterfuge so that other prisoners on the landing would not be aware that this prisoner was giving information.

6   In evidence to the Inquiry it was estimated that 15–20 officers could have held the main prison (Woolf and Tumim, 1991: para. 3.143, 62).

Chapter 7

The Siege of Strangeways

Introduction

The main reason why the riot at Strangeways lasted for 25 days and came to signify the chronic problems inherent in the prison system is explained in large measure by the reactions of the authorities to the protest. The chapter begins with an account of how the prisoners were able to take over one of the largest prisons in Europe, and also carried out some horrific attacks on Rule 43 (a) (own protection) prisoners who were understood to be sex offenders or informers. There then follows an outline of the actions surrounding the controversial cancellation of a proposed plan to retake the prison on the second day of the disturbance, once the majority of the prisoners had been evacuated. After this discussion the state of siege is described. This period is characterised by negotiation, some staff interventions into the prison, and the use of pressure tactics to weaken the resolve of the prisoners remaining in the prison. The steady trickle of surrendering prisoners continued up to 13 April at which point there were only a handful of prisoners remaining in the prison. Strangeways was recaptured some 12 days later, in an operation involving over 100 staff to recover a prison, which was by then controlled by six prisoners. The chapter concludes with a discussion of Woolf's comments on the events at the prison. Although they are not described as such, his findings reside in the deprivation and disorganisation perspectives and I indicate that these, on their own, are not enough to adequately explain why the riot occurred when it did. This requires a deeper understanding of the nature of institutional power, social order and contingent drift, matters that I attend to in the final chapter.

Expansion

From the Chapel and Beyond

The disturbance began shortly after 11.00 in the chapel, yet by noon prisoners had seized control of almost the entire prison. The reason for this success is a direct consequence of staff abandoning the fourth landing gates outside the chapel, which 'effectively handed the prison to the prisoners' (Woolf and Tumim, 1991: para. 3.154, 64). Initially the prisoners barricaded themselves in the chapel, fully expecting an imminent staff attack, whilst a few other prisoners were managing to get into the roof area through an unprotected gap in the roof protection. At first they went to A Wing and from there to the other wings of the main prison. Access to the wings was gained by making a hole in the ceiling of an office on the top floor of A Wing which, like similar offices on other wings, was not fully protected. Once on the wings the prisoners were able to release all the other prisoners.

One of the first prisoners to leave the chapel has described his initial progression to the roof as follows:

> On reaching the back of the church ... I exited with other inmates ... I was even more taken aback to find no confrontation by any warders; the place seemed completely deserted ... After going three-quarters of the way round the rotunda, my attention was automatically drawn to the scaffolding and I felt this compulsion to enter and climb it to the roof. So on quickly gazing through the meshing which covers the rotunda, I noticed to my delight that some had already made an opening near the church. I joined the few people going through. After entering the mesh I quickly scaled the scaffolding... On finally reaching this roof I admittedly began to vent my ten years of frustration and anger over my illegal treatment and that of many other lifers who I know who've been subjected to the same brutal force, both mentally and physically, not just in Strangeways but many other institutions around the British Isles ... So this relative freedom naturally brought a reaction and I began to disassemble the roof with complete joy and frustration. (Jamieson and Allison, 1995: 21–2)

In the meantime, Deputy Governor Wallace, who was responsible for the prison in O'Friel's absence,[1] was in his office on F wing. Shortly before the service was due to finish at 11.00 he decided to go and observe the preparations being made for prisoners to leave the chapel. Just as he was leaving his office he heard the noise which signified trouble had started and he went to take charge in the communications room, which was in a building near to the chapel, and arrived at 11.05, by which time the police and fire brigade had been notified, and the Regional Office were informed. At 11.07 reports were received that prisoners were on the E and F/chapel wing roofs, and by 11.08 Brendan O'Friel had been paged (Woolf and Tumim, 1991: para. 3.156, 64–5).

The passage of events in the rest of the prison is as follows. In charge of A wing that weekend was Acting Senior Officer Richardson. When the disturbance started he was waiting for the prisoners to come out of the chapel and he ran with other staff towards the chapel. Those prisoners in A Wing who had not attended the service were secure in their cells. As a result of hearing a voice saying the prisoners were getting on to the forecourt, Richardson and the group of staff went to this area, which was near the vestry door, where they 'milled about' (Woolf and Tumim, 1991: para. 3.157, 65). The other officers on A Wing appear also to have evacuated the wing at an early stage. So when the prisoners from the chapel came one at a time through the roof space, they found A Wing unsupervised, and could release prisoners there at will. It would seem that B Wing was also without officers. Prison Officer Andrews had locked up the last prisoners before the service had begun. He found no other officers present, apart from a Senior Officer. Andrews was in the tea room on A Wing when the disturbance began and was told to hold the back door of the chapel to cut prisoners off if they attempted to break out onto the forecourt (Woolf and Tumim, 1991: para. 3.160, 65).

Meanwhile, Senior Officer Collins was in charge of the 1st landing on C Wing where the majority of prisoners who were separated for their own protection under Rule 43 of the Prison Rules were confined and in serious danger as they were regarded as sex offenders. At the time of the disturbance two officers were with him. Following Principal Officer Zegveldt's instructions he advised the Rule 43s not to go to chapel, but allowed 15 to have exercise. When a message had been received of a disturbance in the chapel and keys taken, the prisoners were taken in and locked up. Though Collins had heard a message on the radio instructing Main prison staff to withdraw, he was concerned about the plight of the 71 Rule 43 prisoners on C1 landing so three officers went back to C1 landing and attempted to evacuate the prisoners. A number of the prisoners were terrified and barricaded themselves in their cells. However, the officers were eventually successful and were able to get the prisoners to safety.

As an example, one prisoner who was on Rule 43 (a) (own request) recalled that:

> We heard windows breaking, a lot of shouting and bawling so we barricaded the doors. The other two lads that was with me, we barricaded the door with our beds, pushed them up against the door. A few minutes later we heard crashing round at the landing. That was the skylights coming in. Officer Duffield pushed the door. He said: 'It's me lads. Shift the beds', so we shifted the beds. He said: 'Run like so-and-so to common' [sic] so we did. They was coming through with scaffolding poles, coming through the skylights ... If it was not for Mr. Ward and Mr. Duffield they would have gone up and got us. (Prisoner H, HO 370/4: 85–6)

There were a further seven Rule 43 prisoners on the second landing of C Wing. Collins thought he could hear prisoners on either the 2s or the 3s, and decided he could not release them in what now must have been harrowing circumstances (Woolf and Tumim, 1991: para. 3.163, 66).

Five Category A prisoners from D wing were having exercise during the chapel service, supervised by Prison Officer Parr. When he heard about the trouble on his radio he tried to bring the exercise to an end but the prisoners refused to return. The three officers decided they could not force them to come in and on hearing the radio message to evacuate the prison they locked the entrance to the exercise yard. At this time prisoners were already on D2 and D3 landings (Woolf and Tumim, 1991: para. 3.164, 66).

On E wing there were two senior officers and a dozen or so basic grade officers. About 100 of the young prisoners on the wing had gone to chapel. There had been no advice given to the officers on E Wing that Rule 43 prisoners should not go to chapel (though in the event none did, presumably as they were aware of the rumours circulating the prison). Since some form of trouble was expected staff went down the E Wing passage to meet the young prisoners but beat a retreat when they saw what was happening. Once back on the wing the passage gates were locked. The officers remained at the gate until they were instructed to evacuate the prison. As opposed to C wing, the Rule 43s were left on the wing on the 4s landing. The danger to them was not recognised until prisoners broke into E Wing (Woolf and Tumim, 1991: paras 3.165–71, 66–7).

Over the weekend of 31 March and 1 April Governor Stewart was responsible for the remand prison and E wing as the Governor 4 was off duty. At the time the disturbance started 37 adults were on exercise in H yard. All the other remand prisoners were locked up in their cells. The Senior Officer and his staff, apart from one officer, in G wing were instructed to report to the communications room. The exercise was allowed to continue, until Governor Wallace telephoned at 11.10 with the instruction to bring the prisoners in, which passed without incident. Stewart instructed all her staff, apart from a principal officer, a senior officer and four or five other staff to go to the Centre. She left the remand prison at about 11.20. Nothing was done to defend the remand prison apart from chaining and padlocking the gate on G1 and doubling the external locks. Only a skeletal staff force were left in the remand prison, although a substantial number of officers were in the vicinity of the main gate waiting to be told what to do. The scale of the disturbance took Stewart completely by surprise: she had not been fully briefed about the warnings and there were no contingency plans advising that the remand prison should be secured in the event of a serious incident in the main prison. The physical defences of the remand from the main prison were limited. While a substantial gate had recently been put inside the wooden door on G1, it could not be doubled. Moreover, it had been positioned part way along the last cell wall on G1, so that it would have been possible to by-pass the gate by making a hole in the wall of the cell (Woolf and Tumim, 1991: paras 3.172–81, 67–8).

Wallace was in command in the communications room until O'Friel arrived just before noon. The room was previously located in the Gate Lodge, where the facilities were totally inadequate, and it had subsequently been moved into temporary accommodation in the building known as the Back Reception; this was linked with the passage which runs between the chapel and E Wing. The communications room provided barely any visibility. Video equipment only surveyed the pedestrian entrance at the main gate. The room had three telephones and an outside direct line to the police. There was also a radio system, but since the prisoners from an early stage had possession of a radio they were able to jam the system and overhear communications for some time. When the prisoners obtained access to offices they were able to tamper with the telephone lines, which meant the communications room could only use a single outside line until a mobile phone was provided. Compounding these problems was the fact that the room was tiny. There were no separate areas from where governors could take charge of the situation or make any executive decisions without being surrounded by everyone else who was in there (Woolf and Tumim, 1991: para. 3.182–4, 68–9).

One of Wallace's concerns was that prisoners coming from the chapel along the corridor to E Wing could attack the communications room. Staff with C&R (control and restraint) training were therefore stationed in MUFTI (minimum use of force and tactical intervention) armour in that corridor and in F wing. Yet no MUFTI squads were sent to the remand prison. At the Inquiry, Wallace's explanation for this was that he thought there was not enough staff. The C&R instructor, Principal Officer Nicholson (who was not yet at the scene), gave contrary evidence to the effect that he thought the remand prison could have been held by one trained C&R trained unit (12 men and a commander).

Woolf (Woolf and Tumim, 1991: para. 3.187, 69) argues that one of Wallace's first priorities should have been to hold the remand prison. But until O'Friel arrived nothing was done, apart from applying the double lock to the external door and putting a padlock and chain on the gate on G1. Six officers remained in the remand prison. The incident log reports that prisoners were seen proceeding to the remand centre at 11.43. Yet it was not until about

12.20 that they actually broke in through the wooden door leading from the kitchen into G1.

O'Friel arrived at the prison at 11.55 and one of the first orders he gave was that steps should be taken to retain the remand prison. Stewart set off to organise this, but she only reached as far as the end of I Wing before the retreating staff met her. It was already too late to salvage the remand prison. Brendan O'Friel [01] subsequently recalled that:

> by 12 o'clock when I came in it looked as if we'd lost control of the whole thing. My first decision was to send a Governor 5 back up to the remand prison to see if we could hold it, but it was too late. That decision, had it been taken half an hour earlier, would have meant we could have started barricading, doubling and getting some staff up there. This might have meant we could have held the remand prison, meaning we could have kept another 400 locked up. Assuming the doors would have held, that sort of thing. But we had about 200 staff on duty, and we must have lost nine or ten casualties of one sort or another and then you lose staff getting the casualties out. We didn't have a lot of the staff come pouring in until about 1 o'clock. I tell you what really bugged us was there was an element of April Fool about it. We rang staff up about it, who said 'You must be joking, is this an April Fool?' That's what happened when they rang up my home, my son thought it was an April Fool.

During the whole of this period Rev. Proctor was in the vestry with a number of other prisoners. At 12.37 the incident log recorded that he had telephoned to say that he and the 10 prisoners wished to be released. At 13.06 it is recorded they were still locked in the vestry but safe. They were eventually rescued by three officers, at around 15.00, who 'faced a barrage of slates and missiles' (Woolf and Tumim, 1991: para. 3.200, 71). A prisoner who was in the remand prison recalled that when:

> it spread to remands it was around 12, 12.30, 12.45 ... about then and when my door got opened I knew by then of course what had taken place in the chapel ... Soon after I got unlocked from my cell on day one the remand wing went up ... set alight ... the halls filled with thick black smoke ... a cry of 'Everyone to the main prison!' went up and loads of us went onto the main prison ... Some kids I know went back to sleep on remand and left the gaol when the MUFTI came in and retook remands on Monday morning. I stayed on the convicted side on Sunday night because it was a sight to behold, a real novelty to sit on the roof with around 200 to 350 people at midnight. All I could think was 'I wonder which section of Rule 47 para. 6 this comes under'. (In Jameson and Allison, 1995: 23–4)

The whole of the prison accommodation had been lost by midday, but all the staff had managed to leave the wings, with some casualties, but no fatalities. The prisoners responded to this situation in all manner of different ways: some stayed in their cells, or only left them to find their way out of the prison and to the authorities. Others set about destroying the fabric of the institution, whilst others watched, enjoying the display and destruction of despised surroundings. A good many prisoners were terrified. Woolf states that:

> as far as the prisoners were concerned, whether they wanted to be or not, they were caught up with what was happening in the prison. If they were one of the unfortunate Rule 43 prisoners who were not evacuated, their position was indeed perilous. (Woolf and Tumim, 1991: para. 3.201, 71)

A number of prisoners gave evidence to the Inquiry, relating their treatment at the hands of other prisoners.

Perhaps the most harrowing experience happened to Prisoner N who was sharing his cell with another inmate on Rule 43 on E4 landing. They barricaded their door but four prisoners, two masked, started breaking the door down, shouting they were going to kill them. When they broke in they found some objects which they believed did not belong to him, and he was then hit with a table leg, stabbed with a pair of scissors and eventually thrown over the balcony from the landing on to the wire netting between the second and first landing. Various objects, including a cell door, were then thrown on him and he lost consciousness. When he came to he found himself being dragged off the netting by prisoners, who threw paint over him. Another prisoner came to his rescue and took him to the A1 landing, where he was able to get out and was carried away on a stretcher (Woolf and Tumim, 1991 para. 3.205, 72).

These attacks raise profound questions about the politics of protest (see also Bosworth and Carrabine, 2001). It is important here to emphasise the knowledgeability of the actors, for one of the central assertions of feminist thought has been that the categorising of the 'use of violence in to instrumental and expressive types overlooks the important contribution of the gendered context, knowledge and the meaning of violence' (Stanko, 1994: 41). It will be recalled that in certain versions of deprivation perspectives violence is regarded as the instrumental, purposive dramatisation of grievances. Yet this avoids confronting the ways in which such acts of violence, outlined here at Strangeways, were a performance of an aggressive, hegemonic masculinity, in terms of overt displays of power and domination against the most vilified group of individuals in the prison community. Equally, the fact that other prisoners were prepared to help those suffering at the hands of these men, illustrates the contested nature of hegemonic masculinity.

In Gramsci (1971), the term hegemony implies struggle and it is this dimension that needs to be emphasised here. For while prisoners bully, intimidate and torture each other, these actions should not be understood simply as contradictory and doomed attempts at resolving the existential problems imposed by imprisonment and social injustice. Instead, the metaphor of transgression offers an important conceptual means of conveying the sheer excess of actions, emotions and meanings associated with prison unrest, in which desire, pleasure and risk-taking are central experiences.

Likewise, the depiction of violence as an expressive, spontaneous, irrational outburst is hard to sustain, as the Rule 43 (a) (own protection) prisoners were actively sought out. Nevertheless, such activities should not be reduced to some form of troublesome masculinity; they need to be located in the context of prisons as organisations which routinely sustain and reproduce cultures of masculinity which emphasise force and domination (Carrabine and Longhurst, 1998). For the fundamental point, which the sociology of the prison has barely begun to address, is that 'it reproduces normal men' (Sim, 1994: 108) and thereby perpetuates gender divisions. Above all else, these acts of violence ought to force an understanding of the contradictions that collective dissent engenders without simplifying complex events and characterising protesters as a homogenous entity, acting with one unified will to resist or destruct. In some respects the violence can be understood as a form of 'protest masculinity', which Connell (1995: 111) defines 'as a response to powerlessness, a claim to the gendered position, a pressured exaggeration (bashing gays, wild riding) of masculine conventions', where physical aggression is expected and admired amongst certain men. This is not to suggest that violence is an intrinsic quality of masculinity, for definitions of 'acceptable' levels of male violence have been contested between 'bourgeois' and 'brutish' men since at least the eighteenth century (Liddle, 1996), but rather that 'the negotiation of everyday violence has played a major role in the construction of everyday masculinities' (Carrabine et al., 2002: 32) – a point that will be returned to in the next chapter.

It is also clear that a number of prisoners wanted to leave the prison and escape the trouble, but were finding it extremely difficult as the exits had been double locked from 13.21. Further hampering the evacuations was the almost continuous bombardment of slates, scaffolding, and bricks raining down from the roofs. To evacuate prisoners, officers eventually formed a cordon of overhead shields under which the inmates could pass. It is also important to recognise that there were a number of incidents which make 'it clear that before the riot, notwithstanding the physical conditions in Strangeways, some of the relationships between prisoners and staff were what they should be' (Woolf and Tumim, 1991: para. 3.214, 73). For instance, a group of Category A prisoners were given keys to release prisoners still trapped in their cells which were either on fire or full of smoke. The number of prisoners that were now surrendering became a major logistical problem of organisation and control. Between 14.00 and 17.00 some 800 prisoners surrendered. Initially they were housed in the visits area. It soon became impossible to accommodate all the prisoners in this location. They were therefore taken out of the prison by the main gate and transported round to the perimeter wall to the Croft area, where they were placed until arrangements could be made to transfer them to other institutions.

National coordination was required to find places in the different parts of the country to which the prisoners could be evacuated. The Deputy Director General of the Prison Service, Brian Emes, opened the headquarters control room at Cleland House, in London, for this purpose. Attempts were made to keep records on the prisoners housed in the Croft area, but conditions were chaotic and it was not possible to do it accurately. The computer was not operating and some prisoners gave the wrong names. The Regional Office made arrangements for staff from other establishments in the Region to provide support. There was initially some confusion over their deployment: some had come with C&R equipment, others had not. It was not clear where they were to go or what they were to do. Principal Officer Nicholson, who was responsible for C&R training in the North Region, arrived at 14.45 and took charge.

The media began to gather at the prison in large numbers by the end of the afternoon. Liaison with the media was far from satisfactory. There was a brief statement at 15.40, and at 17.00 a further press statement was issued which said 500 prisoners had already surrendered, and steps were being taken to transfer them to other prisons. No escapes were known to have occurred but the serious disturbance was continuing. It was too early to report on casualties or on the extent of the damage, but this was thought to be considerable. In the following days it was reported that between 12 and 20 prisoners had been murdered, with accompanying lurid stories of castration and mutilation. The sensational banner headlines and detailed accounts of gruesome events within the prison were later to be found to be fictitious (see the Press Council, 1991, for a fuller discussion of the actions of the media during the disturbance), but as the above has indicated what actually happened was grim enough. Nevertheless, it is clear that the massive media presence surrounding the prison encouraged the prisoners to remain on the roof and perform for the cameras while as will now be seen also influencing the actions of authorities.

Plans to Recapture

By about 20.00 O'Friel and Nicholson agreed that prison officers should enter E Wing. Approximately ten C&R units of 12 men each were used. E Wing was retaken without any great difficulty or casualties. It commenced at 20.05, and by 20.10 all four landings were secured. Whilst it was not intended for the incursion to go beyond E Wing, at least one C&R unit had entered the main Centre, where some fighting took place. O'Friel instructed them not to move beyond E Wing doors when this was reported. Some staff believed that the Centre could have been retaken. If this had taken place the progress of the disturbance would have been very different (Woolf and Tumim, 1991: para. 3.228, 75). The staff from time to time came under attack from the roof area above the fourth landing with scaffold poles and other objects. The staff withdrew at about 00.22 on 2 April when inmates broke onto the Wing; Nicholson argued that 'while it would have been possible for the units to have remained, it would clearly have been uncomfortable for them to have done so' (Woolf and Tumim, 1991: para. 3.229, 75).

Governor Boon, the Governor 1 from Risley who had been sent to assist O'Friel, relieved him from duty at 00.10, which was shortly before it was decided to retreat from E Wing, at which point O'Friel spoke with the Regional Office to say that he intended trying to retake the prison early the following morning. At 05.44 Emes, the Deputy Director General, had a long discussion with Boon over the prospects of retaking the prison. Boon was very pessimistic and informed Emes that:

> the risks are considerable. Primarily because in E Wing prisoners have got those very long scaffolding poles which they were able to poke through the wire netting which is lining the roof ... C&R people really cannot say whether they could withstand that but they certainly would have to. (In Woolf and Tumim, 1991: para. 3.232, 75)

Emes thought there were would be staff fatalities, and said he wanted to reflect on the situation and not put an operation into effect without discussing it with him.

O'Friel came back on duty at 07.00, at which time it was estimated there were 142 prisoners still inside the prison. After discussions between O'Friel and Emes, C&R units entered the remand prison at 10.00 and retook it without any great difficulty and seized six prisoners in the process. There was extensive damage, but no bodies were found – though the prisoners thought that two prisoners were dead in the Main prison, one hanged in the Centre and another thrown on to the netting in E Wing. These, and other rumours, fuelled the sense of urgency over retaking the prison. Because of the seriousness of the disturbance and the difficulties with communications, the operations room at Headquarters and O'Friel were in direct communication with each other. In a conversation at 12.57, O'Friel told Emes that there were still 120 prisoners as yet unaccounted for and they were trying to ensure there were enough forces to make the 'operation as risk free as possible, but the trouble was that the longer they waited the more opportunity the inmates had for reinforcing their defences' (Woolf and Tumim, 1991, para. 3.235, 76).

By 14.00 O'Friel and his C&R commanders had worked out and agreed a plan. It involved entering the chapel by the two lower doors and making their way through the chapel to the doors at the top end of the chapel, giving access to the 4s landing of the Centre. 12 units of 150 C&R-equipped officers would use this route. Prior to this, a number of diversionary attacks would be made from different points. These were to be on F Wing (below the chapel) and from the remand Wing through the kitchen in order to take the Centre at ground level. A further attack was to be made through the hospital into E Wing. It was intended for the diversionary attacks to draw prisoners on to the low ground so that the main attack would trap prisoners below roof level. The main thrust through the chapel would have an additional 70 C&R-trained staff to deal with the captured or surrendering prisoners (Woolf and Tumim, 1991: para. 3.236, 75).

Headquarters, through the Regional office, were initially informed that it was hoped the attack would take place at 14.30. O'Friel was confident that the plan would be authorised by Emes and he gave Nicholson permission to brief the three other C&R commanders (who all thought the plan would be successful) and to form the units up ready to implement the plan as soon it was authorised. Woolf asserts that in coming to the conclusion that:

> the plan should be implemented, Mr. O'Friel was naturally influenced by the views of the C&R commanders. But he was also in a position to form his own judgement of the merits of the attack. He had not before had operational command in a riot situation, but he had previous experience of a number of prison riots and had to deal with a disturbance which took place in the Chapel at Strangeways in 1986. Mr. O'Friel was an extremely experienced Governor

1 and the current chairman of the Prison Governors' Association. He was widely regarded as one of the most able governors in the Prison Service. He was entitled to expect that his opinion of the prospects of the intervention being successful would carry great weight with Mr. Emes. (Woolf and Tumim, 1991: para. 3.241, 77)

O'Friel knew he would not be able to speak to Emes immediately because he was seeing the Home Secretary at 13.30.

Instead Assistant Regional Director Rudgard, who had been sent to the prison to liaise with the Governor and if necessary Headquarters, was told the plan. He then informed Acting Regional Director Bone. In the absence of Emes, Bone spoke to Leonard, a Governor 2 at Headquarters, at 14.09. The record of this conversation does not make it clear that the main attack would be through the chapel and wrongly notes two teams, not 12, would be involved. Additionally, it is not emphasised that part of the plan was to draw prisoners from the high ground so they would be cut off when the main thrust was made through the chapel. Leonard spoke to Emes at 14.18, and Emes stressed he would not authorise any plan until he had spoken to the Governor. The instruction from him at this stage was to be 'No'. The log records: 'Mr. Emes would initiate'. Bone passed this message on to O'Friel, who replied that he was still in favour of an early intervention as the prisoners were busy building fortifications. They both agreed that the risks involved would increase if the operation was left until the following day (Woolf and Tumim, 1991: paras 3.243–4, 77–8).

A further report was made by Bone to Headquarters. Again the record of the telephone conversation misrecords the proposed action, as it implied that the attack on the chapel was the diversion and not the main attack. It also indicates a clear difference of opinion between Bone and Leonard. The latter said there was no chance of 'grabbing' the 119 prisoners then thought to be in the main prison, to which Bone replied that if they did not intervene the riot would be more protracted. It was emphasised that O'Friel needed a decision by 16.00 otherwise it would be too late, as it would be too dark (Woolf and Tumim, 1991: para. 3.245, 78).

Bone regarded himself as an intermediary in relation to the attack that he considered a good plan. When he spoke to Leonard, he then formed the impression that Emes was likely to disapprove of the plan, which he conveyed to O'Friel. As a result O'Friel briefed the C&R commanders that, if permission were not given for the attack on the prison, then a raid would be made on the kitchen, to prevent prisoners obtaining food. At 14.55 O'Friel instructed the staff to draw back. Leonard spoke to Emes again, and reported back to Bone at 14.57, informing him that Emes had posed two questions. The first concerned the chances of success, which Leonard thought were better than 50 per cent. This was not good enough for Emes who, according to Woolf wanted a 100 per cent guarantee. The second question was: Why was it necessary for the attack to take place today, and would it not be more advisable to wait a couple of days? Leonard answered that 'it was going to be increasingly difficult because of the size and geography of the place' (in Woolf and Tumin, 1991: para. 3.249, 78).

The decision not to retake the prison obviously had profound consequences and the Woolf report commits a considerable degree of analysis to the cancellation of the plan, which is briefly summarised here. The reason why Emes was unable to speak directly to O'Friel, and why messages were passed in such an inadequate manner, was that Emes, for the second time that day, was with ministers at the Home Office rather than in the command room at Prison Service Headquarters. However, just before 15.00 O'Friel received a call from Emes, at the Home Office. The call was taken in a former cell that had been converted into an office behind the communications room, where there were also a number of officers. From O'Friel's recollection the conversation began with Emes saying he knew there was a plan for a major attack on the prison, which O'Friel confirmed. He was then asked about the prospects of staff casualties, to which he replied that there was a strong possibility in an operation of this size. He also believes he stressed the number of staff and the size of the operation, involving 382 staff, notwithstanding supporting groups. The conversation turned to weapons and the previous night's difficulties on E Wing. O'Friel stressed that the position would be different because of the scale of the plan, though he could not rule out fatalities. Emes then told him not to launch the attack. In his version, O'Friel's assessment of the prospects of success and his reasoning were never properly discussed. In evidence, he said he was concerned there would be a morale and management problem for the forces if the major attack did not proceed. Anxious that they should be seen to achieve something, he therefore told Emes about his plan to attack the kitchen and Emes agreed to this (Woolf and Tumim, 1991: paras 3.250–54, 78–9).

Woolf notes that the telephone conversation was not recorded because it was made from the Home Office. However, Emes later made a note of it, which points to a lack of accuracy and a general misunderstanding of O'Friel's thinking. In Woolf's view the note

> provides useful confirmation as to how Mr Emes was assessing the question of intervention. What is significant is that he was concentrating on what

would be the advantages and disadvantages in a Manchester context. He was not attaching importance in reaching his decision to the impact on the prison system as a whole. In particular, he did not consider the effect on other vulnerable establishments of prisoners for the first time demonstrating that not only could they take control of virtually the whole of the largest prison in the country, but that they could continue to hold it. (Woolf and Tumim, 1991: para. 3.244, 78)

The report suggests that what misled Emes was O'Friel's lack of advocacy for the plan and his rapid development of an alternative plan to attack the kitchen. This can be partly explained by the circumstances in which the conversation was held. A crowded converted cell is not an ideal place to argue with the Deputy Director General. It is also possible, from earlier conversations, that O'Friel recognised Emes would be hostile to the plan even before he spoke with him.

Woolf (Woolf and Tumim, 1991: para. 3.261, 81) is highly critical of Emes, as he 'was primarily interested in obtaining information of the decision to which he had already come, a decision which was based on inadequate, inaccurate and out of date information'. During this period Emes regarded it as his role to make the decision, rather than limiting himself to scrutinising a decision made by O'Friel and only intervening if he felt it was a wrong decision. Instead he regarded the decision as his to take. This distinction is stressed because in the later disturbances at other institutions that month he adopted the monitoring role.

Perhaps, more than anything else, this exposed to Woolf the full extent of the organisational crisis in the Prison Service, which was characterised by a very strong top-down structure with a high level of centralised control exercised by the Home Office. As is clear the governor of Strangeways was severely hampered as he continually had to consult upwards, often with superiors who had no operational experience. Woolf went on to criticise the deep gulf that had long existed between Home Office ministers, Prison Headquarters staff and those working in the service itself, and the severe levels of 'dissension, division and distrust' that existed throughout the service (Woolf and Tumim, 1991: paras 12.1–4).

In abandoning the attack an opportunity to test the reaction of the prisoners and to regain at least part of the prison was lost. It sent a message to the prisoners that they did not need to fear a full attack by staff or an attempt to regain at least part of the prison. The later negotiations were seriously handicapped since the prisoners were not under threat of the storming of the prison (Woolf and Tumim, 1991: paras 3.266–72, 81–3). It is also important to recognise that if the plan had gone ahead and been successful, there would have been less outside scrutiny of the prison system, there would have been no Woolf Inquiry, and no improvement in prison conditions generally. It is also the case that there would have been casualties, including the distinct possibility of deaths on either side. It is also quite likely that Emes was anxious about the public outcry that would inevitably follow, given the media presence at the prison, should the plan result in a bloodbath. While it is possible to speculate on likely scenarios the more important point is that this decision reveals that the dynamics of prison disorder are by no means solely determined by the actions of the protesters. In fact much depends on the reactions of the authorities – no matter how disorganised these appear to be it was, ultimately, the authorities that allowed the prisoners to remain in the prison until 25 April.

Of course, responses at the time to the news of the cancellation were far from sanguine and had a devastating effect on staff morale, which was already at a low ebb as a result of the loss of their prison and what this meant to their collective identity. However, more recent interviews with staff reveal that those in the front line of the assault were relieved that the plan was cancelled. For instance, when one governor [04] was asked specifically about the effects of the cancellation of the plan on the staff, he replied that he thought it was best summed up by 'a PE Officer, a young man – macho, pumped up', who said to him that:

> I don't know what anyone else thinks, but I was in the first section to go into the chapel; I was looking up against the gate, looking up into the chapel, looking up over the barricades, the rows of seats and the prisoners with scaffold poles … I didn't mind when it was called off [the retake plan]. I breathed a sigh of relief, I would be lying if I said I didn't … I thought it was going to be very dangerous.

The relevance of this anecdote is made clear, in light of a more general question asked about the prevailing atmosphere in the subsequent days:

> I think people were obviously angry or upset, and I'm sure that would include some of the participants and some of the C&R troops, but I think the people who weren't going in were a little bit more upset about it, shall we say. You could be angry about it, if you weren't going in yourself. As with all these things there's a lot of bullshit floating around.

These insights are important as they imply a far more complex set of reactions involved in the gung-ho atmosphere that surrounded the prison during the following days and weeks, which were articulated forcefully over a couple of nights, as will be discussed below.

Once the main plan had been vetoed O'Friel gave instructions for the attack on the kitchen to proceed as a means of mobilising some of the troops prepared for the full-scale assault. This began at 15.30. It involved a diversionary attack on F Wing deploying six C&R units which met no resistance. However, the staff had to withdraw from the kitchen at about 15.40, because fires in the kitchen were causing considerable smoke and there was a risk of the roof collapsing. Shortly after this the staff re-entered the kitchen, supported by a diversionary attack on F Wing. This time the kitchen was held until the remaining food and stores had been removed or destroyed. The staff withdrew at 16.15. While the kitchen operation was continuing the diversionary attack on F Wing met serious resistance from prisoners throwing missiles from the chapel roof. The staff had to withdraw at 15.50. Though the operation had been reasonably successful, only a fraction of the staff who had been assembled for the main task of retaking the prison were involved. The cancellation of the main attack was a very serious blow to staff morale. It was not understood why Headquarters had cancelled the attack, and although O'Friel tried to explain the reasons, it was clear he was far from happy about the decision (Woolf and Tumim, 1991: paras 3.273–7, 83).

Strangeways under Siege: Negotiations and Pressure Tactics

The pace of events progressed slowly after this operation up to 25 April, when the prison was eventually recaptured. In response to media accounts purporting a large number of prisoner deaths, a banner was unfurled which pronounced there were 'No Dead' at 16.30 on 2 April and a little after 17.15 discussions with the remaining prisoners resumed. Between then and 20.30, 15 prisoners surrendered. It was vainly hoped that a large-scale surrender would take place and there were negotiations to this effect, but they broke down. That evening it was calculated there were still 102 prisoners in the prison. One of the problems facing the authorities was that the staff were finding it impossible to keep accurate records in the confusion. Consequently the Prison Service was not sure how many prisoners had surrendered, how many were still in the prison and whether any prisoners were missing.

Just after 11.00 on Tuesday 3 April prisoners in the chapel dug a hole in the floor in an attempt to enter F Wing. Staff holding the barricades which led from F Wing into the Centre were attacked with scaffolding poles and other weapons.[2] There was a danger of being outflanked from above and the confidential records relating to prisoners stored in F Wing were at risk. It was decided to counter-attack and try to retake the chapel. However, over the previous night the prisoners had strengthened the barricades and the C&R teams were unable to enter the chapel. The plan was consequently changed. Under the command of Nicholson an attack was made on E Wing. For the next one and a half hours staff controlled all four landings on E Wing up to the Centre, though they were under attack from the roof. This attack diverted the attention of prisoners who had been attempting to enter F Wing. During this incident, one of the prisoners recognised Nicholson. He shouted he 'did not want this sort of situation' (Woolf and Tumim, 1991: para. 3.286, 84). Nicholson replied they should pack it in then, and the attacks upon the staff gradually ceased. For a time there was a truce and it seemed as though a large number of prisoners might be prepared to surrender and arrangements were made for this. Twelve prisoners surrendered on A Wing at about 13.30, but the large-scale surrender never took place.

As a result of the attacks on staff in E Wing, four officers had to be taken to hospital. Despite the viciousness of the attacks, Nicholson believed the abandoned plan of the previous day would have been successful, because it would have involved entering the prison from a number of different points. One prisoner recalled that:

> on the third day we were all busy talking and sorting out YPs [Young Prisoners] who were scared and wanted to leave but thought they would get done in. We got their solicitors and parents up and the ones who wanted to leave left. Because we were doing this we were told there would be no disturbance towards us that day but in the afternoon about 250–300 riot police and screws came storming into the gaol with force and were setting fire to offices on E wing to smoke it out, so we couldn't see them and where they were coming from. They were everywhere, banging on their shields, shouting … they were just getting through the main part of E wing when we started to rebuild the barricades to keep them out. Some scaff bars were thrown at them to keep them out too. (Jameson and Allison, 1995: 43)

At 15.00 one of the Rule 43 (a) (own protection) prisoners, Derek White, who had been evacuated from A wing on Sunday night, died in hospital from a severe coronary attack. He had been a remand prisoner, and had been admitted to hospital with a dislocated shoulder and head injuries.

Earlier in the day, prisoners unfurled a 'media contact' banner and a *Manchester Evening News* reporter volunteered the editor's name. Michael Unger [18] was allowed into the prison at 11.10 and he recalled that they 'had two main concerns, one was to make sure that when they gave themselves up they would be treated properly and second, that their demands were published'.

The demands and grievances were published in the next day's edition of the *Manchester Evening News* and related to mental and physical brutality, misuse of drugs in controlling prisoners, poor food and cramped conditions. Unger [18] explained that initially negotiations were difficult as he was on the ground level having to shout up to the men up on the roof:

> but he went into a cell at one stage with two prisoners and the prison people were absolutely terrified for me because they thought I would be kidnapped. I just had to trust them. I could easily have been taken, but when I went along this landing there were prison officers everywhere. The prison officers had closed off some areas and let them run riot in these areas. It was actually very dangerous because huge pieces of masonry were being thrown at people and of course they splintered and bounced when they hit the ground.

In addition to Unger, who left the prison at around 23.00, local solicitors also assisted in the negotiations and by about 18.00, 26 prisoners had surrendered. During the evening five further prisoners surrendered. At 19.44 O'Friel reported progress to Emes. In addition to holding E Wing, other staff were patrolling at ground level under cover of the landings in B and D Wings. There was concern over the possibility of booby traps and structural dangers, due to the weakened fabric of the buildings. Because of this the staff were pulled back to a holding position at the access points to the first and second landings. The staff did not re-enter E Wing again until the end of the siege. Over the night of 3/4 April, Boon was again the governor in charge and he organised the recovery of the records and other documents from F Wing in the early hours. The staff were subjected to some attacks from the roof. Up to this point 26 staff members had received injuries, and one officer who had been on duty on 1 April died in hospital from pneumonia on 4 April (Woolf and Tumim, 1991: para. 3.295, 85).

By Wednesday 4 April it was thought there were at least 35 prisoners remaining in the prison. However, later analysis of the inmate roll indicated there were still 54 prisoners present. The Governor decided that the policy should be to carry on negotiations. During the day another 29 prisoners surrendered. There was still doubt over the number of prisoners left. The highest figure suggested was 25 (26 was the correct number). During that night, 11 of the remaining prisoners were identified by name. For the second night running there 'was little activity on the part of prisoners' (Woolf and Tumim, 1991: para. 3.297, 85).

On Thursday 5 April there was concern over information received from the negotiators that the prisoners might stage a dramatic incident, such as setting fire to the whole prison or breaking out. In response, for the first time, areas of the prison were doused with water by the fire service. No other active steps were taken. Staff remained in control of the remand prison and guarded the access points to the main prison. The main event of the day, at the prison,[3] was the efforts of a prisoner to address the public and media using a loud hailer. The governor and staff responded 'devising methods of making a noise in an attempt to drown out what the prisoner was trying to communicate' (Woolf and Tumim, 1991: para. 3.299, 86).

Over the next two nights the prison adopted tactics to prevent the prisoners from sleeping. These involved the use of powerful lights and noise, including officers hammering on their shields. On the second night, during this 'psychological' exercise, some officers shouted and jeered at the prisoners, including calling the prisoners beasts.[4] These tactics were part of the techniques of attrition devised by the negotiators to weaken the resolve of the protesters. Yet as one of the negotiators [03] subsequently recalled, they 'were put in a ridiculous role when you look back on it, though at the time it seemed quite sensible, of organising, if you like, the "dirty tactics"; so the conflict between the negotiators was quite immense', and far from weakening their resolve it is clear that the prisoners were well prepared and in good spirits, with striking banners on prominent display, including one that memorably proclaimed 'Plebeius of the Common People', capturing the solidarity amongst the remaining men. One of the prisoners recalled that:

> when the riot started, inmates who were staying to put forward their say about the system, went round getting plenty of food and stacking it into big carrier-bags and putting them in spare cells or up high on the scaffolding. There was always food. When they stopped the water we had cartons of orange and other drinks. When the meat went off we carried on eating biscuits and chocolate and Complan. Even if the protest had gone on longer than 25 days there wouldn't have been any problem with the food. (Jameson and Allison, 1995: 53)

During the next week and over the following Easter weekend (Sunday 8 April to Easter Monday 16 April) the principal tactics adopted were continued negotiations, with considerable quantities of water sprayed to avoid fires, and to dampen the prisoners' spirits, from Green Goddesses (army fire-fighting vehicles). Authorisation was given by the Regional Director, Mr Papps, for water to be used above ground level. This was to create a barrier to prevent prisoners entering an area where they might cause injury to staff or further damage to the prison. The 'discussions between Headquarters and Region made it clear that it did not matter if prisoners became wet in the process, as long as water was not being used on them directly in a position where they could slip and fall' (Woolf and Tumim, 1991: para. 3.306, 87). Initially noise, including loud music, ranging from Wagner's *Valkyrie* to rock music, was relied on to disturb the prisoners at night. From 9 April a ministerial decision decreed that music was no longer to be used. Instead it was intended to use 'mechanical means' to generate noise (sirens), accompanied by the constant hum of the low-flying police helicopter and the strafing of the roof with spotlights and strobes. One of the more sinister of these strategies was the use of female prison officers imitating the prisoners' girlfriends and mothers encouraging them to surrender at night.

Occasional limited entries were made into the prison to gather information. In one operation officers received injuries from attacks made by inmates. These caused concern, as there were rumours that the prisoners had crossbows and darts. There was also a fear of booby traps, and many staff thought one prisoner was HIV positive and might attempt to infect them. One of the last six prisoners to capitulate states that these rumours were deliberately spread by surrendering prisoners:

> at no time whatsoever were booby traps laid within the prison; however, we were using our very own psychological warfare in that we convinced the authority of the prison service that we had in fact laid many booby traps on the landings. I touched upon that fact in negotiation by inviting prison officers to come into the prison, to storm the prison at any time they cared to, with of course the awareness of the precarious problems they would have in coming along landings, where I would not explain what traps had been laid ... We asked prisoners leaving to appear reluctant at first to speak about booby traps, then to tell the Prison Service chiefs that sections of the landings had been taken out on each landing with lino covering the several foot gap, making effectively a lion-trap. Also that there were weights on the underside of landings attached to string-rope on the upper levels to bring them crashing down on the riot squad. None of these things were actually implemented; however, to give foundation further to our claims, we put chairs and tables up against the 'ones' landing doors which prison officers had access to at all times, with eating trays on top so that whenever a sneak-squad came along and through, having opened the door by pulling them, the trays would clatter to the ground and alert those of us remaining to be cautious and pose a threat where they would simply back off in retreat again. (In Jameson and Allison, 1995: 60–61)

On Wednesday 11 April, Emes and Papps visited the prison and had discussions with the Governor. It was agreed that the tactics of negotiation together with measures to probe the prison and put pressure on the remaining prisoners should continue.

The steady surrender of prisoners continued up to Good Friday, 13 April; by then 11 had surrendered, when the intermittent surrenders ceased. On 16 April a prisoner suffering from gastroenteritis was brought out of the prison by two other inmates. All three were then seized. After that, no further prisoners were captured or surrendered until 23 April. Until then, the number of prisoners at large remained at seven. Although negotiations continued after 13 April, they were not having any serious affect on the prisoners. Nevertheless the same tactics continued to be used and for over a week no prisoner surrendered; two of the negotiators have written that:

> from the perpetrator viewpoint, although some degree of fatigue, physical deprivation and reduced enthusiasm for continuation of the siege had become apparent, morale and commitment remained at a generally high level. This was augmented by continued relative invulnerability, sound logistical organisation (food, water, sleep, tobacco, etc.) combined with no diminution of media interest or public support ... A clear leadership structure had emerged and been maintained, with defection having the potential for considerably greater discomfort and loss of credibility than remaining in occupation. The evident exasperation of the authority representatives within the perimeter of the siege area (prison staff) provided sufficient doubt as to reasonableness under surrender conditions to encourage continued occupation ... At the mid-point of the siege there prevailed a feeling of powerlessness among those used to the exercise of authority under normal circumstances. Somewhat naturally, feelings of animosity became directed towards both perpetrators and negotiators who were attempting to resolve the siege without resort to the use of force. (Cornwell and Boag, no date: 113)

At the Inquiry, Emes was asked why this strategy of negotiation and pressure was being pursued in the face of such limited success. In his reply he suggests this was an oversight, because Headquarters were focusing on the disturbances occurring at other institutions. O'Friel's reason for not taking the initiative was due to the decision not to launch a major attack meant his only option was negotiation and pressure tactics. However, as early as 5 April, O'Friel had made it clear, in discussions with the minister of state, that he and the Acting Regional Director were of the view that due to structural problems at the prison, the fire risk, and booby traps, intervention was impractical with the available forces. The C&R-trained staff were returning to their establishments, whilst his own C&R staff were exhausted (Woolf and Tumim, 1991: paras 3.313–16, 87–8).

The strategy of alternative periods of negotiation and pressure is one employed in hostage taking situations. For negotiations to be effective in a riot situation the negotiators must be able to make it clear to prisoners that if they do not surrender within a limited period of time then a forceful intervention will occur. This was not possible at Strangeways because the C&R forces that had been assembled were subsequently dispersed. It was not until Friday 20 April that an intervention was made into the chapel by four C&R units. They took down a barricade that contained large quantities of combustible material. They advanced as far as the Centre where they met prisoners and used water pumped from Green Goddesses to prevent the prisoners attacking them. Another C&R unit also dismantled the barricade in F Wing. The following morning a further incursion was made into the chapel and F Wing to remove material.

A conference was held at the Prison Service Staff College, chaired by Emes, on Sunday 22 April in which a group of experts (including the police and army) discussed what tactical intervention might be possible.

Recapture: The Final Six

On Monday 23 April the Home Secretary, who had been briefed about the meeting which had taken place the previous day, 'agreed that the time had come to take the initiative to bring the incident to a conclusion' (Woolf and Tumim, 1991: para. 3.327, 89). In the afternoon the C&R commanders were instructed to devise a plan whilst at the same time negotiators enticed a leading member of one group of prisoners to the door of E Wing for discussions. C&R officers were lying in ambush and he was captured. C&R units later entered C Wing as far as the Centre at ground level, the barricades on B Wing were removed and D Wing was also explored. After the units had withdrawn, the prisoners started a large fire that continued to burn from 16.25 to 18.00 on 23 April, when it was brought under control. During the night, other C&R units removed most of the barricades in F Wing.

On Tuesday 24 April, the intervention plan was rehearsed in the remand prison. Other prisons provided seven additional C&R units and four more Green Goddesses were provided (a total of seven were now available). The plan of attack involved two units entering C Wing. One unit would go to the 4s landing and climb through a hole in the wire grid which had already been cut and advance along the wire to the Centre. The other unit was to block off the lower landings at the Centre end of the Wing. Two units would enter E Wing and go up to the 4s landing using a ladder and then on to the wire grid with the aid of a step-ladder. One unit was then to move on to D Wing. Three C&R units were to enter the chapel, and one of the units was to gain access to A Wing via the left hand chapel roof space (via the ceiling of the projection room). The other unit was to gain access by the right hand chapel roof space and proceed to B Wing. The last unit was to secure the entrance from F Wing using hosepipes in support. Woolf (1991: 90) ironically remarks that this 'was a fairly complex strategic exercise involving over 100 staff to recover a prison which was by then held by six prisoners' (Woolf and Tumim, 1991: para. 3.329, 90).

At 08.55 on Wednesday 25 April O'Friel gave the instruction for the planned operation to commence. After 25 minutes the staff had managed to secure the planned positions on the wire grid. However, five prisoners managed to escape to the roof from where they were able to throw down planks and hinder staff. At 10.02 the sixth prisoner surrendered in B Wing as he had become separated from the others. Meanwhile attempts were made to isolate the prisoners on the chapel roof. The initial efforts were unsuccessful and the staff came under heavy bombardment. There were then attempts to build a barricade, but a prisoner impeded them. Water was used to drive him away. Meanwhile, a large hole was made inside the Rotunda that effectively prevented prisoners moving from the chapel roof. At 18.13 the prisoners made it known they would come down if three named officers were present. At 18.20 all five remaining prisoners were brought down using a hydraulic platform. Whilst on the roof, some staff placed their own irony-free banner which read: 'HMP in charge – No visits'.

In total, 147 prison staff were injured in the course of the riot and one officer died. One prisoner received injuries and subsequently died, whilst 47 other prisoners were injured. Damage to the prison was estimated to be in the region of £60 million. Fifty-one rioters were taken to court and trials took place in 1992 and 1993 on charges of riot, conspiracy to cause grievous bodily harm, violent disorder, criminal damage and in six cases the murder of a prisoner. The murder charge was subsequently dropped through lack of evidence. Nevertheless, 23 prisoners received additional sentences, with some as much as ten years, for their part in the disturbance (Jameson and Allison, 1995: 11). One of the rioters, a young man aged 19 who had been in Strangeways on remand, killed himself at Hindley prison two months after the riot ended (Stern, 1993: 252).

Conclusion

At this point it is useful to summarise the conclusions that Woolf draws in relation to the events at Strangeways that have been detailed in this and the preceding chapter. There is little doubt that a protest had been planned, yet no more than a dozen prisoners went to the chapel with the intention of creating a disturbance to draw attention to injustices, some of which were long-standing and concerned their treatment by the Prison Service, the conditions they had to live under and the lack of any alternative means of effectively airing their grievances. It is extremely unlikely that they intended taking over the whole prison, yet this was achieved remarkably easily. Other prisoners felt, with some justification, that they had been abandoned by staff. The reason why the disturbance developed so quickly was in particular due to the inept handling of the early stages of the disturbance, not least because the training the prison staff and management had received was completely inadequate for handling a disturbance of this type and scale. Moreover, the fact that there were relatively junior and inexperienced governors on duty at weekends further contributed to the riot spreading to the whole prison.

However, the rapid expansion of the disturbance was not simply due to the disordered responses of the staff and management, but was also a consequence of the widespread support the instigators received from other prisoners who were also aggrieved at the conditions of their confinement. The prison was overcrowded, with too few activities and association, which meant that prisoners were spending far too long in insanitary cells with scarcely any opportunity to wash and change their clothes. A large number of the prisoners had come to expect to benefit from the recent improvements that had taken place in the prison, but these benefits were reduced or withdrawn in the weeks leading up to the disturbance because of overcrowding and problems relating to staffing levels, which increased feelings of discontent and injustice. Nevertheless, it is clear that the management and staff of the prison were faced with immense problems due to the failure of previous Governments to give the necessary resources to provide for an increased prison population in anything approaching a humane manner (Woolf and Tumim, 1991: para. 3.432, 104–12).

These conclusions clearly articulate both deprivation and disorganisation perspectives on prison unrest, in a manner that is similar to Useem and Kimball's (1989) analysis. For instance, there is the acknowledgement that the prisoners who planned the disturbance intended it to be a demonstration against injustices, which chimed with the feelings of a significant number of other prisoners, who had seen the regime deteriorate over the recent weeks. Yet the reason why the disturbance was allowed to spread has less to do with the guile of the prisoners and rather more to do with the disorganised handling of the early stages of the protest by the authorities. Furthermore, the subsequent passage of events over the next few weeks was indelibly characterised by deep distrust and intense divisions between the Home Office, Prison Headquarters and local management that revealed the extent of the organisational and leadership crisis within the penal system.[5] Nevertheless, Woolf's (1991) analysis shares similar limitations in that there is an implicit assumption that those prisons which experience some form of collective disturbance are pathological to the extent that it masks the degree to which 'normal' prisons routinely face chronic legitimating deficits without erupting into riots, and it is to such matters that the book now turns.

Notes

1   Brendan O'Friel was not normally on duty at the prison on weekends, though he was at Strangeways on Saturday morning as Wallace was on leave, and he 'did not notice anything amiss' (Woolf and Tumim, 1991: para. 3.93, 54). In a more recent interview [01] he said, 'I had actually walked around on the Saturday morning and not one member of staff said to me things were bad'.

2   There were two major trials following Strangeways. The first was for riot and murder, held from 14 January to 16 April 1992, the second was for conspiracy to commit GBH with intent, from 5 October 1992 to 1 March 1993. These latter charges arise from this skirmish in which prison officers alleged they were assaulted with scaffolding poles.

3   Whilst in the House of Commons, the Home Secretary (Kenneth Baker) announced the setting up of the Inquiry.

4   The use of the term 'beast' was, no doubt, a result of *The Sun* publishing a story on Friday 5 April claiming that one of the remaining prisoners had been convicted of rape.

5   The crisis was to return as farce by the mid-1990s with the much publicised sacking of the then Director General of the Prison Service, Derek Lewis, by the Home Secretary, Michael Howard in the wake of acutely embarrassing prison escapes from Whitemoor and Parkhurst high security dispersal prisons.

Chapter 8

Conclusions

Introduction

This final chapter draws together the various threads of argument running through the book and reflects on the contribution that a genealogical approach brings to understanding prison unrest. Although there are a number of different styles of genealogical analysis (for overviews, see Gordon, 1986: 77–80; Dean, 1999: 41–8), there is an important sense in which the perspective involves a commitment to exposing the limits of established systems of thought so that it is possible to think differently and disturb certainties. In other words, the point of a genealogical analysis is to problematise social and political phenomena to reveal the inadequacies of existing practice. Despite the increasing tendency over the last 15 years for 'Anglo-Foucauldian' work to distance itself from what it disdainfully describes as 'criticism' (O'Malley et al., 1997: 505), especially in the governmentality studies, one of the central tasks of this book is to strengthen the critical orientation of genealogical work. Nevertheless, there are long-running and deep-seated divisions between Nietzschean and Marxist thinking, the latest manifestation of which is Habermas' critique of Foucault over the character of Modernity[1] (for commentary see the essays in Kelly, 1994; Ashenden and Owen, 1999), and the intention here is not to minimise or ignore these tensions, but rather to preserve the significance of critique through the diagnosis of difference. For it is through 'becoming clear on how regimes of practice operate, we become clear on how forms of domination, relations of power and kinds of freedom and autonomy are linked, how such regimes are contested and resisted, and thus how it might be possible to do things differently' (Dean, 1999: 37).

Even though the term genealogy is used here as a shorthand for generating an interpretation that is both a critique of and advance over orthodox explanations of prison unrest, it should be emphasised that Useem and Kimball's (1989) explicit and Woolf's (1991) implicit arguments over the significance of legitimacy ought to locate the study of prison riots in the broader problem of order familiar to social and political theorists. By doing so the implication is that there are no simple answers to the question of why prisoners rebel in the ways that they do. In fact, it raises the pressing issue of how such matters as age, class, gender, race, religion and sexuality challenge a universalising notion like legitimacy (Bosworth, 1999: 62). Yet, the conclusion to be drawn from these accounts is that prison riots ought to happen more often. Explaining why they do not involves recognising that prisons typically generate diverse forms of social order in spite of frequently illegitimate distributions of institutional power. Consequently, the chapter begins with a discussion of the relationships between institutional power, penal discourse and social order and examines the overlooked contribution that fatalism makes to the problem of order in prisons. There then follows a consideration of the distinctive qualities that the genealogical analysis undertaken in this book offers through addressing the issues of necessity and contingency in historical interpretation, and the chapter concludes with some comments on the importance of understanding prisons as gendered organisations.

Institutional Power, Penal Discourse and Social Order

A central argument of the book is that the problem of order is multi-faceted and any account that relies on a singular solution to the neglect of others is unlikely to grasp the variable ways in which the elementary forms of power combine to produce stable and orderly patterns of institutional life. As Chapter 3 indicated, though most sociological discussions of imprisonment tend to privilege one solution over others. For instance, in Scraton et al.'s (1991) analysis of the protests at Peterhead prison in 1986 and 1987 the emphasis lay firmly centred on state coercion, whereas Colvin's (1992) examination of the 1980 riot at the Penitentiary of New Mexico recognised the role of force in securing compliance but he argues that the institution maintained order through manipulating material rewards and that disorder becomes likely if the inducements offered by the authorities are withdrawn. Of course, this understanding has a long and distinguished sociological pedigree as it was initially advanced by Sykes (1958) in his classic study of Trenton maximum security prison, where he argued that order is maintained through a system of compromises and accommodations between the keepers and the kept.

Although these studies do provide a sense of how order is negotiated, there remains the pervasive sociological assumption that power in prisons is non-legitimate and relies purely on corrective influence, of either a coercive or manipulative cast. It is at this point that some of the arguments from Chapter 2 on the question of power require revisiting to illustrate the limitations of such an understanding. Scott's (2001) discussion of the diverse accounts of social power identifies two traditions (the 'mainstream' and 'second-stream') that have produced the leading understandings of power and emphasise either corrective or persuasive influence. It will be recalled that further analytical distinctions can be made, as corrective influence can involve force and manipulation, whereas persuasive influence operates through forms of signification and legitimation, as it causes 'subalterns to believe that it is appropriate to act in one way rather than another' (Scott, 2001: 14). The fundamental elements of power are force, manipulation, signification and legitimation, which combine in different and variable ways so as to give rise to concrete patterns of domination and resistance.

Consequently, the recognition of legitimacy in recent prison sociology addresses an important absence and Sparks et al.'s (1996) account is the most developed – more so than Useem and Kimball (1989) and Woolf (1991) where the concept plays a pivotal role. Their argument is based on Beetham's (1991) insistence that all systems of power seek legitimation and Tyler's (1990) empirical account of conditions of legitimacy in people's encounters with criminal justice agencies. They conclude that 'prisoners (any more than anyone else) can hardly be expected to take the state's pretensions to moral authority and concern seriously unless the *representations* of that authority and those concerns, which they receive from the activities of prison administrators and staff, give them reason to do so' (Sparks et al., 1996: 308, emphasis in original). Clearly this formulation is touching on the importance of signification in persuading the confined to accept the institutional arrangements in which they find themselves. Nevertheless, 'even the most assiduous work of prison staff can hardly overcome a failed or unprincipled policy' (Sparks et al., 1996: 308).

The overall implication of their understanding of legitimacy is that it relies on normative compliance and the moral involvement of prisoners in their subordination. Additionally, Sparks et al. (1996: 303) insist that while 'prisons embody some version of a normative order it is not in any sense intended to imply consensualism', yet as I argued in Chapter 3 it is here that accounts of legitimacy run into difficulty. There is, as they are aware, a fine distinction 'between the "taken-for-granted" and the "accepted-as-legitimate"' (Sparks et al., 1996: 89). This distinction is crucial, for it could be argued that, in a number of ways, power in prisons represent an inevitable, 'external fact' for prisoners – in which the experience of confinement is endured without any reference to some version of legitimacy. It is unfortunate that Sparks et al. (1996) chose not to pursue the implications of the distinction as it recalls Mann's (1970: 425) characterisation of order in liberal democracies where he draws the contrast between 'pragmatic acceptance, where the individual complies because he perceives no realistic alternative, and normative acceptance, where the individual internalises the moral expectations of the ruling class and views his own position as legitimate'.

It is at this point that a fourth approach to the question of order becomes crucial as a central argument of the book is that prisons generate diverse forms of social order in spite of frequently illegitimate distributions of institutional power. Especially important in this regard is Durkheim's (1966) overlooked concept of fatalism, which is developed by Lockwood (1992) and offered as a solution to the problem of order. As he puts it:

> the concept of fatalistic order can dispense with the view that widespread agreement on the ultimate values legitimating institutions is a prerequisite of social stability. A sufficient condition of order is simply that the structure of power, wealth, and status is believed to be inevitable. (Lockwood, 1992: 43)

There is an important difference between fatalistic beliefs that arise when an individual believes they are caught in a situation beyond their control and those beliefs that result from the internalisation of a discourse that explains why their inferiority is legitimate. Lockwood (1992: 46) explains that the extent to which 'subordinate strata regard their position as legitimate, as opposed to simply accepting them as unalterable, is a matter that is closely bound up with the question of whether social cohesion is based principally on beliefs or rituals'. Durkheim is again significant for in his discussion of elementary forms of religious life he drew a contrast between the external constraints of ritual in ancient religions and the internal constraints of conviction in modern religions. Clearly the difference is overstated, but the point remains a salient one. If the main source of cohesion is ritual rather than belief this bears directly on fatalism as it 'forces a distinction between a social order that is based on a commitment to ultimate values that legitimate it, and one that rests on the rather less secure foundation of beliefs in its unalterability' (Lockwood, 1992: 49).

In the prison context the importance of ritual can scarcely be exaggerated, which would range from symbolic 'degradation ceremonies' (Garfinkel, 1956) to the mundane repetitiveness of routines that serve to reinforce the loss of autonomy that a prison sentence entails. Moreover, the fact that such rituals are based on the routinisation of conduct goes some way to explaining why prisoners fatalistically accept or pragmatically put up with prison regimes even when the distribution of institutional power is patently illegitimate. As one former prisoner [07] explained in Chapter 5, most prisoners 'want to get in, do their time, and get out'. It is this dimension of experience that is crucial to understanding social order in prison. Yet, it also needs to be emphasised that in developing this characterisation of ritual the intention is not to imply that prisoners are rendered 'docile' (Foucault, 1977) through a form of passive resignation to the disciplinary power of the institution, for as was seen in Chapter 6 a 'mood of fatalism' (Matza, 1964) can also provoke unrest, which will be returned to below. Rather it is to draw attention to the distinction that needs to be made between ritual and belief in securing order, which can now be addressed through reflecting on the fourth element of power.

Scott (2001: 15) argues that where the persuasive form of power 'operates through cognitive symbols – ideas and representations that lead people to define situations in certain ways – it takes the form of signification' and it is in the context of indicating how penal discourse shapes, guides and directs the conduct of the powerful that the distinction between belief and ritual can be further developed. In Chapter 2, the concept of discourse was defined as a way of both structuring knowledge and organising practice; as such the various discourses that have been identified in this book ideologically incorporate the agencies of the powerful, meaning administrators, governors and staff who are firmly committed to the norms, values, sensibilities and appropriate forms of conduct articulated by particular discursive formations – a point also recognised by Sparks et al. (1996: 302) who have similarly noticed the ways in which prison officials are continually preoccupied with the 'legitimation of their own practice'. In addition, as the evidence from Chapter 5 suggests, there are considerable struggles amongst powerful actors over how to govern the confined, with much of the antagonism driven by deep convictions over the moral purpose of imprisonment and the proper way to interact with prisoners.

Adler and Longhurst (1994b) have argued that such struggles oscillate between ideological and utopian positions. Drawing on the work of Levitas (1990), Mannheim (1991) and Ricoeur (1986) they identify a number of themes relevant to the use of the terms of ideology and utopia in the interpretation of discursive struggles. The most pertinent to the discussion here is that utopian impulses seek to break the existing order, whilst ideological ones seek to preserve it. Moreover, 'utopias are in the process of being realized and the problem for utopians is partly the way in which to do this, whilst ideology attempts to legitimate that which already exists' (Adler and Longhurst, 1994b: 6). One of the objections raised by Levitas (1990: 75–8) against this characterisation is that it is an exceptionally crude division between those who defend and those who seek to change an existing order. This is a trenchant criticism against the approaches in Ricoeur (1986) and Mannheim (1991).

However, if ideology and utopia are understood in relational terms – that is as tendencies or capacities within discursive systems of thought and practice – then it becomes empirically possible to identify ideological and utopian forces in the field of penal power relationships. The clearest example of this in Strangeways is the struggles between 'old' and 'new school' prison officers in the late 1980s. The 'old school' officers can be regarded as an ideological movement seeking to maintain the status quo, whereas the attempts to liberalise the regime through the discourses of normalisation and professionalism can be characterised as a utopian force that sought to break the existing order. There is, of course, an extensive debate over Marxist theories of ideology and post-structuralist understandings of discourse that will not be entered into here, but it is hoped that the arguments in this book will be of some use to this debate as there is a tendency to conflate the two terms without specifying precisely which practices and processes belong to ideological or discursive domains.

Another reason why the book has concentrated on the importance of penal discourse lies with integrating the lived detail of microsociological studies of particular prisons with a macrosociological focus on the systematic elements that endure beyond the personal, local and everyday encounter. In Chapter 5 the particular discursive alignments that occupied institutional hegemony over 25 years were discussed in this context to indicate how general political rationalities and governmental technologies were translated in Strangeways and to provide a sense of the diverse patterning of interactions in the prison over an extended period of time. In other words, it is important to recognise that a prison, like any other complex organisation, will be a place possessing a unique history, with a distinctive tradition that informs the actions and beliefs of the keepers and the kept. By excavating this longer history it becomes clear that the sharp distinction drawn between 'normal' and 'pathological' prisons found in various explanations of riots needs to be eroded and replaced with a more nuanced accent on the diversity of institutional practice, as it is important not to exaggerate the extent to which those prisons which do experience some form of collective discontent are fundamentally different from other prisons. As Vaughan (1996: 200) has argued, with respect to Perrow's (1992) account of engineering accidents, that if 'non-accidents were investigated, the public would discover that the messy interior of engineering practice which after an accident looks like an "accident waiting to happen", is nothing more or less than "normal technology"'. It is significant that this point is not only an injunction against retrospective determinism but also echoes Mathiesen's (1965) finding that social relations in prisons are typically far more 'disrupted' than usually understood.

Explaining why crises of disorder are not more frequent and widespread involves recognising the ignored contribution that fatalism makes in generating a form of order even when social relations are especially fractured. Of course, this is not to imply that prisons can do without legitimacy as the overall argument of this book is that the problem of order is multifaceted and any account that relies on a singular solution to the neglect of others will fail to grasp the variable ways in which force, manipulation, signification and legitimation combine to give rise to distinctive patterns of domination, acquiescence and resistance. For instance, a clear contrast can be drawn between the authoritarian regime at Strangeways and the subsequent attempt to liberalise the prison in a more 'active' direction, which gave rise to different discursive practices, organisational priorities and subject positions for prisoners. In addition, as Sparks et al. (1996: 326) recognise, 'in liberal democratic societies the range of possible states of order in prisons is quite wide' and can range from super-maximum security prisons in the United States where prisoners who are defined as the 'worst of the worst' (King, 1999: 163) are confined in near-total lockdown situations to the Barlinnie Special Unit in Scotland, which was 'founded on a measure of internal deomocratization and consultation' (Sparks et al., 1996: 327).

Clearly the spectrum is fairly broad, yet it must be emphasised that in other accounts of prison riots the argument is that unjust deprivation in tandem with administrative disorganisation produces anomic tensions that lead prisoners to withdraw their consent and rebel. However, this explanation not only effaces the significance of force and manipulation in maintaining order but also ignores how forms of social order based on fatalism are generated when power relations lack, or have lost, normative justification – a point which is also neglected in Sparks et al.'s (1996) discussion of order. Although fatalism does generate stability, in prisons it does so largely through the dull compulsion of rituals that serve to signify the inevitability of the social structure, as few prisoners embrace an ideology of fatalism that maintains they are inferior and deserve their fate. Instead prisoners tend to develop, as Cohen and Taylor (1981: 139) observed several years ago, 'an uneasy tolerance often combined with a sardonic distancing of themselves which takes the edge off any aggression', in which denigrating staff through conversations, wind-ups, foot-dragging and other 'weapons of the weak' (Scott, 1985) forms a routine hindrance to institutional hegemony.

Consequently, the fatalism that arises through ritual rather than belief is a somewhat fragile solution to the problem of order as it does not rest on the prisoners' ideological incorporation into a dominant value system that justifies their subordination but relies instead on their grudging acceptance that the perceived despotism is a given and unalterable feature of the prison regime. Of course, there is an important sense in which for prisoners this is not a pessimistic resignation but is an entirely realistic assessment of their situation, for as Chapters 5 and 6 indicated, the hierarchical structure of prisons is not unlike mediaeval states with prisoners occupying practically the same status as serfs (see also Goldstone and Useem, 1999: 987–8, who develop Mathiesen's, 1965, original insights here).

In conclusion then there are four principal reasons why prisoners obey, which can be summarised as a variable combination of: (i) sheer fear; (ii) calculated expediency; (iii) moral commitment; and (iv) ritualistic fatalism. Each of these closely corresponds with the fundamental elements of power, so that prisons combine the elements of physical coercion, material inducement, moral persuasion, and dull compulsion in different ways giving rise to distinctive patterns of domination. Although regimes can be classified according to whether they are predominantly coercive, remunerative, normative or fatalistic, it is important to recall that structuring every power relationship there is a 'dialectic of control', which means that 'all forms of dependence offer some resources whereby those who are subordinate can influence the activities of their superiors' (Giddens, 1984: 16). There will be times when prisoners withdraw from, intensely resent, or actively disrupt the institutional routine as well as occasions when they sardonically tolerate, pragmatically conform or even willingly cooperate in the reproduction of order out of expediency, fear, commitment or ritual. The overall point is that the social order in prisons is a delicate, messy and variable *process* as prisoners are rarely rendered docile through the disciplinary power of the institution, and the next section draws out the significance of these arguments through a discussion of the small beginnings that culminated in the near month-long siege of Strangeways.

Genealogical Analysis, Contingent Drift and Gendered Prisons

To speak of small beginnings is to deliberately invoke one of the central tenets of genealogical analysis, which is that rather than reducing a dynamic series of interchanges down to a singular foundational moment one looks to the multiplicity of competing forces that give birth to events. In doing so it is necessary to recall Mathiesen's (1965) important finding that social relations in prisons are normally disrupted as prisoners often perceive penal power to be arbitrary, unpredictable and crushing, a situation he defines as 'illegitimate patriarchalism'. It is also the case that the level of violent incidents in prisons indicates that intimidation, assaults and abuse form part of the everyday routine to the extent that they 'are woven into the fabric of prison life' (Edgar et al., 2003: 185). Although violence, victimisation and fear are widespread they also contribute in significant ways to the uneasy social order that persists in prisons most of the time. The fact that this ordinary violence supports an aggressive culture of masculinity will be returned to below. Here it is important to begin by emphasising that even though major riots are rare events they do not abruptly occur in an otherwise tranquil vacuum and it is in this sense that Matza's (1964) concept of drift is important for it manages to convey the contingent, dynamic and fluid aspects of prison disorder. Moreover, it is able to explain why riots do not happen more often as drift 'is a gradual process of movement, unperceived by the actor, in which the first stage may be accidental or unpredictable ... and deflection from the delinquent path may be similarly accidental or unpredictable' (Matza, 1964: 29).

One of the key implications then is that 'drift may be initiated or deflected by events so numerous as to defy codification', and they are in any case 'accidental and unpredictable', so that the central task is identifying the conditions that make 'drift possible and probable' (Matza, 1964: 29). Crucial in this regard, as Chapter 7 indicated, were the widespread feelings that the social relations between prisoners, officers and governors had become arbitrary, personalised and unpredictable to the extent that an oppressive mood of fatalism hung over Strangeways. Of course, as I have argued there was nothing especially unusual in this 'illegitimate patriarchalism' and fatalism can be a compelling force promoting stability as it relies on prisoners accepting it as an inevitable feature of the regime. In such situations feelings of desperation, as Matza (1964: 188) defines it, can take hold and in an effort to undo this crushing sense of hopelessness actors can aspire to creating new and dramatic gestures that reassure them that they can 'still make things happen'. However, the will is 'not easily activated' and he goes so far as to argue that:

> drift is not likely to culminate in new or previously unexperienced infraction unless the will to crime receives massive activation. Such activation may be provided by a feeling of desperation. (Matza, 1964: 188)

At this point, Matza (1964) comes very close to advocating a version of strain theory, but as Box (1981: 119) has also recognised, 'this type of theory is the object of his attack'. Instead what needs further elaboration here are how feelings of desperation combine with the seductive qualities of transgression in the drift toward disorder.

The distinction that Katz (1988: 313) draws between 'foreground' experience and 'background' factors in criminological theory is now well known and is worth developing in this context. Although Matza (1964) inadvertently retains some structural elements of 'sentimental materialism' there is an important sense in which his focus on will manages to grasp something of the immediate, intoxicating and alluring spell that delinquency casts, which he would later describe as the 'invitational edge' that deviancy offers (Matza, 1969: 111). It is this dizzying edge that Katz (1988) attempts to capture in his work through concentrating on the experiential foreground of crime across a diverse range of acts that include juvenile 'sneaky thrills', armed robbery and cold-blooded, 'senseless' murder. Each specific crime offers distinctive ways of overcoming the mundane routines of everyday life through presenting unique emotional attractions that offer 'a dialectic process through which a person empowers the world to seduce him to criminality' (Katz, 1988: 7). Whilst Katz's work has been influential it has not escaped criticism on the grounds that it disregards the wider social context in which all action takes place (O'Malley and Mugford, 1994), fails to secure 'serious distance' and lacks any 'systematic explanation' of the various 'motivational' accounts (Taylor, 1999: 224). Yet, as Hayward (2002: 83) suggests, these forms of objection ignore 'the failure of "background" structural theories of crime to address the fundamental question of why (under shared social conditions) one person rather than another commits crime'. This crucial point returns us to a central theme of this book, which concerns specifying how human agency, institutional history and social structure are articulated without resorting to reductionism, determinism or overprediction.

The importance of Katz's (1988) work lies not so much in privileging agency over structure, but in highlighting the place of emotion in the romance of crime; and by emphasising the existential dilemmas confronted through wrongdoing it challenges two widely held views: that crime is either a 'rational activity' or a 'social pathology' (Hayward, 2002: 82). Instead, he poses the question of 'why are people who were not determined to commit a crime one moment determined to do so the next?' (Katz, 1988: 4). In building up his answer he provides a picture of the sensual dynamics of criminal events that is crucial to understanding how the 'assailant must sense, then and there, a distinctive constraint or seductive appeal that he did not sense a little while before in a substantially similar place' (Katz, 1988: 4). Subsequent developments in cultural criminology, where Katz's work has been particularly influential, have seen the 'thrills and spills of edge-work' (Presdee, 2000: 62) assume increasing prominence in explorations of the 'carnival of crime' that have immediate relevance for understanding the libidinal attractions of disorder.

If these overall arguments are extended to an institutional context they strongly caution against assuming that riots are caused by a combination of organisational incompetence and perceived injustice, not least since these 'background' factors are sufficiently widespread to suggest that they provide the routine rather than the exceptional structure of life in prisons and they ignore the seductive qualities of transgression. Crucially, neither do these arguments imply that prison riots are totally spontaneous or entirely arbitrary events sparked by some relatively trivial event or incident. Instead, a genealogical approach needs to reconcile how, as Raymond Aron (1965: 242) has put it, historical events are always 'born of general causes [and] completed, as it were, by accidents'. As explained in Chapter 1, Aron (1965) comes to this conclusion through a consideration of Alexis de Tocqueville's unfinished study of the origins of democracy in France that was published as *The Ancien Régime and the Revolution* (1856). In this book Tocqueville posed what will now appear as a familiar question, which is: Why did the revolution only occur in France when, across Europe, the old regimes were collapsing? His initial answer provides no surprises as he describes the disintegration of the privileged classes, the absence of a healthy body politic and the increasing bureaucratic centralisation of the state, all of which conspired to fragment French society. Yet paradoxically by the end of the *ancien régime* it was, out of all European societies, the most democratic in terms of social equality but it was also the one where political freedom was the most severely curtailed. Prompting his famous insight that 'this kind of revolution will occur not when things are going worse, but when they are going better' (Aron, 1965: 212).

Although this statement would now be regarded as an expression of relative deprivation, in that sudden good fortune can be as just as distressing for the social equilibrium as bad luck or miserable circumstances (see Lockwood, 1992: 72–6 for a discussion of how the concept is developed in Durkheim), it is the tension between necessity and contingency in Tocqueville's historical analysis that is particularly important here. Of course, he did not endorse either of these extremities. The French Revolution was not simply a historical accident and it was only necessary in the sense that 'the democratic movement was bound eventually to sweep away the institutions of the old regime; but it was not necessary in the precise form it assumed and in the details of its episodes' (Aron, 1965: 213). In the published preparatory notes for his planned second volume of *The Ancien Régime and the Revolution*, Tocqueville wrote that:

> I am less struck by the genius of those who made the Revolution because they desired it than by the singular imbecility of those who made it without desiring it. When I consider the French Revolution, I am amazed at the prodigious magnitude of the event, at the glare it cast to the extremities of the earth, at its power, which more or less stirred every nation.
>
> When I, then, turn to that court which had so great a share in the Revolution, I see there some of the most trivial scenes in history: hare-brained or narrow minded ministers, dissolute priests, futile women, rash or mercenary courtiers, a King with peculiarly useless virtues. (Cited in Aron, 1965: 218)

Although these are nostalgic words condemning a reckless aristocracy and forcefully reminding us that revolutions happen in spite of the revolutionaries' best laid plans, there is an attempt to grasp the essence of historical analysis, which is not to show that nothing could have happened otherwise but to 'discover the combination of general and secondary causes that weave, as it were, the web of history' (Aron, 1965: 244).[2]

This discussion illuminates a central contention of genealogical analysis, which is, as Nietzsche put it, that in history there is only 'the iron hand of necessity shaking the dice-box of chance' (cited in Foucault, 1986: 89). Moreover, he insists that owing to our 'grammatical custom that adds a doer to every deed' (Nietzsche, 1968: 268) we succumb to a spurious division between cause and effect, which he attempts to overcome through the doctrine of perspectivism that sets out to 'reveal the multiplicity of factors behind an event and the fragility of historical forms' (Sarup, 1993: 59). Consequently, it is important to emphasise that in his concept of drift Matza (1964: 5) is careful to distinguish between positivist 'hard determinism' in which every 'event is caused' and his own preferred 'soft determinism' that still permits free will but not freedom. Through advocating the latter he manages to capture the crucial experience of a 'distinctive constraint' or 'seductive appeal' that Katz (1988: 4) would subsequently identify as the decisive factors that lie at the 'foreground' of transgression. These insights can be further developed through recalling that common to all the pre-riot situations in Useem and Kimball's (1989: 209) study was 'a period during which the tempo of conflict escalated and the rebellious side won some sort of battle demonstrating the vulnerability of its opponents', which would in Matza's (1964: 184) sense of the term, be regarded as 'preparation', for once rebellious acts are learnt, performed successfully and are easily repeated they remind prisoners of their potential power. Useem and Kimball (1989: 209) recognise that 'preparation' is a dynamic process for they suggest that an 'act of resistance in prison that fails may teach inmates that the prison is secure, the guards really are alert, and that future, more serious action would be foolish'.

Nevertheless, as has been documented, at Strangeways during the second half of March 1990 there were a number of incidents that suggested there was an increasingly tense atmosphere in the prison. This encouraged prisoners to speculate over the weaknesses in the institution at a time when the regime improvements that had steadily taken place over the recent years suddenly seemed to vanish, which provoked discontent not so much with the resulting hardship but because the deterioration undermined the persuasive power of legitimacy. This is one of the conclusions that Woolf (1991) arrives at and is also anticipated in Useem and Kimball's (1989) synthesis of theoretical perspectives on prison unrest. However, it is important to recognise that administrative disorganisation combined with dashed expectations following a period of reform are, in Tocqueville's sense, necessary factors that make a prison riot likely rather than inevitable. Moreover, these factors do not determine the course that events will take. In fact, the closer one gets to the historical evidence the events seem to be governed not out of necessity but through increasing contingency. This is not to say that the riot was simply an accident, but that Strangeways, despite its ominous name, did not differ drastically from other local prisons at this time, so that the problem of specificity raised in this book is ultimately one of reconciling necessity and contingency through genealogical analysis. Especially since one of the inescapable conclusions to be drawn from the last two chapters is that the riot was not so much a result of the guile of prisoners but a consequence of the reactions of the authorities.

The evidence from Chapters 6 and 7 strongly suggests that the combination of disorganisation (various management failures) and deprivation (widespread prisoner grievance) were important factors causing the riot – as orthodox explanations of prison disorder attest. However, the critical problem is that these necessary conditions are so widespread that they need to be supplemented by an understanding of how institutions contingently drift into and out of heightened periods of conflict. It is clear that Strangeways every so often faced times when social order was especially threatened yet somehow managed to muddle through. In other words, the argument of this book follows Mathiesen's (1965) point that social relations in prisons are far more 'disrupted' than conventionally understood. The previous chapters have clearly indicated that disruption is present not only horizontally among prisoners (not least as the pace of change in local prisons severely limits the development of prisoner subcultures) but is also a characteristic feature of vertical relations between administrators, governors and staff over the appropriate way to run prisons.

Nevertheless, the intermittent character of drift should not conceal the inescapable conclusion that the tempo of events at Strangeways suggest that there is, once drift is set in motion, an 'escalating determinism' (Katz, 1988: 6) toward collective confrontation. For instance, the increasing signs of tension during March paved the way for a planned disturbance in the Chapel and while other actions (such as cancelling the service) may well have prevented a large-scale uprising that day, the discontent and anticipation would have been such that other forms of disorder would have occurred until an uneasy peace returned – through transferring identifiable 'ringleaders', for example, as had occurred in the previous year. This did not happen. Instead, once the lines of action were drawn up they acted as alluring constraints and enchanting prompts to further unruly activity in an effort to achieve mastery over destiny. As Matza (1964: 189) recognised, such mastery celebrates 'the virtues of manliness' and offers creative ways of transcending the demeaning feeling of being 'pushed around'.

  Consequently, another aim of the book is an attempt to push the sociology of imprisonment into comprehending the ways in which prisons, as organisations, are routinely gendered, and as such contribute to the reproduction of unequal power relations between men and women, as order within prisons is sustained through 'deeply embedded discourses around masculinity and femininity' (Sim, 1995: 102). For instance, the charting of governmental rationalities in Chapter 5 sought to indicate how these discursive formations articulated distinctive understandings of gender, not least since in the uneven transition from authoritarianism to professionalism there were quite significant struggles over the appropriate way to govern the prison and an aggressive, confrontational approach to prisoners continued to characterise interactions. Moreover, it is important to emphasise that everyday violence plays a significant role in structuring prison life (Edgar et al., 2003). Rather than interrupting the social order, the level of violent incidents in prisons indicates that assaults, abuse and intimidation form part of the fabric of institutional interactions and shape the expectations that participants have of one another (Bottoms, 1999).

  It is in this context that the violence described in Chapter 7 should be approached as it was neither an outburst of pathological fury nor a misguided dramatisation of grievances. Instead, the attacks against prisoners regarded as sex offenders and informers were overt displays of power and domination against the most vilified groups in the prison community, yet the fact that other prisoners helped those suffering strongly reminds us that masculinity is contested. Moreover, the fact that such activities regularly occur in prison riots (Useem and Kimball, 1989), accompanied by the more general point that riots are overwhelmingly concentrated in male prisons, suggest that forms of 'protest masculinity' are significant elements structuring unrest (Bosworth and Carrabine, 2001: 508–9). This point was established by Matza (1964: 189) when he argued that in 'any setting in which manliness is stressed, celebrated and regularly probed or sounded, the mood of fatalism will yield something approximating a sense of desperation', and as will be clear by now there are few institutions that idealise aggressive forms of masculinity so routinely as prisons.

However, it is important not to lose sight of the ways in which women can and do seriously disrupt institutional regimes. For instance, historically 'outbreaks of "smashing up", where girls [in reformatories and borstals] would seriously damage their rooms and their contents' (Cox, 2002: 98) were not uncommon in the interwar period in Britain, while research in contemporary prisons has further indicated the versatile ways in which women resist institutional power (Bosworth, 1999) and damage each other through violence (Edgar et al., 2003). So while gender differences might structure the sheer amount of collective prison unrest, it is vital that the distinctions between the ways in which women and men experience imprisonment are not overstated as this can serve to reinforce stereotypes that men are 'active' and women are 'passive' in how they cope with prison life. For instance, although women have 'responded to the pain of confinement through self-mutilation, attempted suicide, and suicide' (Sim, 1992: 108) such acts are far from unusual in male prisons. In other words, one of the important tasks that prison sociology has yet to fully appreciate is how the institution reproduces gender divisions that sustain the unequal power relations between women and men. It is hoped that this book is a small beginning along these lines.

The final conclusion to be drawn is a short comment on what the genealogical analysis provided here does and does not offer. Genealogy does not give the answer to everything. Yet the fact that other perspectives are available does 'not make each perspective equally valuable' (Spinks, 2003: 144). In this book there has been an explicit attempt to unsettle explanations of prison riots so that the limits of existing thinking are revealed and an alternative framework developed that offers a more convincing account of this social phenomenon. In doing so it has sought to restore a critical edge that has been lost in much of the recent work in governmentality. The distinctive contribution the book makes is that it emphasises the signification of power through discourse and advances the fatalistic solution to the problem of order as crucial, but overlooked, elements in the sociology of imprisonment. The extent to which this, or any other book, has been successful or not rests in the last analysis with 'the wider community of social scientists [who] form the *ultimate tribunal of truth* for social science investigation' (Howarth, 2000: 142, emphasis in original). Of course, one cannot appeal to a 'value-neutral' science in this final judgement but it is to be hoped that new, or more refined, ways of approaching social phenomena can at least be articulated. Nevertheless, the book will have achieved its main purpose if it has helped to show that central problems in social theory are vital to understanding the complexities of prison life.

Notes

1   Callinicos (1999: 56) provides an excellent summary of the three basic positions on Modernity produced in the aftermath of the French Revolution. The first stance is taken up by Marx, who insisted that the Enlightenment dream of creating an authentically rational society in which every individual could realise freedom required a further social revolution since the alienating reality of capitalist exploitation stunted human self-consciousness. The second position, most readily associated with modern liberalism, broadly accepts that contemporary bourgeois society is the best that can be hoped for – even though there are clear enough understandings of the dangers posed by Modernity. For instance, Weber writes as if the 'probable future of capitalist bureaucracy promises to be only marginally more appealing than that of a socialist bureaucracy' (Gordon, 1986: 78). The third position, advocated by Nietzsche, involves the radical rejection of Modernity and Western rationality, through his claim that all forms of reason are particular expressions of the will to power and that all forms of interpretation are necessarily selective. So for Habermas (1985) the Enlightenment remains an unfinished project as the possibilities of communicative rationality have yet to be realised, whereas Foucault (1984b: 45) rejects the 'intellectual blackmail of "being for or against the Enlightenment"' and instead he advocates 'a version of Nietzsche's perspectivism according to which every body of knowledge must be scrutinized for the particular will to power which it embodies' (Callinicos, 1999: 279).

2   The details of the Revolution are brought brilliantly to life in Steel's (2003: 118) history, which includes the revelation that the fleeing King was arrested only because the son of a local postmaster recognised him as the face printed on banknotes.

Bibliography

Abercrombie, N., S. Hill and B. Turner (1980), *The Dominant Ideology Thesis*, London: Allen and Unwin.

Adams, R. (1992), *Prison Riots in Britain and the USA*, London: Macmillan.

Adler, M. and B. Longhurst (1994a), *Discourse, Power and Justice: Towards a New Sociology of Imprisonment*, London: Routledge.

Adler, M. and B. Longhurst (1994b), 'Progressive Rhetoric is Not Enough: The Ideological Fate of Utopian Prison Reform North of the Border', paper to *Prisons 2000*, University of Leicester 8–10 April.

Advisory Council on the Penal System (chaired by Sir Leon Radzinowicz) (1968), *The Regime for Long-term Prisoners in Conditions of Maximum Security*, London: HMSO.

Arendt, H. (1959), *The Human Condition*, New York: Anchor Books.

Aron, R. (1965), *Main Currents in Sociological Thought 1*, Harmondsworth: Penguin.

Ashenden, S. and D. Owen (1999), *Foucault contra Habermas*, London: Sage.

Bachrach, P. and M. Baratz (1962), 'Two Faces of Power', *American Political Science Review*, Vol. 56, pp. 947–52.

Bahktin, M. (1984), *Rabelais and His World*, Bloomington, IN: Indiana University Press.

Barbalet, J.M. (1987), 'Power, Structural Resources and Agency', *Current Perspectives in Social Theory*, Vol. 8, pp. 1–24.

Barry, A., T. Osborne, and N. Rose (1996) (eds), *Foucault and Political Reason*, London: University College London Press.

Beetham, D. (1991), *The Legitimation of Power*, London: Macmillan.

Bosworth, M. (1999), *Engendering Resistance: Agency and Power in Women's Prisons*, Dartmouth: Ashgate.

Bosworth, M. and E. Carrabine (2001), Reassessing Resistance: Race, Gender and Sexuality in Prison', *Punishment and Society*, Vol. 3, No. 4, pp. 501–15.

Bottoms, A. (1977), 'Reflections on the Renaissance of Dangerousness', *Howard Journal of Criminal Justice*, Vol. 16, pp. 70–96.

Bottoms, A. (1980), 'An Introduction to "The Coming Crisis"', in A. Bottoms and R. Preston (eds), *The Coming Penal Crisis*, Edinburgh: Scottish Academic Press.

Bottoms, A. (1987), 'Limiting Prison Use: Experience in England and Wales', *The Howard Journal of Criminal Justice*, Vol. 26, No. 3, pp. 177–202.

Bottoms, A. (1994), 'The Philosophy and Politics of Punishment and Sentencing', in R. Morgan and C. Clarkson (eds), *The Politics of Sentencing Reform*, Oxford: Clarendon Press.

Bottoms, A. (1999), 'Interpersonal Violence and Social Order in Prisons', in M. Tonry and J. Petersilia (eds), *Crime and Justice: A Review of Research*, Vol. 26, Chicago, IL: University of Chicago Press.

Bottoms, A. and R. Sparks (1995), 'Legitimacy and Order in Prisons', *British Journal of Sociology*, Vol. 46 No. 1 pp. 45–62.

Bottoms, A., W. Hay, and R. Sparks (1995), 'Situational and Social Approaches to the Prevention of Disorder in Long-Term Prisons', in T.J. Flanagan (ed.), *Long-term Imprisonment: Policy, Science and Correctional Practice*, London: Sage.

Box, S. (1981), *Deviance, Reality and Society*, 2nd edn, London: Holt, Rinehart and Winston.

Bracewell, M., R. Montgomery, and L. Lombardo (eds) (1994), *Prison Violence in America*, Cincinnati: Anderson Publishing.

Brody, S. (1976), *The Effectiveness of Sentencing*, Home Office Research Study No. 35. London: HMSO.

Bryans, S. (2000), 'Governing Prisons: An Analysis of Who is Governing Prisons and the Competencies Which they Require to Govern Effectively', *The Howard Journal of Criminal Justice*, Vol. 39, No. 1, pp. 14–29.

Burchell, G., C. Gordon and P. Miller (eds) (1991), *The Foucault Effect: Studies in Governmentality*, Hemel Hempstead: Harvester Wheatsheaf.

Burrell, G. (1998), 'Modernism, Postmodernism and Organizational Analysis: The Contribution of Michel Foucault', in A. McKinlay and K. Starkey (eds), *Foucault, Management and Organization Theory*, London: Sage.

Butler, J. (1993), *Bodies that Matter*, London: Routledge.

Cahnman, W. (1964), 'Max Weber and the Methodological Controversy in the Social Sciences', in W. Cahhman and A. Boskoff (eds), *Sociology and History*, London: Macmillan.

Callinicos, A. (1999), *Social Theory: A Historical Introduction*, Cambridge: Polity Press.

Callon, M. (1986), 'Some Elements of a Sociology of Translation: Domestication of the Scallops and Fishermen of St. Brieuc Bay', in J. Law (ed.), *Power, Action and Belief: A New Sociology of Knowledge?*, London: Routledge and Kegan Paul.

Callon, M. and B. Latour (1981), 'Unscrewing the Big Leviathan: How Actors Macrostructure Reality and Sociologists Help Them to Do So', in K. Knorr-Cetina and A. Cicourel (eds), *Advances in Social Theory and Methodology: Towards an Integration of Micro- and Macro-Sociologies*, London: Routledge and Kegan Paul.

Callon, M., J. Law and A. Rip (eds) (1986), *Mapping out the Dynamics of Science and Technology: Sociology of Science in the Real World*, London: Macmillan.

Carrabine, E. (2000), 'Discourse, Governmentality and Translation: Towards a Social Theory of Imprisonment', *Theoretical Criminology*, Vol. 4, No. 3, pp. 309–31.

Carrabine, E. and B. Longhurst (1998), 'Gender and Prison Organisation: Some Comments on Masculinities and Prison Management', *The Howard Journal of Criminal Justice*, Vol. 37, No. 2, pp. 161–76.

Carrabine, E., M. Lee and N. South (2000), 'Social Wrongs and Human Rights in Late Modern Britain: Social Exclusion, Crime Control and Prospects for a Public Criminology', *Social Justice*, Vol. 27, No. 2, pp. 193–211.

Carrabine, E., P. Cox, M. Lee and N. South (2002), *Crime in Modern Britain*, Oxford: Oxford University Press.

Cavadino, M. and J. Dignan (1992), *The Penal System: An Introduction*, London: Sage.

Clegg, S. (1989), *Frameworks of Power*, London: Sage.

Clemmer, D. (1958), *The Prison Community*, New York: Rhinehart and Co.

Cohen, A. (1976), 'Prison Violence: A Sociological Perspective', in A. Cohen, G. Cole and R. Bailey (eds), *Prison Violence*, Lexington, MA: Lexington Books.

Cohen, S. (1980), *Folk Devils and Moral Panics: The Creation of the Mods and Rockers*, Oxford: Blackwell.

Cohen, S. (1985), *Visions of Social Control*, Cambridge: Polity Press.

Cohen, S. and L. Taylor (1976), *Escape Attempts: The Theory and Practice of Resistance to Everyday Life*, London: Allen Lane.

Cohen, S. and L. Taylor (1978), *Prison Secrets*, London: National Council for Civil Liberties/Radical Alternatives to Imprisonment.

Cohen, S. and L. Taylor (1981 [1972]), *Psychological Survival: The Experience of Long-term Imprisonment*, Harmdonsworth: Penguin.

Colvin, M. (1992), *The Penitentiary in Crisis: From Accommodation to Riot in New Mexico*, Albany: State University of New York Press.

Committee for the Prevention of Torture (1991), *Report to the United Kingdom Government on the visit to the United Kingdom carried out by the CPT from 29 July 1990 to 10 August 1990*, Strasbourg: Council of Europe.

Connell, R. (1987), *Gender and Power*, Cambridge: Polity Press.

Connell, R. (1995), *Masculinities*, Cambridge: Polity Press.

Conway, D. (1999), 'Pas de deux: Habermas and Foucault in Genealogical Communication', in S. Ashenden and D. Owen (1999), *Foucault contra Habermas*, London: Sage.

Cornwell, D. and D. Boag (no date), 'The Multi-perpetrator Dimension in Prison Siege Negotiation: Psycho-strategic Considerations', paper supplied by HMCIP.

Cox, P. (2002), *Gender, Justice and Welfare: Bad Girls in Britain, 1900–1950*, London: Palgrave.

Cressey, D. (ed.) (1961), *The Prison: Studies in Institutional Organization and Change*, New York: Holt, Rhinehart and Winston.

Dahl, R. (1957), 'The Concept of Power', *Behavioural Science*. Vol. 2, pp. 201–5.

Dahl, R. (1961), *Who Governs? Democracy and Power in an American City*, New Haven: Yale University Press.

Dean, M. (1999), *Governmentality: Power and Rule in Modern Society*, London: Sage.

DiIulio, J.J. Jr (1987), *Governing Prisons: A Comparative Study of Correctional Management*, New York: Free Press.

DiIulio, J.J. Jr (1991a), *No Escape: The Future of American Corrections*, New York: Basic Books.

DiIulio, J.J. Jr (1991b), 'Understanding Prisons: The New Old Penology', *Law and Social Inquiry* Vol. 16, No. 1, pp. 65–99.

Downes, D. and R. Morgan (1997), 'Dumping the "Hostages to Fortune"? The Politics of Law and Order in Post-War Britain', in M. Maguire, M. Morgan and R. Reiner (eds), *The Oxford Handbook of Criminology*, 2nd edn, Oxford: Oxford University Press.

Dreyfus, H. and P. Rabinow (1983), *Michel Foucault: Beyond Structuralism and Hermeneutics*, Chicago: University of Chicago Press.

Dunbar, I. and A. Langdon (1998), *Tough Justice: Sentencing and Penal Policies in the 1990s*, London: Blackstone.

Durkheim, E. (1933 [1893]), *The Division of Labour in Society*, New York: Free Press.

Durkheim, E. (1966 [1897]), *Suicide: A Study in Sociology*, New York: Free Press.

Durkheim, E. (1973 [1925]), *Moral Education: A Study in the Theory and Application of the Sociology of Education*, New York: Free Press.

Durkheim, E. (1964 [1912]), *The Elementary Forms of Religious Life*, London.

Durkheim, E. (1983), 'The Evolution of Punishment', in S. Lukes and A. Scull (eds), *Durkheim and the Law*, Oxford: Martin Robertson.

Dyrberg, T. (1997), *The Circular Structure of Power: Politics, Identity, Community*, London: Verso.

Edgar, K., I. O'Donnell and C. Martin (2003), *Prison Violence: The Dynamics of Conflict, Fear and Power*, Devon: Willan.

Etzioni, A. (1970), 'Compliance Theory', in O. Grusky and G. Miller (eds), *The Sociology of Organizations*, New York: Free Press.

Evans, P. (1980), *Prison Crisis*, London: George Allen and Unwin.

Fairclough, N. (1992), *Discourse and Social Change*, Cambridge: Polity Press.

Feely, M. and J. Simon (1992), 'The New Penology: Notes on the Emerging Strategy of Corrections and its Implications', *Criminology*, Vol. 30, No. 4, pp. 449–474.

Feely, M. and J. Simon (1994), 'Actuarial Justice: The Emerging New Criminal Law', in D. Nelken (ed.), *The Futures of Criminology*, London: Sage.

Fielding, N. and T. Fowles (1990), 'Penal Policy File No. 39 (April–June 1990)', *The Howard Journal of Criminal Justice*, Vol. 29, No. 4, November, pp. 279–90.

Fine, R. (1985), *Democracy and the Rule of Law*, London: Pluto Press.

Fitzgerald, M. (1977), *Prisoners in Revolt*, Middlesex: Penguin.

Fitzgerald, M. and J. Sim (1982), *British Prisons*, 2nd edn, Oxford: Basil Blackwell.

Foucault, M. (1972), *The Archaeology of Knowledge*, Tavistock.

Foucault, M. (1977), *Discipline and Punish: The Birth of the Prison*, Harmondsworth: Penguin.

Foucault, M. (1979), *The History of Sexuality: An Introduction, Volume 1*, Harmondsworth: Penguin.

Foucault, M. (1980), *Power/Knowledge: Selected Interviews and Other Writings 1972–1977*, New York: Pantheon Books.

Foucault, M. (1982), 'The Subject and Power', in H. Dreyfuss and P. Rabinow (eds), *Michel Foucault*, Chicago: University of Chicago Press.

Foucault, M. (1984a), 'Nietzsche, Genealogy, History', in P. Rabinow (ed.), *The Foucault Reader*, Harmondsworth: Penguin.

Foucault, M. (1984b), 'What is Enlightenment?', in P. Rabinow (ed.), *The Foucault Reader*, Harmondsworth: Penguin.

Foucault, M. (1988), 'Technologies of the Self', in L. Martin, H. Gutman, and P. Hutton (eds), *Technologies of the Self: A Seminar with Michel Foucault*, Amherst, MA: University of Massachusetts Press.

Foucault, M. (1991), 'Governmentality', in G. Burchell, C. Gordon and P. Miller (eds), *The Foucault Effect: Studies in Governmentality*, Hemel Hempstead: Harvester Wheatsheaf.

Fowles, A. (1990), 'Monitoring Expenditure in the Criminal Justice System', *Howard Journal*, Vol. 29, No. 2, pp. 82–100.

Fox, V. (1971), 'Why Prisoners Riot', *Federal Probation*, Vol. 35 No. 1, pp. 9–14.

Fox, V. (1973), *Violence Behind Bars: An Explosive Report on Prison Riots in the United States*, Westport, CT: Greenwood Press.

Gamson, W. (1975), *The Strategy of Social Protest*, Homewood, IL: Dorsey Press.

Garfinkel, H. (1956), 'Conditions of Successful Degradation Ceremonies', *American Journal of Sociology*, Vol. 61, pp. 420–24.

Garfinkel, H. (1963), 'A Conception of, and Experiments with, "Trust" as a Condition of Stable Concerted Actions', in O. Harvey (ed.), *Motivation and Social Interaction*, New York: Ronald Press.

Garland, D. (1985), *Punishment and Welfare: A History of Penal Strategies*, Hampshire: Gower.

Garland, D. (1990), *Punishment and Modern Society: A Study in Social Theory*, Oxford: Clarendon Press.

Garland, D. (1991), 'Sociological Perspectives on Punishment', in M. Tonry (ed.), *Crime and Justice: A Review of Research*, Vol. 14, pp. 115–65.

Garland, D. (1996), 'The Limits of the Sovereign State', *British Journal of Criminology*, Vol. 36, No. 4, pp. 445–71.

Garland, D. (1997), "Governmentality' and the Problem of Crime', *Theoretical Criminology*, Vol. 1, No. 2, pp. 173–214.

Garland, D. (2001), *The Culture of Control: Crime and Social Order in Contemporary Society*, Oxford: Oxford University Press.

Garland, D. and P. Young (eds) (1983), *The Power to Punish*, London: Heinemann.

Gateway Exchange (1987), *The Roof Comes Off: The Report of the Independent Committee of Inquiry into the Protests at Peterhead Prison*, Edinburgh: Gateway Exchange.

Geertz, C. (1973), *The Interpretation of Cultures*, New York: Basic Books.

Genders, E. and E. Player (1995), *Grendon: A Study of a Therapeutic Prison*, Oxford: Clarendon.

Giddens, A. (1976), *New Rules of Sociological Method*, London: Hutchinson.

Giddens, A. (1979), *Central Problems in Social Theory*, London: Macmillan.

Giddens, A. (1981), *A Contemporary Critique of Historical Materialism, Vol. 1*, London: Macmillan.

Giddens, A. (1984), *The Constitution of Society*, Cambridge: Polity Press.

Giddens, A. (1987), 'Structuralism and Post-structuralism and the Production of Culture', in A. Giddens and J. Turner (eds), *Social Theory Today*, Cambridge: Polity Press.

Giddens, A. (1987), *Social Theory and Modern Sociology*, Cambridge: Polity Press.

Giddens, A. (1990), *The Consequences of Modernity*, Cambridge: Polity Press.

Giddens, A. (1991), 'Structuration Theory: Past, Present and Future', in C. Bryant and D. Jary (eds), *Giddens' Theory of Structuration: A Critical Appreciation*, London: Routledge.

Gilroy, P. and J. Sim (1987), 'Law, Order and the State of the Left', in P. Scraton (ed.), *Law, Order and the Authoritarian State*, Milton Keynes: Open University Press.

Goffman, E. (1961), *Asylums: Essays on the Social Situations of Mental Patients and other Inmates*, Harmondsworth: Penguin.

Goldstone, J. and B. Useem (1999), 'Prison Riots as Microrevolutions: An Extension of State-Centred Theories of Revolution', *American Journal of Sociology*, Vol. 104, No. 4, pp. 985–1029.

Gordon, C. (1986), 'Question, Ethos, Event: Foucault on Kant and Enlightenment', *Economy and Society*, Vol. 15, No. 1, pp. 73–87.

Gordon, C. (1991), 'Governmental Rationality: An Introduction', in G. Burchell, C. Gordon and P. Miller (eds), *The Foucault Effect: Studies in Governmentality*, Hemel Hempstead: Harvester Wheatsheaf.

Gouldner, A. (1973), 'Foreword' to I. Taylor, P. Walton and J. Young (1973), *The New Criminology: For a Social Theory of Deviance*, London: Routledge & Kegan Paul.

Gramsci, A. (1971), *Selections from the Prison Notebooks*, London: Lawrence and Wishart.

Habermas, J. (1984), *The Theory of Communicative Action, Volume 1: Reason and the Rationalization of Society*, Cambridge: Polity.

Habermas, J. (1985), 'Modernity – An Incomplete Project', in H. Foster (ed.), *Postmodern Culture*, London: Pluto.

Habermas, J. (1987a), *The Theory of Communicative Action, Volume 2: The Critique of Functional Reason*, Cambridge: Polity.

Habermas, J. (1987b), *The Philosophical Discourse of Modernity*, Cambridge: Polity.

Hale, C. (1989), 'Economy, Punishment and Imprisonment', *Contemporary Crises*, Vol. 13, pp. 327–49.

Hall, S. (1980), 'Race, Articulation and Societies Structured in Dominance', in UNESCO (eds), *Sociological Theories: Race and Colonialism*, Paris: UNESCO.

Hall, S. (1988), *The Hard Road to Renewal: Thatcherism and the Crisis of the Left*, London: Verso.

Hall, S. (1996b), 'On Postmodernism and Articulation: An Interview with Stuart Hall', in D. Morley and K. Chen (eds), *Stuart Hall: Critical Dialogues in Cultural Studies*, London: Routledge.

Hall, S. (1996b), 'For Allon White: Metaphors of Transformation', in D. Morley and K. Chen (eds), *Stuart Hall: Critical Dialogues in Cultural Studies*, London: Routledge.

Hall, S. and T. Jefferson (1976), *Resistance Through Rituals: Youth Subcultures in Post-War Britain*, London: Hutchinson.

Hall, S. and M. Jacques (1983) (eds), *The Politics of Thatcherism*, London: Lawrence and Wishart.

Harding, C., B. Hines, R. Ireland and P. Rawlings (1985), *Imprisonment in England and Wales: A Concise History*, London: Croom Helm.

Hayward, K. (2002), 'The Vilification and Pleasures of Youthful Transgression', in J. Muncie, G. Hughes, and E. McLaughlin (eds), *Youth Justice: Critical Readings*, London: Sage.

Hey, V. (1986), *Patriarchy and Pub Culture*, London: Tavistock.

HMCIP (1982), *Report on HM Prison Manchester by HM Chief Inspector of Prisons*, London: HMSO.

HMCIP (1982b), *HM Chief Inspector of Prisons, Annual Report*, Cmnd 8532, London: HMSO.

HMCIP (1990a), *Report on HM Prison Manchester*, London: HMSO.

HMCIP (1990b), *Report on HM Prison Wandsworth*, London: HMSO.

HMCIP (1990c), *Report on HM Prison Birmingham*, London: HMSO.

HMCIP (1996), *Report on HM Prison Manchester*, London: HMSO.

Hobsbawm, E. (1995), *Age of Extremes: The Short Twentieth Century 1914–1991*, London: Abacus.

Home Office (1965), *The Adult Offender*, Cmnd 2852, London: HMSO.

Home Office (1966), *Report of the Inquiry into Prison Escapes and Security by Admiral of the Fleet, the Earl Mountbatten of Burma*, Cmnd 3175. London: HMSO.

Home Office (1979), *Committee of Inquiry into the United Kingdom Prison Services* (The May Inquiry), Cmnd 7673, London: HMSO.

Home Office (1981), *Prison Statistics England and Wales 1980*, Cmnd 8372, London: HMSO.

Home Office (1982), *Prison Statistics England and Wales 1981*, Cmnd 8654, London: HMSO.

Home Office (1983), *Prison Statistics England and Wales 1982*, Cmnd 9027, London: HMSO.

Home Office (1984), *Prison Statistics England and Wales 1983*, Cmnd 9363, London: HMSO.

Home Office (1985), *Prison Statistics England and Wales 1984*, Cmnd 9622, London: HMSO.
Home Office (1986), *Prison Statistics England and Wales 1985*, Cmnd 9903, London: HMSO.
Home Office (1987), *Prison Statistics England and Wales 1986*, Cmnd 210, London: HMSO.
Home Office (1988), *Prison Statistics England and Wales 1987*, Cmnd 547, London: HMSO.
Home Office (1989), *Statistics of Offences Against Prison Discipline and Punishments England and Wales 1988*, Cmnd 929, London: HMSO.
Home Office (1990), *Statistics of Offences Against Prison Discipline and Punishments England and Wales 1989*, Cmnd 1236, London: HMSO.
Home Office (1991), *Custody, Care and Justice: The Way Ahead for the Prison Service*, Cmnd 1647, London: HMSO.
Home Office (1992), *Prison Statistics England and Wales*, Cmnd 1800, London: HMSO.
Home Office (1993), *Digest 2: Information on the Criminal Justice System in England and Wales*, Home Office Research Study No. 85, London: HMSO.
Howarth, D. (2000), *Discourse*, Buckingham: Open University Press.
Howarth, D. and Y. Stavrakakis (2000), 'Introducing Discourse Theory and Political Analysis', in D. Howarth, A. Norval and Y. Stavrakakis (eds), *Discourse Theory and Political Analysis*, Manchester: Manchester University Press.
Hoy, D. (ed.) (1986), *Foucault: A Critical Reader*, Oxford: Basil Blackwell.
Hudson, B. (1993), *Penal Policy and Social Justice*, London: Macmillan.
Jacobs, J.B. (1977), *Stateville: The Penitentiary in Mass Society*, Chicago: University of Chicago Press.
Jacobs, J.B. (1983), *New Perspectives on Prisons and Imprisonment*, Ithaca: Cornell University Press.
Jameson, N. and E. Allison (1995), *Strangeways 1990: A Serious Disturbance*, London: Larkin.
Jefferson, T. (2002), 'For a Psychosocial Criminology', in K. Carrington and R. Hogg (eds), *Critical Criminology: Issues, Debates, Challenges*, Devon: Willan.
Jenkins, C and J. Perrow (1977), 'Insurgency and the Powerless: Farm Workers Movements', *American Sociological Review*, Vol. 42, pp. 249–68.
Jewkes, Y. (2002), *Captive Audiences: Media, Masculinity and Power in Prisons*, Devon: Willan.
Katz, J. (1988), *The Seductions of Crime: Moral and Sensual Attractions in Doing Evil*, New York: Basic Books.
Kelly, M. (ed.) (1994), *Critique and Power: Recasting the Foucault/Habermas Debate*, Cambridge, MA: MIT Press.
Kimmel, M. (1990), *Revolution: A Sociological Interpretation*, Cambridge: Polity Press.

King, R. (1985), 'Control in Prisons', in M. Maguire, J. Vagg and R. Morgan (eds), *Accountability in Prisons: Opening up a Closed World*, London: Tavistock.

King, R. (1999), 'The Rise and Rise of Supermax: An American Solution in Search of a Problem', *Punishment and Society*, Vol. 1, No. 2, pp. 163–86.

King, R. and K. McDermott (1989), 'British Prisons 1970–1987: The Ever Deepening Crisis', *The British Journal of Criminology*, Vol. 29, No. 2, pp. 107–28.

King, R. and K. McDermott (1995), *The State of Our Prisons*, Oxford: Clarendon Press.

King, R. and R. Morgan (1980), *The Future of the Prison System*, Aldershot: Gower.

King, R., R. Morgan, J. Martin and J. Thomas (1980), *The Future of the Prison System*, Hampshire: Gower.

Laclau, E. (1977), *Politics and Ideology in Marxist Theory*, London: New Left Books.

Laclau, E. (1990), *New Reflections on the Revolution of Our Times*, London: Verso.

Laclau, E. and C. Mouffe (1985), *Hegemony and Socialist Strategy*, London: Verso.

Latour, B. (1986), 'The Power of Association', in J. Law (ed.), *Power, Action and Belief: A New Sociology of Knowledge?*, London: Routledge and Kegan Paul.

Latour, B. (1994), *We Have Never Been Modern*, Hemel Hempstead: Harvester Wheatsheaf.

Law, J. (1994), *Organising Modernity*, Oxford: Blackwell.

Law, J. and J. Hassard (1999), *Actor Network Theory and After*, Oxford: Blackwell.

Layder, D. (1985), 'Power, Structure and Agency', *Journal for the Theory of Social Behaviour*, Vol. 15, No. 2, pp. 131–49.

Layder, D. (1994), *Understanding Social Theory*, London: Sage.

Le Bon, G. (1960 [1895]), *The Crowd*, London: Viking Press.

Lea, J. and J. Young (1993 [1984]), *What is to be Done about Law and Order?*, London: Pluto Press.

Leech, M. (1995) (ed.), *The Prisoners' Handbook 1995*, Oxford: Oxford University Press.

Levi, P. (1988), *The Drowned and the Saved*, New York: Summit Books.

Levitas, R. (1990), *The Concept of Utopia*, Hemel Hempstead: Phillip Allan.

Liddle, M. (1996), 'State, Masculinities and Law: Some Comments on Gender and English State Formation', *British Journal of Criminology*, Vol. 36, No. 3, pp. 361–80.

Liebling, A. (2000), 'Prison Officers, Policing and the Use of Discretion', *Theoretical Criminology*, Vol. 4, No. 3, pp. 333–57.

Lindholm, C. (1990), *Charisma*, Cambridge, MA: Basil Blackwell.

Lipton, D., R. Martinson, and J. Wilks (1975), *Effectiveness of Treatement Evaluation Studies*, New York: Praeger.

Lockwood, D. (1992), *Solidarity and Schism: 'The Problem of Disorder' in Durkheimian and Marxist Sociology*, Oxford: Clarendon Press.

Lukes, S. (1974), *Power: A Radical View*, London: Macmillan.

Lyng, S. (1990), 'Edgework: A Social Psychological Analysis of Voluntary Risk Taking', *American Journal of Sociology*, Vol. 95, pp. 851–86.

Maguire, M. (1997), 'Crime Statistics, Patterns, and Trends: Changing Perceptions and their Implications', in M. Maguire, M. Morgan and R. Reiner (eds), *The Oxford Handbook of Criminology*, 2nd edn, Oxford: Oxford University Press.

Mann, M. (1970), 'The Social Cohesion of Liberal Democracy', *American Sociological Review*, Vol. 35, pp. 423–39.

Mannheim, K. (1991), *Ideology and Utopia: An Introduction to the Sociology of Knowledge*, London: Routledge.

Marsh, A., J. Dobbs, J. Mont and A. White (1985), *Staff Attitudes in the Prison Service*. London: HMSO.

Marshall, G. (1982), *In Search of the Spirit of Capitalism: An Essay on Max Weber's Protestant Ethic Thesis*, New York: Columbia University Press.

Martin, R. and S. Zimmerman (1994), 'A Typology of the Causes of Prison Riots and an Analytical Extension to the 1986 West Virginia Riot', in M. Bracewell, R. Montgomery, and L. Lombardo (eds), *Prison Violence in America*, Cincinnati: Anderson Publishing Company.

Martinson, R. (1974), 'What Works: Questions and Answers about Prison Reform', *The Public Interest*, No. 35, Spring, pp. 22–54.

Marx, G. and J. Wood (1975), 'Strands of Theory and Research in Collective Behaviour', in A. Inkeles and J. Short (eds), *Annual Review of Sociology*, Palo Alto: Annual Reviews.

Marx, K. (1963), *The Eighteenth Brumaire of Louis Bonaparte*, New York: International Publishers.

Mathiesen, T. (1965), *The Defences of the Weak*, London: Tavistock.

Mathiesen, T. (1974), *The Politics of Abolition*, Oxford: Oxford Martin Robertson.

Mathiesen, T. (1990), *Prison on Trial*, London: Sage.

Matza, D. (1964), *Delinquency and Drift*, New York: Wiley.

Matza, D. (1969), *Becoming Deviant*, Englewood Cliffs, NJ: Prencice Hall.

May Committee (1979), *Report of the Committee of Inquiry into the United Kingdom Prison Services*, Cmnd 7673, London: HMSO.

McAdam, D. (1982), *Political Powerless and the Development of Black Insurgency 1930–1970*, Chicago: University of Chicago Press.

McCarthy, J. and M. Zald (1977), 'Resource Mobilization and Social Movements: A Partial Theory', *American Journal of Sociology*, Vol. 82, No. 6, pp. 1212–41.

McConville, S. (1998), 'The Victorian Prison: England, 1865–1965', in N. Morris and D. Rothman (eds), *The Oxford History of the Prison: The Practice of Punishment in Western Society*, Oxford: Oxford University Press.

McDermott, K. and R. King (1988), 'Mind Games: Where the Action is In Prisons', *British Journal of Criminology*, Vol. 28, No. 3, pp. 357–77.

McLaughlin, E. and J. Muncie (1994), 'Managing the Criminal Justice System', in J. Clarke, A. Cochrane, and E. McLaughlin (eds), *Managing Social Policy*. London: Sage.

McLaughlin, E. and K. Murji (2001), 'Lost Connections and New Directions: Neo-liberalism, New Public Managerialism and the "Modernization" of the British Police', in K. Stenson and R. Sullivan (eds), *Crime, Risk and Justice: The Politics of Crime Control in Liberal Democracies*, Devon: Willan.

McNay, L. (1992), *Foucault and Feminism: Power, Gender and the Self*, Cambridge: Polity Press.

McRobbie, A. (1978), 'Working Class Girls and the Culture of Femininity', in Women's Studies Group, Centre for Contemporary Cultural Studies, *Women Take Issue: Aspects of Women's Subordination*, London: Hutchinson.

Miller, D. (1985), *Introduction to Collective Behaviour*, Belmont, CA: Wadsworth.

Miller, P. and Rose, N. (1990a), 'Political Rationalities and Problematics of Government', in S. Hanniken and K. Palonen (eds), *Text, Contexts, Concepts: Studies on Politics and Power and Language*, Helsinki: Finish Political Science Association.

Miller, P. and N. Rose (1990b), 'Governing Economic Life', *Economy and Society*, Vol. 19, pp. 1–19.

Miller, P. and N. Rose (1995), 'Political Thoughts and the Limits of Orthodoxy: A Reply to Curtis', *British Journal of Sociology*, Vol. 46, No. 4, pp. 590–97.

Mills, C.W. (1959), *The Sociological Imagination*, Oxford: Oxford University Press.

Mills, S. (1997), *Discourse*, London: Routledge.

Montgomery, R. and G. Crews (1998), *A History of Correctional Violence: An Examination of Reported Causes of Riots and Disturbances*, Lanham, ND: American Correctional Association.

Morgan, D.H. (1992), *Rediscovering Men*, London: Routledge.

Morgan, R. (1991), 'Woolf: In Retrospect and Prospect', *Modern Law Review*, Vol. 54 pp. 249–258.

Morgan, R. (1992), 'Following Woolf: The Prospects for Prisons Policy', *Journal of Law and Society*, Summer, Vol. 19, No. 2, pp. 231–50.

Morgan, R. (1994), 'Imprisonment', in M. Maguire, R. Morgan and R. Reiner (eds), *The Oxford Handbook of Criminology*, Oxford: Clarendon Press.

Morgan, R. (1997), 'Imprisonment: Current Concerns and a Brief History since 1945', in M. Maguire, M. Morgan and R. Reiner (eds), *The Oxford Handbook of Criminology*, 2nd edn, Oxford: Oxford University Press.

Morgan, R. (2002), 'Imprisonment: A Brief History, the Contemporary Scene, and Likely Prospects', in M. Maguire, M. Morgan and R. Reiner (eds), *The Oxford Handbook of Criminology*, 3rd edn, Oxford: Oxford University Press.

Morris, T. (1989), *Crime and Criminal Justice since 1945*, Oxford: Basil Blackwell.

Newburn, T. (1995), *Crime and Criminal Justice Policy*, Essex: Longman.

Newburn, T. and E. Stanko (eds) (1995), *Just Boys Doing Business?*, London: Routledge.

Newton, C. (1994), 'Gender Theory and Prison Sociology: Using Theories of Masculinities to Interpret the Sociology of Prisons for Men', *The Howard Journal of Criminal Justice*, Vol. 10, No. 2, pp. 193–202.

Nietzsche, F. (1961), *Thus Spoke Zarathustra*, London: Penguin.

Nietzsche, F. (1968), *The Will to Power*, New York: Vintage.

Nietzsche, F. (1977), *A Nietzche Reader*, Harmondsworth: Penguin.

Nietzsche, F. (1996), *On the Genealogy of Morals*, Oxford: Oxford World's Classics.

Nixon, S. (1997), 'Exhibiting Masculinity', in S. Hall (ed.), *Representation: Cultural Representations and Signifying Practices*, London: Sage.

Oberschall, A. (1973), *Social Conflict and Social Movements*, Englewood Cliffs, NJ: Prentice Hall.

Oberschall, A. (1978), 'Theories of Social Conflict', *Annual Review of Sociology*, Vol. 4, pp. 291–315.

Ohlin, L. (1956), *Sociology and the Field of Corrections*, New York: Russell Sage Foundation.

O'Malley, P. (1999), 'Volatile and Contradictory Punishment', *Theoretical Criminology*, Vol. 3, No. 2, pp. 175–96.

O'Malley, P. and S. Mugford (1994), 'Crime, Excitement and Modernity', in G. Barak (ed.), *Varieties of Criminology: Readings from a Dynamic Discipline*, Westport, CT: Praeger.

O'Malley, P., L. Weir and C. Shearing (1997), 'Governmentality, Criticism, Politics', *Economy and Society*, Vol. 26, No. 4, pp. 501–17.

Park, R. (1972 [1904]), *The Crowd and the Public*, Chicago: University of Chicago Press.

Park, R. and E. Burgess (1921), *Introduction to the Science of Sociology*, Chicago: University of Chicago Press.

Parkin, F. (1982), *Max Weber*, London: Routledge.

Parsons, T. (1952), *The Social System*, London:

Parsons, T. (1960), *Structure and Process in Modern Society*, New York: Free Press.

Pashukonis, E. (1978 [1924]), *Law and Marxism: A General Theory*, London: Ink Links.

Pearson, G. (1976), '"Paki-bashing" in a North Eastern Lancashire Cotton Town: A Case Study and Its History', in G. Mungham and G. Pearson (eds), *Working Class Youth Culture*, London: Routledge and Kegan Paul.

Perrow, C. (1992), 'Accidents in High Risk Systems', *Technology Studies*, Vol. 1, No. 1, pp. 11–13.

Player, E. and M. Jenkins (1994), *Prisons After Woolf: Reform Through Riot*, London: Routledge.

Pratt, J. (2002), *Punishment and Civilization: Penal Tolerance and Intolerance in Modern Society*, London: Sage.

Presdee, M. (2000), *Cultural Criminology and the Carnival of Crime*, London: Routledge.

Press Council (1991), *Press at the Prison Gates: Report of the Inquiry by the Press Council into Press Coverage of the Strangeways Prison Riot and Related Matters*, Press Council Booklet No. 8, London: Press Council.

Pugh, R. (1968), *Imprisonment in Medieval England*, Cambridge: Cambridge University Press.

Quinn, P.M. (1995), 'Adjudications in Prisons: Custody, Care and a Little Less Justice', in M. Leech (ed.), *The Prisoners Handbook 1995*, Oxford: Oxford University Press.

Remy, J. (1990), 'Patriarchy and Fratriarchy as Forms of Androcacy', in J. Hearn and D. Morgan (eds), *Men, Masculinities and Social Theory*, London: Unwin Hyman.

Ricouer, P. (1986), *Lectures on Ideology and Utopia*, New York: Columbia University Press.

Rock, P. (1996), *Reconstructing a Woman's Prison: The Holloway Redevelopment Project*, Oxford: Clarendon Press.

Rogers, D. (1988), *Men Only: An Investigation into Men's Organisations*, London: Pandora.

Rose, N. (1996), 'Governing "Advanced" Liberal Democracies', in A.Barry, T. Osborne, and N. Rose (eds), *Foucault and Political Reason*, London: University College London Press.

Rose, N. (1999), *Powers of Freedom: Reframing Political Thought*, Cambridge: Cambridge University Press.

Rose, N. (2000), 'Government and Control', in D. Garland and R. Sparks (eds), *Criminology and Social Theory*, Oxford: Clarendon Press.

Rose, N. and P. Miller (1992), 'Political Power Beyond the State: Problematics of Government', *British Journal of Sociology*, Vol. 43, No. 2, pp. 173–204.

Rothman, D. (1971), *The Discovery of the Asylum: Social Order and Disorder in the New Republic*, Boston: Little Brown.

Rudé, G. (1964), *The Crowd in History*, New York: Wiley.

Rusche, G. and O. Kirchheimer (1968 [1939]), *Punishment and Social Structure*, New York: Russell and Russell.

Rutherford, A. (1986), *Prisons and the Process of Justice*, Oxford: Oxford University Press.

Rutherford, A. (1993), 'Penal Policy and Prison Management', *Prison Service Journal*, Issue 90.

Ryan, M. (1983), *The Politics of Penal Reform*, Essex: Longman.

Ryan, M. (1992), 'The Woolf Report: on the Treadmill of Prison Reform', *Political Quarterly*, Vol. 63, No. 1, pp. 50–56.

Ryan, M. and J. Sim (1998), 'Power, Punishment and Prisons in England and Wales, 1975–1996', in N. South and R. Weiss (eds), *Comparing Prison Systems: Toward A Comparative and International Penology*, Reading: Gordon and Breach.

Sarup, M. (1993), *An Introductory Guide to Post-structuralism and Postmodernism*, London: Harvester Wheatsheaf.

Scokpol, T. (1979), *States and Social Revolutions: A Comparative Analysis of France, Russia, and China*, Cambridge: Cambridge University Press.

Scokpol, T. (1994), *Social Revolutions in the Modern World*, Cambridge: Cambridge University Press.

Scott, J. (2001), *Power*, Cambridge: Polity.

Scott, J.C. (1985), *Weapons of the Weak: Everyday Forms of Peasant Resistance*, New Haven, CT: Yale University Press.

Scraton, P., J. Sim and P. Skidmore (1991), *Prisons Under Protest*, Milton Keynes: Open University Press.

Seidler, V. (1989), *Rediscovering Masculinity: Reason, Language and Sexuality*, London: Routledge.

Sheldon, R. (1982), *Criminal Justice in America: A Sociological Approach*, Boston: Little Brown.

Shils, E. (1975), *Center and Periphery: Essays in Macrosociology*, Chicago: University of Chicago Press.

Sim, J. (1986), 'Watching the Prison Wheels Grind: The 1984 Report of Her Majesty's Chief Inspector of Prisons', *The Abolitionist*, Vol. 21, No. 1, pp. 6–9.

Sim, J. (1990), *Medical Power in Prisons: The Prison Medical Service in England 1774–1989*, Milton Keynes: Open University Press.

Sim, J. (1991), 'We are not Animals, we are Human Beings: Prisons, Protest and Politics in England and Wales 1969–1990', *Social Justice*, Vol. 18, No. 3, pp. 107–29.

Sim, J. (1992), '"When You Ain't Got Nothing You Got Nothing To Lose": The Peterhead Rebellion, the State and the Case for Prison Abolition', in K. Bottomley, T. Fowles, R. Reiner (eds), *Criminal Justice: Theory and Practice*, Vol. 2, London: British Society of Criminology.

Sim, J. (1995), 'Tougher than the Rest? Men in Prison', in T. Newburn and E. Stanko (eds), *Just Boys Doing Business?*, London: Routledge.

Sim, J., P. Scraton and P. Gordon (1987), 'Introduction: Crime, the State and Critical Analysis', in P. Scraton (ed.), *Law, Order and the Authoritarian State*, Milton Keynes: Open University Press.

Simon, J. (2000), 'The "Society of Captives" in the Era of Hyper-incarceration', *Theoretical Criminology*, Vol. 4, No. 3, pp. 285–308.

Skolnick, J. (1969), *The Politics of Protest*, New York: Simon and Schuster.

Slack, J. (1996), 'The Theory and Method of Articulation in Cultural Studies', in D. Morley and K. Chen (eds), *Stuart Hall: Critical Dialogues in Cultural Studies*, London: Routledge.

Smelser, N. (1962), *Theory of Collective Behaviour*, London: Routledge and Paul.

Smith, D. (1996), 'Introduction', in F. Nietzsche (1996), *On the Genealogy of Morals*, Oxford: Oxford World's Classics.

Sofsky, W. (1997), *The Order Of Terror: The Concentration Camp*, Princeton: Princeton University.

Sparks, R.F. (1971), *Local Prisons: The Crisis in the English Penal System*, London: Heinemann.

Sparks, R. (1993), 'Book Review: Robert Adams, *Prison Riots in Britain and the USA*', *Crime, Law and Social Change*, Vol. 20, pp. 177–79.

Sparks, R. (1994), 'Can Prisons be Legitimate? Penal Politics, Privatization, and the Timeliness of an Old Idea', *British Journal of Criminology*, Special Issue, Vol. 34, pp. 14–28.

Sparks, R. (1996), 'Prisons, Punishment and Penality', in E. McLaughlin and J. Muncie (eds), *Controlling Crime*, London: Sage.

Sparks, R. and A. Bottoms (1995), 'Legitimacy and Order in Prisons', *British Journal of Sociology*, Vol. 46, No.1, pp. 45–62.

Sparks, R., A. Bottoms, and W. Hay (1996), *Prisons and the Problem of Order*, Oxford: Clarendon Press.

Spinks, L. (2003), *Friedrich Nietzsche*, London: Routledge.

Stallybrass, P. and A. White (1986), *The Politics and Poetics of Transgression*, Ithaca, NY: Cornell University Press.

Stanko, E. (1994), 'Challenging the Problem of Men's Individual Violence', in T. Newburn and E. Stanko (eds), *Just Boys Doing Business?*, London: Routledge.

Steel, M. (2003), *Vive la Revolution: A Stand-up History of the French Revolution*, London: Scribner.

Stenson, K. (1999), 'Crime Control, Governmentality and Sovereignty', in R. Smandych (ed.), *Governable Places: Readings on Governmentality and Crime Control*, Aldershot: Ashgate.

Stenson, K. (2001), 'The New Politics of Crime Control', in K. Stenson and R. Sullivan (eds), *Crime, Risk and Justice: The Politics of Crime Control in Liberal Democracies*, Devon: Willan.

Stern, V. (1993), *Bricks of Shame: Britain's Prisons*, 3rd edn, Harmondsworth: Penguin.

Stevenson, J. (1992), *Popular Disturbances in England and Wales: 1700–1832*, Essex: Longman.

Sykes, G. (1958), *The Society of Captives*, Princeton, NJ: Princeton University Press.

Taylor, I. (1999), *Crime in Context*, Cambridge: Polity.

Taylor, I., P. Walton and J. Young (1973), *The New Criminology: For a Social Theory of Deviance*, London: Routledge and Kegan Paul.

Thomas, J. (1972), *The English Prison Officer: A Study in Conflict*, London: Routledge & Kegan Paul.

Thomas, J. and R. Pooley (1980), *The Exploding Prison*, London: Junction Books.

Thrasher, F. (1927), *The Gang*, Chicago: University of Chicago Press.

Tilly, C. (1978), *From Mobilization to Revolution*, Reading, MA: Addison-Wesley.

Tilly, C., L. Tilly and R. Tilly (1975), *The Rebellious Century: 1830–1930*, London: J.M. Dent.

Torfing, J. (1999), *New Theories of Discourse: Laclau, Mouffe and Žižek*, Oxford: Blackwell.

Tosh, J. (1991), 'Domesticity and Manliness in the Victorian Middle Class: The Family of Edward White Benson', in M. Roper and J. Tosh (eds), *Manful Assertions: Masculinities in Britain since 1800*, London: Routledge.

Tyler, T. (1990), *Why People Obey the Law*. New Haven: Yale University Press.

Useem, B. (1985), 'Disorganization and the New Mexico Prison Riot of 1980', *American Sociological Review*, Vol. 50, pp. 677–88.

Useem, B. (1990), 'Correctional Management: How do we Govern our "Cities"?', *Corrections Today*, February, pp. 88–94.

Useem, B. and J. Goldstone (2002), 'Forging Social Order and its Breakdown: Riot and Reform in U.S. Prisons', *American Sociological Review*, Vol. 67, August, pp. 449–525.

Useem, B. and P. Kimball (1989), *States of Siege: US Prison Riots, 1971–1986*, Oxford: Oxford University Press.

Vaughan, D. (1996), *The Challenger Launch Decision: Risky Technology, Culture, and Deviance at NASA*, Chicago: University of Chicago Press.

Waddington, D. (1992), *Contemporary Issues in Public Disorder*, London: Routledge.

Waddington, D. (1998), 'Waddington Versus Waddington: Public Order Theory on Trial', *Theoretical Criminology*, Vol. 2, No. 3, pp. 373–94.

Waddington, D., K. Jones and C. Critcher (1989), *Flashpoints: Studies in Public Disorder*, London: Routledge.

Waddington, P. (1991), *The Strong Arm of the Law: Armed and Public Order Policing*, Oxford: Clarendon Press.

Waddington, P. (1994), *Liberty and Order: Policing Public Order in a Capital City*, London: UCL.

Waddington, P. (2000), 'Orthodoxy and Advocacy in Criminology', *Theoretical Criminology*, Vol. 4, No. 1, pp. 93–111.

Walmsley, R., L. Howard, and S. White (1992), *The National Prison Survey: Main Findings*, Home Office Research Study No. 128, London: HMSO.

Weber, M. (1968a), *Economy and Society: An Outline of Interpretative Sociology, Volume 1*, New York: Bedminster Press.

Weber, M. (1968b), *Economy and Society: An Outline of Interpretative Sociology, Volume 3*, New York: Bedminster Press.

Welch, M. (1996), *Corrections: A Critical Approach*, New York: McGraw Hill.

Wilde, O. (1999), *Collins Complete Works of Oscar Wilde*, Glasgow: HarperCollins.

Williams, G. (1999), *French Discourse Analysis: The Method of Post-Structuralism*, London: Routledge.

Windelsham, Lord (1993), *Responses to Crime, Volume 2: Penal Policy in the Making*, Oxford: Clarendon Press.

Wodak, R. (1996), *Disorders of Discourse*, London: Longman.

Woolf, H. and S. Tumim (1991), *Prison Disturbances April 1990*, Cmnd 1456, London: HMSO.

Wrong, D. (1994), *The Problem of Order: What Unites and Divides Society*, New York: Free Press.

Young, J. (1999), *The Exclusive Society*, London: Sage.

Young, P. (1987), 'The Concept of Social Control and its Relevance to the Prisons Debate', in A. Bottoms and R. Light (eds), *Problems of Long-Term Imprisonment*. Aldershot: Gower.

Name Index

Useem, Bert 6, 11, 17, 49, 51–4, 56, 68n, 117, 126–7, 137, 175, 177, 179, 184, 188–90

Vaughan, Diane 97–98, 100, 142, 182

Waddington, David (Home Secretary) 14, 164
Waddington, David 49–50, 54–5
Waddington, Peter 54–7
Wallace, Deputy Governor 153, 155–6
Walmsley, R. 87
Walton, Paul 43n
Waterhouse, Alfred 151n
Weber, Max 5, 23, 27, 117, 192
Welch, Michael 85
Weir, L. 177
White, Allon 46, 57
White A. 85–7
White, Derek 168

White, S. 87
Whitelaw, William 80
Wilde, Oscar 45
Wilkes, J. 90
Williams, Glyn 34, 37, 44n
Wilson, Harold 125
Windelband, Wilhelm 4
Windelsham, Lord 94
Woolf, Lord (The Woolf Report) 1, 2, 6, 14–17, 19, 22, 53, 62, 65, 70, 98–101, 120–22, 127, 133–5, 138–9, 141–58, 160–65, 169–76, 189
Wrong, Dennis 62–3, 67, 126

Young, Jock 43n, 49, 72, 73

Zald, M. 68n
Zegfield, Principal Officer 143–4, 148–9, 153
Zimmerman, S. 48

Subject Index